Trudi Bissom

W9-CAI-300

Jerry Baker's Flowering Garden

OTHER BOOKS BY JERRY BAKER

Jerry Baker's Lawn Book
The Impatient Gardener
Jerry Baker's Happy, Healthy House Plants
Jerry Baker's Fast, Easy Vegetable Garden

Jerry Baker's Flowering Garden

✺ ✺

by Jerry Baker
America's Master Gardener

Illustrations by Susan Johnston Carlson

COLLIER BOOKS
MACMILLAN PUBLISHING COMPANY *New York*
COLLIER MACMILLAN PUBLISHERS *London*

Copyright © 1989 by Jerry Baker
Illustrations by Susan Johnston Carlson

All rights reserved. No part of this book may
be reproduced or transmitted in any form or by
any means, electronic or mechanical, including
photocopying, recording or by any information
storage and retrieval system, without permission
in writing from the Publisher.

Collier Books
Macmillan Publishing Company
866 Third Avenue, New York, NY 10022
Collier Macmillan Canada, Inc.

Library of Congress Cataloging-in-Publication
Data

Baker, Jerry.
  [Flowering garden]
  Jerry Baker's flowering garden/by Jerry
Baker; [illustrations by Susan Johnston Carlson].
    p. cm.
  Includes index.
  ISBN 0-02-030375-0
  1. Flower gardening. 2. Flowers. 3. Flowering
trees. 4. Flowering shrubs. 5. Landscape
gardening. I. Title.
EB405.B247   1000   89-9948   CIP
635.9—dc20

Macmillan books are available at special
discounts for bulk purchases for sales
promotions, premiums, fund-raising, or
educational use. For details, contact:

Special Sales Director
Macmillan Publishing Company
866 Third Avenue
New York, N.Y. 10022

10 9 8 7 6 5 4 3 2 1

Printed in the United States of America

To my wife, Ilene, the sunshine of my life

Contents

Preface

This book is all about flowers, outdoor flowers. Most homeowners confine their use of these flowers to the most popular annuals, like petunias, zinnias, marigolds, and impatiens, while their choice of perennials, as a rule, only include chrysanthemums. It is my hope that I can inspire you to venture further into the beautiful and exciting world of home gardening to discover the challenges, beauty, and rewards of a well-planned and well-planted yardscape.

Have you ever wondered what kind of folks create those gardens that you see every time you open the pages of the more popular and prestigious garden and landscape magazines? People, just like you, who are curious and think, What would happen if I planted this or built that? and then put their curiosity into action and discover they can have a work of growing, colorful art year-round, no matter where they live.

A home yard, lawn, and garden can be planned to provide a different face for each season, even when the grass withers and the flowers fade. There are evergreens that change color in the winter, and shrubs and trees with interesting and colorful bark to show off after their leaves have dropped, not to mention the broad-leaved evergreens, like rhododendrons and mountain laurel, that retain foliage and berries throughout the year. Even in the short-season areas of zones 2 and 3 to the north and east, where you are lucky to get ninety frost-free days, you can plan and plant combinations of flowers that will fill your days with beauty.

I am going to try very hard to give you all the information I can recall to help you create a flowerscape that will be the envy of the neighborhood and make you button-poppin' proud to be its keeper.

As most of you already know, if you and I have been gardening together for very long, my methods may seem rather nontraditional, bordering on irreverent, when it comes to chemicals, fertilizers, and techniques. The reason for this is simply that I don't like you to waste your money on tools, equipment, and material you don't want or need when, in fact, the solution to your problem is probably in a box, bottle, bag, or can of some product you already have around the house. As silly as my suggestions may sometimes seem, please try them for your garden's sake.

I am going to discuss the various families of flowers in the order of their importance, as I see them in relation to longevity, return on time and money invested, ease of maintenance, and, of course, beauty. Unlike most books on flowers, I am including flowering trees and shrubs, since they are an important part of any garden.

You do not have to be rich nor have a large piece of property to have a garden that would make anyone proud to say, "Welcome to my garden." A few simple seeds, properly placed and lovingly cared for, will soon become a garden, and you, who have planted and cared for them, will become a gardener, and my friend forever.

Jerry Baker

Jerry Baker's Flowering Garden

1

Flowering Trees
A Splash of Color

I t may seem unusual to begin a book on flower gardens with a chapter on trees, but that is only because most North American home gardeners, unlike their European, Asian, and Oriental counterparts, are not used to reading about trees in most Canadian and American flower gardening books. Yet they are, as a rule, the first plants to be placed in a new landscape planting. And for good reason, too—when properly selected and sited, flowering trees contribute beauty, balance, and stability to any garden.

BEFORE YOU BUY YOUR TREE

How to Choose

After you have decided to include a flowering tree in your landscape plan, you must take several factors into consideration when making your selection: (1) the size of the tree's root system—how much garden space you are willing to give up to a large root ball that must be covered with shredded wood for two years, preventing you from planting flowers in that area; (2) the density of the tree's foliage when mature—this will affect what or whether you can plant under it; (3) the tree's height and width when mature—you need to make sure your tree doesn't overshadow your flower garden, your living room window, or your house, for that matter; and (4) the tree's hardiness—there's nothing worse than planting a tree that doesn't survive the winter, unless it's a tree that takes five years to die miserably and slowly.

Remember, all plant roots are competing for the same food source, and tree roots have a distinct advantage over those of annuals, perennials, or bulbs. Some trees are companionable, but others have a very dense and vigorous root growth that will crowd out other plants within a certain radius—check with your nurseryman before making a final selection.

Secondly, all flowering plants need varying amounts of light, and the future density of the foliage and the height and circumference of your flowering tree will have a direct bearing on the flowers you will be able to plant beneath it and nearby, for your tree will be throwing shade in several directions.

If I sound like I'm trying to discourage you from planting trees, you're wrong—it's just the opposite. I want you to have a well-balanced and integrated flowerscape that enhances and flatters your home. A balanced landscape is seldom plagued with disease, insects, or discontented plants or garden tenders (that's you!).

When you select a flowering tree for your flowerscape, you have to think ahead. Search out pictures of mature examples of the variety you are considering and check the accompanying plant tag for final height and width information when you are at the garden center. Remember, the tree that is the perfect size right now may overwhelm your garden in five years. Moving a tree, shrub, or evergreen because it has outgrown its space after it has been in the ground for a year or two can cause severe damage, not only to the plant you are moving, but also to the dozens of others that have become quite comfortable growing underneath it.

Finally, please heed this last bit of advice when selecting a flowering tree or, as a matter of fact, any tree for your home landscape. Many of you have a habit of looking through mail order catalogs, seeing an attractive picture, and then ordering that plant to be delivered at planting time to your home, seldom checking its hardiness zone to make sure it has a chance for survival in your garden. Removing any tree for any reason causes problems for the surrounding plants, but when a tree or shrub dies and its decayed trunk and roots remain in the ground for a period of time, insects and diseases tend to move in and make it home, attacking or infecting neighboring plants, trees, shrubs, or flowers.

TREE FORM. Garden trees are one of three forms:

Freestanding—the tree is growing as it normally would in its natural habitat, with some pruning to control its growth.

Espalier—this is accomplished by severely pruning, bending, and binding the branches of a tree to grow flat against a surface, usually a garden wall. Many flowering trees, as well as fruit trees, are espaliered. They look terrific and produce well when fruit-bearing, but also take more of your time than you may wish to invest, which brings up another point. As a rule, the initial cost of an espalier tree is

FREESTANDING   **ESPALIER**   **DWARF**

3 to 4 times that of a standard variety of the same species and, I must add, worth every penny of it. Having an espalier flowering tree or two in your flowerscape will make it special, but be aware of its special demands.

Dwarf Form—Many flowering and fruit trees are grafted onto a low-growing root stock, which inhibits height but not head size. Dwarf trees are great where your vertical space is limited by overhead wires, a roof overhang, or patio cover.

Type of Planting Containers

When you purchase a flowering tree, you can receive it either bare root from a mail source, pre-potted, field grown, field potted, balled and burlapped, or machine dug and planted.

Bare Root—This is the most chancy way of purchasing and planting trees, as the roots can dry out if you miss even one day of watering. If you have a choice, pass this one up.

Pre-Potted—Bare-root stock has been planted in permanent growing media in a plastic container or a corrugated or a paper-mâché container, both of which will rot in the ground. This type of packaging is reasonably safe.

Field Grown—Young whips are planted directly into a plastic, metal, or paper-mâché container and grown aboveground for one to three years before you buy them. These are about the safest and best.

Field Potted—This is chancy, since the young tree is dug up by machine or hand and placed into a container, watered, put on a truck, and shipped to you. I avoid this type of tree stock if I can.

Balled and Burlapped—Up until a few years ago this was the popular way to buy trees, but the cost of labor and freight has just about done away with this practice. A freshly dug and balled tree in early spring or late fall (when the tree is dormant), especially if the ball is large, is pretty safe; if the tree's had a year in the ball and has been allowed to heal aboveground, it's better. If the tree is summer-dug, balled, and delivered, don't buy it.

Machine-Dug and Planted—This is the most expensive but the best way to buy a tree if you need, want, or can afford a mature tree. The tree is dug up and replanted the same day with a huge root ball; if done properly, the tree may never even know it's been moved.

If you dedicate yourself to your tree's safety and comfort, you can handle any of these methods with great success, but if you don't plan to participate in your yard's care and comfort, don't take a chance—go with machine-dug and planted.

FLOWERING TREE FAVORITES

Here are my picks for the most beautiful flowering trees that can be used in your flowerscape. I have provided their zone hardiness as well as their blossom color. I'm also giving you the botanical names of these trees—this is how they are known to professional nurserymen. Asking for your tree by its botanical name will, in most cases, insure that you get what you want, as many trees have several common names or two different trees may be known by the same common name.

PROFESSIONAL NAME (BOTANICAL)	HOMEOWNER NAME	FLOWER COLOR	ZONE
Acacia baileyana	Cootamundra wattle	yellow	10
Acacia decurrens dealbata	Silver wattle	yellow	9
Acer platanoides columnare	Columnar Norway maple	yellow	3
Acer platanoides 'Crimson King'	Crimson King maple	yellow	4
Acer platanoides 'Emerald Queen'	Emerald Queen maple	yellow	3
Acer platanoides schwedleri	Schwedler maple	yellow	3
Acer platanoides 'Summershade'	Summershade maple	yellow	3
Albizia julibrissin	Silk tree	purple	6
Albizia julibrissin 'Charlotte'	Charlotte silk tree	purple	6
Albizia julibrissin rosea	Hardy silk tree	purple	5
Albizia julibrissin 'Tryon'	Tryon silk tree	purple	6
Amelanchier canadensis	Shadblow serviceberry	white	4
Amelanchier grandiflora	Apple serviceberry	white	4
Arbutus unedo	Strawberry tree	white	8

PROFESSIONAL NAME (BOTANICAL)	HOMEOWNER NAME	FLOWER COLOR	ZONE
Bauhinia variegata	Purple orchid tree	lavender	10
Bauhinia variegata 'Candida'	White orchid tree	white	10
Castanea mollissima	Chinese chestnut	white	5
Ceratonia siliqua	Carob	red	10
Cercis canadensis alba	Whitebud	white	5
Cercis canadensis 'Withers Pink Charm'	Withers Pink Charm redbud	purple	5
Citrus species	Citrus fruits	white	9
Cladrastis lutea	Yellowwood	white	4
Cornus florida	Flowering dogwood	white	4
Cornus kousa	Kousa dogwood	white	5
Cornus nuttallii	Pacific dogwood	white	7
Crataegus mollis	Downy hawthorn	white	4
Crataegus phaenopyrum	Washington hawthorn	white	4
Eucalyptus ficifolia	Crimson eucalyptus	red	9
Halesia carolina	Carolina silver bell	white	4
Heteromeles arbutifolia	Toyon	white	7
Jacaranda acutifolia	Sharp-leaved jacaranda	lavender	10
Koelreuteria paniculata	Goldenrain tree	yellow	5
Laburnum x watereri 'Vossii'	Golden chain tree	yellow	5
Lagerstroemia indica 'Ingleside Pink'	Ingleside Pink crape myrtle	purple	7
Lagerstroemia indica 'Wm. Toovey'	Wm. Toovey red crape myrtle	red	7
Ligustrum lucidum	Glossy privet	white	7
Liriodendron tulipifera	Tulip tree	yellow	4
Magnolia denudata	Yulan magnolia	white	5
Magnolia grandiflora	Southern magnolia	white	7
Magnolia stellata	Star magnolia	white	5
Magnolia virginiana	Sweet bay	white	5
Malus 'Almey'	Almey crab apple	red	4
Malus x arnoldiana	Arnold crab apple	white	4
Malus x astrosanguinea	Carmine crab apple	red	4
Malus baccata	Siberian crab apple	white	2
Malus floribunda	Japanese flowering crab apple	white	4

PROFESSIONAL NAME (BOTANICAL)	HOMEOWNER NAME	FLOWER COLOR	ZONE
Malus 'Hopa'	Hopa crab apple	red	4
Malus hupehensis	Tea crab apple	white	4
Malus 'Katherine'	Katherine crab apple	purple	4
Malus 'Prince George'	Prince George crab apple	purple	4
Malus pumila	Common apple	white	3
Malus sargentii	Sargent crab apple	white	5
Oxydendrum arboreum	Sorrel tree	white	4
Photinia serrulata	Hardy orange	white	5
Prunus cerasifera nigra 'Thundercloud'	Thundercloud plum	white	4
Prunus persica	Peach	purple	5
Prunus sargentii	Sargent cherry	purple	4
Prunus serrulata 'Amanogawa'	Amanogawa cherry	purple	6
Prunus serrulata 'Kwanzan'	Kwanzan cherry	purple	5
Prunus serrulata 'Shirofugen'	Shirofugen cherry	white	6
Prunus serrulata 'Shirotae'	Mount Fuji cherry	white	6
Prunus subhirtella 'Autumnalis'	Autumn flowering cherry	purple	5
Prunus subhirtella 'Pendula'	Weeping Japanese Higan cherry	purple	5
Prunus yedoensis	Yoshino cherry	white	5
Pyrus calleryana 'Bradford'	Bradford Callery pear	white	5
Pyrus communis	Common pear	white	5
Sophora japonica	Japanese pagoda tree	white	4
Sorbus alnifolia	Korean mountain ash	white	5
Sorbus americana	American mountain ash	white	2
Sorbus aucuparia	European mountain ash	white	3
Sorbus decora	Showy mountain ash	white	2
Stewartia pseudocamellia	Japanese stewartia	white	5
Styrax japonica	Japanese snowbell	white	5
Syringa amurensis japonica	Japanese tree lilac	white	4
Tilia cordata	Littleleaf linden	yellow	3
Tilia cordata 'Greenspire'	Greenspire linden	yellow	3
Tilia euchlora	Crimean linden	yellow	5
Tilia tomentosa	Silver linden	yellow	4
Tilia tomentosa 'Princeton'	Princeton silver linden	yellow	4

Color Selection

While it is true that general growth habits and weather hardiness are important parts of the selection process, the color should be too. A hodgepodge of unmatching colors in the garden indicate poor planning and often can result in a reverse objective, an unappealing lawnscape. Following is a color guide to flowering trees:

White

Baumann horse chestnut
Black locust
Bradford pear
Carolina silver bell
Catalpa
Dogwood
Dove tree
Flowering ash
Fragrant epaulette tree
Franklinia
Fringe tree
Japanese pagoda tree
Japanese snowbell
Japanese tree lilac
Kapok tree
Lavalle hawthorn
Loblolly bay gordonia
Mazzard cherry
Saucer magnolia
Serviceberry
Shirotae Oriental cherry
Siebold viburnum
Snowdrift crab apple

Sorrel tree
Stewartia
Yellowwood

Yellow

Cornelian cherry
Florida yellow trumpet
Goldenrain tree
Golden shower
Golden shower senna
Japanese cornel
Jerusalem thorn
Moreton bay chestnut
Russian olive
Scotch laburnum
Silk-oak grevillea
Silver linden
Silver wattle (acacia)
Sweetshade
Tree of heaven
Tulip tree
Watereri laburnum
Yellow cucumber tree

Red

Arnold crab apple
Bell flambeau tree
Bonita Japanese apricot
Carmine crab apple
Carob
Crape myrtle
Flame bottle tree
Lemoine purple crab apple
Paul's scarlet hawthorn

Professor C. S. Sargent camellia
Royal poinciana
Ruby horse chestnut

Purple

Aldenham purple crab apple
Buddhist bauhinia
Chinaberry
Chinese redbud
Eastern redbud
Empress tree
European smoke tree
Idaho locust
Pawpaw
Sharp-leaved jacaranda

Pink

Blireiana plum
Dawn Japanese apricot
Flowering peach
Katherine crab apple
Kwanzan Oriental cherry
Pink English hawthorn
Pink flowering dogwood
Pink perfection camellia
Pink star magnolia
Sargent cherry
Saucer magnolia
Silk tree
Yoshino cherry

When to Buy

The offhand advice given by most folks who sell landscape plants is that you can plant any time you can get a shovel into the ground. Unfortunately, they forget to add, "That doesn't mean it will live."

In most parts of the country, early fall, after the dry hot weather has passed, is the very best time to plant. When the evenings are cool, but the days remain warm, most newly planted trees quickly acclimate themselves and begin to develop the needed root mass for winter survival. This is even more important if your flowering tree has a root ball that is wrapped in burlap.

The second best time to plant is as early in the spring as you can get a spade into the ground and not have the soil stick to the spade in a muddy mass. An early spring planting allows the tree to get a root source started and get a good supply of drinking water before the hot weather comes along.

The worst time to consider planting trees or shrubs is at the beginning of or during the heat season, unless you have professional training in tree care or are willing to take the precautions of wrapping the trunks and spraying the foliage with an anti-desiccant, a spray designed to retain moisture within the plant by coating it with a polymer-type material. (Read further in this chapter for more information on both.) But ultimately it is better to *wait* than *worry.*

One last thing—ask the person selling you the tree what his or her replacement policy is and ask for a copy of it; also keep your receipt. You will seldom find a professional member of the American or Canadian Association of Nurserymen recommending an improper planting time, so check to see if the person you are dealing with is a member.

PLANTING YOUR FLOWERING TREE

DIGGING THE HOLE. The planting hole for a new tree should be at least a foot wider than its present root system, and 6 to 8 inches deeper. Remember, as strange as this may seem, the best time to plant or transplant is in the evening from 6:00 P.M. on. It is more comfortable for both you and the tree or other plants and gives them a chance to get settled before the sun comes up and they must crank up the food factory.

SUBSURFACE DRAINAGE. After the hole has been dug, it should be partially filled with water. Check closely on the time it takes the water to be absorbed into the soil. If it takes more than a few hours, the subsurface drainage is likely to be inadequate and should be improved. The soil will become waterlogged in such a planting hole, resulting in unsatisfactory growth and the possible death of the tree. If this condition is a result of compaction caused by construction in your yard, deep digging may restore the drainage, also known as percolation. If the lack of subsurface drainage is due to some other condition, you might

try to improve the drainage by ditching or by installing drain tiles. To install a drain tile, dig a ditch 12 to 14 inches deep and 12 inches wide leading from the wet spot to a drier area where the water can drain. Make sure that you pitch the ditch so that it is deeper on the drier end (this will facilitate the flow of water through the drain). Lay down a 2-inch layer of gravel about the size of golf balls in the

LAYING A DRAIN TILE

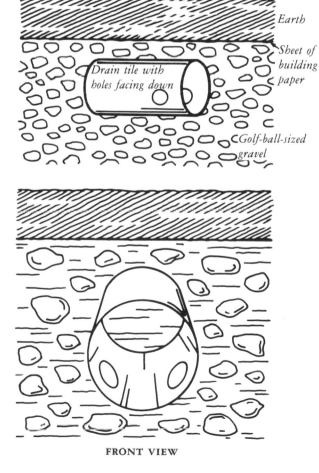

Earth

Sheet of building paper

Drain tile with holes facing down

Golf-ball-sized gravel

FRONT VIEW

bottom of the ditch, then set down the drain tile, making sure the holes are facing down. Fill in with more of the gravel on either side of the tile and then cover the top of it with 4 inches of the golf-ball-sized stones. Finally, cover the gravel with a sheet of building paper (this will prevent earth from filtering down and clogging up the drain) and then refill the remainder of the ditch with the excavated earth. Be sure to overfill the hole, as rain and the elements will eventually pack it down to normal ground level.

A layer of rocks in the bottom of the holes does not do anything to improve subsurface drainage. A layer of gravel in the bottom of a hole does not improve subsurface drainage.

Another good method of overcoming inadequate drainage is to plant the tree in a raised bed. You simply dig a very shallow hole in the existing ground and then pile soil into a large mound over the top of it. Pack the soil down and then dig the planting hole. The raised bed of soil should be high enough above the ground level to permit normal root functioning. You may leave it simply as a raised mound or build a retaining wall around it.

If a raised bed is impractical, trees may still be planted in such soil, provided nothing is done to increase water contact in the root area. The addition of peat moss or compost increases the moisture retentiveness of soil and improves its structure, but if the drainage is poor, using these materials as backfill soil will tend to make the planting hole a reservoir, or pool. If such materials are not added to the planting hole, the likelihood of waterlogged conditions is reduced. Conversely, the addition of vermiculite, perlite, sand, or cinders to the backfill could help improve drainage.

The soil used to fill in the hole around the roots should be well prepared. Except where drainage is poor, the addition of peat moss, compost, or other forms of humus is highly desirable. A third by volume of these materials should be added and thoroughly mixed into the soil so that when the tree is in place, the hole may be quickly filled. I also add a liberal amount of bone meal mixed with Epsom salts (3 parts bone meal to one part Epsom salts)—the Epsom salts will stimulate root and leaf growth. Sprinkle this mixture into the hole and on top of the soil after the hole has been filled.

Compost Making—the Smith Method of Composting

There are many methods of composting. Magazines and newspapers frequently carry articles on the subject, and one book devoted exclusively to composting explains at least a dozen methods in its 800 pages. This vast body of information confuses many gardeners, particularly new ones. I would suggest that you adopt one method and practice it for a season. Then, if you're not satisfied, you can read up on other methods and do some experimenting. My method is a simple one. Because it has worked well for me, I have found no reason to try other ones.

My composting pile consists entirely of

leaves. My kitchen waste—*vegetable only*—is buried in a bare area that will be planted the following year. My grass clippings—*dried on the driveway*—are used as mulch about the yard. The use of leaves exclusively eliminates the possibility of picking up any weed seeds and results in a compost pile that breaks down at a fairly even rate.

Before leaves are collected, compost bins must be built. My lot is 50' × 160'. To screen my bins from the neighbors, I put them behind the garage. The first bin is about 4' × 6' × 4'. I used chain-link fencing for the sides, but you can use boards or even concrete blocks. Whatever material is used, air spaces must be provided—air is an absolute necessity for the breakdown of the leaves. You will also need a cover for your bins. A sheet of exterior plywood, painted or wrapped in plastic, will last three or four years. My second bin is approximately 3' × 4' × 4'. The sides of this bin are solid except for a drilled row of one-inch holes on all 4 sides to provide air. These two bins provide enough compost for my size lot. If you have a larger lot, you may need more than two bins, or bigger bins. You may also want to set aside a corner of your lot for compost bins and screen the area with evergreens.

My compost program begins in the fall. I rake several times during the fall so that my compost heap builds gradually. I discard any twigs that I encounter. The raked leaves are collected and placed in the 4' × 6' × 4' bin. The pile should never be tightly packed. If the leaves are dry, I water them with a few buckets of water—moisture is necessary for the breakdown—and cover the pile. Avoid

overwatering—soggy leaves will not decompose. I keep adding leaves throughout the fall. With the last raking my compost work is over for the year.

One caution—oak leaves in large numbers should be composted separately. Oak leaves are acid and the compost made from them should be used only on acid-loving plants. The only leaves I throw away are the oaks because I have few acid-loving plants.

In early spring—late March or early April in the Detroit area—I use a spading fork to invert the pile. If the pile is dry, I add water and replace the cover. If I had a larger area, I would have a divided bin about 4' × 12' × 4'. Then I could simply move the pile from one bin to the other.

The more times the compost pile is turned, the quicker it will decompose. I don't hurry the process because the leaves I collected in the fall of 1987 will not be used until the spring of 1989. For the person who needs immediate compost, however, turning the pile weekly should result in usable compost in a month or two. After I spade the pile in spring, I turn it every three or four weeks, adding water if necessary. By the end of August my pile is fairly well decomposed, and I transfer the leaves to my 4' × 4' × 4' bin. I add water and make sure the cover is on. When fall comes and I start filling the larger bin again, the leaves in the small bin are reduced to the consistency of coffee grounds and are ready for spring use. The only chore I have in the spring is to screen the material to remove any stones, twigs, or scrap.

To avoid interrupting my step-by-step method of composting, I have waited until now to mention a time-saving product. I see no need for the gardener to buy special mixtures to put on the compost to hasten. the process, special sticks to poke air holes in the pile, etc. These products are, in my opinion, expensive and needless, and in many cases, probably useless. The time-saving product I referred to is The Leaf Eater, an electric leaf grinder. This grinder weighs about 25 pounds and can be placed over a 30-gallon trash can. Instead of steel blades, the unit uses inexpensive nylon line, the stuff used in weed trimmers. The usefulness of this grinder is that it reduces the bulk of the leaves by at least half. As a result, I get twice as many leaves into my bin, and because more surface area is exposed, the leaves decompose more rapidly. If my leaves are dry or just a little moist, I grind them at the curb and then dump them into my larger bin. Soggy leaves, however, do not grind easily, so, if I encounter an extremely wet fall, I put them into the large bin unground and grind them late in the summer of the next year before putting them into the small bin. At a price of about $100, I find the grinder saves enough work to justify the expense.

In conclusion, I wish to emphasize that my compost method is not the only one, maybe not the best one, but it has been adequate for me. Let me give you an example. I wanted a screen at the back of my lot to give both my neighbors and myself some privacy. According to my nursery catalog, the viburnums I had chosen for screening had a mature height of 7 to 8 feet. In planting I used generous amounts of compost. The viburnums were 7 to 8 feet tall in three or four years and today

they are about 15 feet and growing into the telephone lines. My method is obviously working!

Planting Depth

On nearly every tree trunk there is a soil line marking the depth at which it grew in the nursery. It is indicated by a discoloration on the bark. Whether the tree is bare root (B.R.) or balled and burlapped (B & B), it should be placed so that, allowing for settling, the soil line will be the same as it was when the tree was growing in the nursery, no deeper.

Your allowance for settling will vary according to the depth of the planting hole and the materials mixed into the soil. The deeper the hole, the greater the amount of settling to be expected. This may be reduced somewhat by thoroughly tamping the soil below the roots or root ball. However, even when that is done, still allow at least one inch for settling. If generous quantities of peat moss or other compacting materials are mixed into the soil, a 2-inch allowance may be safer.

Remove All Air Pockets

For bare-rooted trees, the soil should be worked in among the roots to avoid any air pockets. You can do this with your hands, but a more common practice is to shovel a quantity of soil into the hole and then lift the tree up and down several times so that the soil filters in among the roots. The soil should be firmed by tamping, but care should be taken not to damage the roots in the process. When the hole is refilled ⅔ to ¾ of the way and the soil firmed, fill the remaining space in the hole with water. This helps to eliminate air pockets and settle the soil, and thoroughly moistens the roots. After the water has percolated into the ground, finish filling the hole. This soil should NOT be packed or tamped. Excess soil can be used to form a slight ridge around the edge of the planting hole to facilitate future watering.

You should not remove the burlap from trees with balled and burlapped roots; the burlap will disintegrate in time.

Staking and Guying

Newly placed trees usually need to be supported to prevent their being whipped about by the wind. They need this support until their roots have had at least one year to become firmly established. Unsupported or unprotected trees frequently are unable to develop an effective root system. Pegs and guylines, stakes, or posts may be used; they should hold the tree firmly in place without injuring the bark. Lengths of old rubber hose can be slipped over the wire where it comes in contact with the tree's bark.

Upright, stout stakes positioned right next to the tree's trunk are the most satisfactory in the home yard, since ground stakes and guy wires interfere with mowing and constitute a hazard (see figure 1).

Mulching the Root Area

A surface mulch is generally recommended for newly planted trees. This not only prevents moisture loss and controls weeds, but it also prevents a crust from forming on the soil over the root area that might exclude air and moisture. A mulch also acts as an insulator and provides nutrients to shallow-rooted trees, such as dogwood, holly, and magnolia. Sphagnum peat moss, sawdust, and woodchips are the three most commonly available mulching materials, but these must be watched, as they will crust under certain conditions. Pine needles, sugar cane bagasse, cranberry straw, slat grass, peanut hulls, and

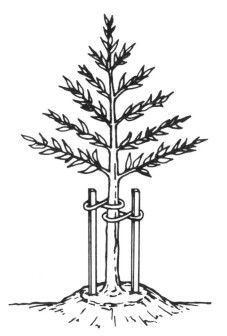

FIGURE 1

many other materials may be used. Coarse gravel works very well, if applied thickly, about 4 inches deep. Vegetative materials are preferred, as they help maintain the humus content of the soil.

The depth of the mulch will vary according to the material used. An inch of sphagnum moss or bagasse will normally be adequate. A 4- to 6-inch layer of rotted compost, straw, or woodchips should be equally effective.

Pruning to Compensate for Loss of Roots

Practically all new planted trees, both evergreens and deciduous, should be pruned at planting time. The major purpose is to compensate for loss of roots in transplanting—its decreased root system will not be able to support the amount of foliage it did before transplanting. The person who plants the tree has little opportunity to know the extent of root loss, except in the case of bare-rooted trees. It is better to err on the side of heavy pruning rather than light pruning. Conifers, as a rule, need less pruning than do deciduous trees and broad-leaved evergreens.

The first step should be to remove all damaged branches by cutting them back to a fork or bud (see figures 1 and 2). The cut should be made just beyond a bud or twig, pointing in the direction in which the new growth should go. In this manner you can help to shape the growth of your tree. The bud immediately below the cut will develop and grow. Next, remove the branches that contribute to weak forks and those that cross over one another.

Injury to the leader or top stem of the tree may require it to be shortened. This need not

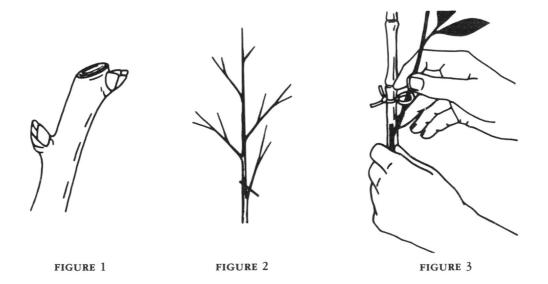

FIGURE 1   FIGURE 2   FIGURE 3

be a cause for concern. Make the cut above a twig or bud. A new leader will grow; once the new shoot has reached a foot or more in length, it may be fastened in a vertical position through the use of a bamboo stake fastened securely to the trunk below the shoot (see figure 3).

Anti-Desiccant Sprays

The anti-desiccant sprays are a boon to transplanting. They reduce moisture loss through leaves so that trees may be moved in full leaf. The protection they give against moisture loss also permits the planting of evergreens later in the fall than was formerly thought possible. (Evergreens planted late in the fall would normally lose a lot of needles to freezing and drying, as they wouldn't have been in the soil long enough to establish feeder roots to supply them with an adequate amount of moisture.)

The anti-desiccant spray forms a transparent coating on the leaf that significantly reduces moisture loss and helps to keep the tree in good condition, even though the root system has been reduced. The coating eventually sloughs off. The sprays have not only proved useful for transplanting, but they can be applied to evergreens in exposed situations, substantially reducing desiccation from drying winds. My favorite anti-desiccant is Cloud Cover.

Wrapping the Trunk of the Tree

The wrapping of a tree trunk to prevent sunscald is frequently overlooked when planting new trees. Many trees suffer irreparable damage from this type of injury. It is especially severe on trees transplanted from a woody area to a sunny situation.

You can reduce the necessity for wrapping by selecting trees that have been growing at the edge of woods or in an open field. Also, if you mark the north side of the tree and take care to maintain the same orientation when you replant, you can lessen the likelihood of injury.

If you must wrap a tree, you can use cheesecloth, old silk stockings, or the prepared wraps available from the garden supply stores. The wrappings are usually left on for a year—the cheesecloth and old silk stockings will have disintegrated by that time. However, the prepared tree wraps are longer lasting, and should be removed in the early spring of the following season, preferably during cloudy weather so that the bark will have time to adjust before the sun gets too bright.

To wrap a tree trunk, begin at the bottom and bandage the trunk like you would your leg with an Ace bandage. Continue this way up to the first branch; secure it there and at the bottom with a piece of nylon stocking.

FEEDING FLOWER TREES

※ ⵉ

Trees cannot live on rain alone; to thrive and survive they must be regularly maintained, and that means fed. I have found over the years that trees fed twice a year constantly perform at peak all season long. To feed flowering trees within an existing flower-scape, I use the Ross Root Feeder in the early spring with the Fruit Tree Cartridges, even though they may not be fruit trees. I also surface-feed with a mixture of:

1 ounce of liquid soap
1 ounce of household ammonia
1 ounce of whiskey
½ can of beer
1 ounce of hydrogen peroxide
1 ounce of dissolved Knox gelatin and
4 tablespoons of instant tea, all dissolved in 2
gallons of warm water.

Each tree should get up to a quart and a half once in the spring and again on June 15, no matter where you live in the United States.

I personally do not feed my trees after August 15 in areas where the temperature drops below freezing in the winter, as the fertilizer will stimulate new growth that will only end up freezing.

General Cleanliness and Care

Plants, like people, cannot properly function if they do not practice good personal hygiene. This means periodic baths. Oh yes, my soil sisters and brothers, your entire garden needs to be bathed regularly with soap and water and a light disinfectant. In the fall of the year, after all of the leaves have fallen from the trees, but before the temperature falls below freezing, you should spray your flowering trees with ½ cup of liquid soap mixed in 10 gallons of water, followed by a Dormant Spray, which is an anti-desiccant and will prevent water loss. In the spring you should repeat the same program as soon as the temperature stays above freezing for twenty-four hours. As soon as the buds have set but before the tree begins to flower, mix together my homemade disinfectant:

½ cup of flea and tick shampoo
½ cup of chewing tobacco
½ cup of Listerine mouthwash

in a 20-gallon hose-end lawn-sprayer jar and wash down your flowering trees, as well as the rest of the dormant flower garden.

Once every three to four weeks, wash everything down in the evening with one cup of liquid soap mixed in 20 gallons of water.

Insect and Disease Control

I find that if you follow my general hygiene program you will seldom have a tree problem, but if you do, spray every fourteen days with a solution of Tomato and Vegetable Dust, mixed at 6 teaspoons per gallon, with an ounce of liquid soap per gallon, and your troubles will go away.

However, there are persistent bugs in any garden and if you are faced with one or more, simply take this safe, sane, aggressive approach:

1. Begin with a light application of diatomaceous earth and paradichlorobenzene crystals (better known for their use in moth balls). Mix one cup crystals with 3 cups earth and sprinkle it on the soil in a 3-foot circle beneath the flowering trees in both the spring and fall.
2. Spray your troubled tree early in the season with a solution of 1/2 cup of liquid soap and 6 tablespoons of Tomato and Vegetable Dust mixed into a paste and then mixed into 6 gallons of water, applied in the evening, every three weeks, with a tree and shrub sprayer.
3. Sprinkle Diazinon granules as directed onto the soil, from the trunk out past the weep line (the line representing the furthest outreach of the tree's longest branch) in spring and fall.

If you have borers, treat your tree with Dexol Borersol as directed.

These few steps can control or head off most insect and disease problems before they get out of hand.

Watering

Trees require a substantial amount of water to carry on their normal functions; however, the amount of water required varies greatly with different species of trees and with different soil conditions.

Many subdivisions in my hometown, Troy, Michigan, have predominantly clay soil; in this area, overwatering is one of the major reasons trees die.

Trees planted in clay should be watered only once a week and then only if there has been no substantial amount of rainfall during the week. When little or no rain has fallen and the soil around the tree's root system has been determined to be dry to a depth of 6 to 8 inches, a hose should be allowed to run at the base of the tree for fifteen to twenty minutes at low pressure.

In areas that have sandy or gravel-rich soil, overwatering is not the problem it is in those areas having clay soil. However, even with the better drainage provided by a sandy soil, trees planted in these conditions should not be watered more than once a week with a hose for fifteen or twenty minutes at low water pressure and should not be watered in weeks in which there has been a heavy rainfall.

Root Prune

Root pruning will stimulate new root growth. This job is done in early spring and should be made part of your feeding program. While the tree is dormant,* plunge a flat-back spade with a sharp edge into the ground out at the weep line (the line around the tree demarcating the furthest extension of its branches) all the way around the tree; now, pour one pound of dry Epsom salts into the cut. Epsom salts will deepen the tree's color, thicken its foliage, petals, and bark, as well as increase its root growth. Next drill holes one inch in diameter 10 to 12 inches deep, 18 inches apart, in a circle 9 inches beyond the weep-line cut. Break tree spikes (fruit tree) into thirds, drop one piece into each hole, and pour in a warm solution of one ounce of liquid soap, 4 tablespoons of instant tea, and a gallon of warm water.

Pruning

Generally speaking, pruning is an annual chore. Putting off or avoiding periodic pruning may not have serious results for a healthy tree, but weaker trees may have dead branches or structural faults (such as low-hanging, contorted, or sharp branches) which may be a hazard for those who pass underneath. Pruning can also, in many cases, promote heavier flowering and fruiting. You'll need pruning shears, a pruning knife, lopping shears, pole pruners, and a pruning saw to prune your trees properly. All of these tools should be sharpened and oiled regularly. It is also a good idea to sterilize the tools with formaldehyde in order to prevent the transfer of possible infectious diseases from one tree to another.

All cuts should be made flush to a larger branch or the trunk. Avoid leaving stubs as they do not heal over and are likely to provide a channel for wood-rotting fungi to enter the heartwood of the tree.

All wounds over one inch in diameter should be covered with pruning paint. A coat of any asphalt varnish base paint or a mixture of 3 drops liquid Sevin to 8 ounces of latex paint will also do a good job.

Flowering trees should be pruned at specific times, as the list on page 22 indicates.

Preparing for Winter

Trees vary in their hardiness. Hardiness may not be so much affected by latitude as it is by exposure to winter winds, sudden drops in temperature, and drought. It is a reasonable precaution to select those kinds of trees that are definitely considered to be hardy to a particular area.

A tree's hardiness can be reduced through overprotection or by applying fertilizer at the wrong time of the year. A tree planted near the home may be sheltered from the cooling fall winds that help induce dormancy. If the

---

*The dormant season is in the autumn after the leaves have fallen and before the sap begins to rise in the early spring.

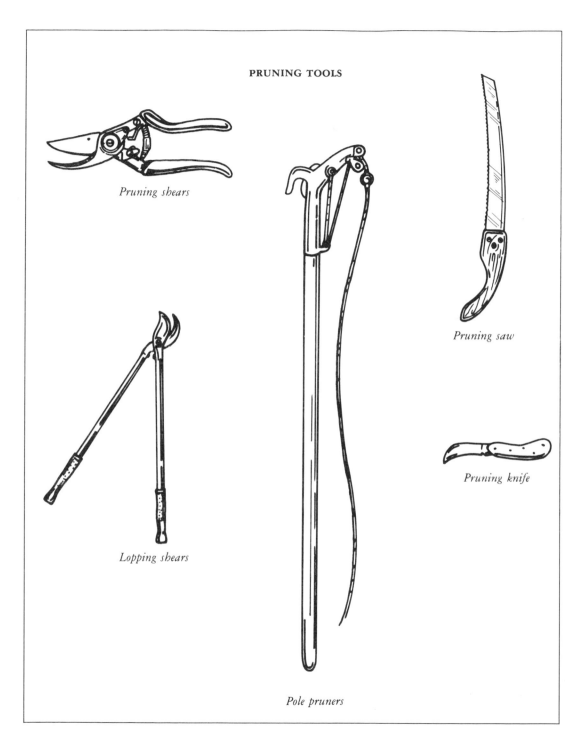

PRUNING TOOLS

Pruning shears

Pruning saw

Lopping shears

Pruning knife

Pole pruners

TREE	WHEN TO PRUNE	HOW TO PRUNE
Carob	After flowering	Repair when necessary
Catalpa	While dormant	Repair when necessary
Chestnut	When necessary	Repair when necessary
Citrus trees	After harvest	Shape and thin occasionally
Eucalyptus	When necessary	Repair when necessary
Flowering cherries, peaches, etc.	After flowering	Shape and thin occasionally
Flowering dogwood	After flowering	Repair when necessary
Fringe tree	After flowering	Repair when necessary
Goldenrain tree	After flowering	Seldom required; repair when necessary
Hawthorn	After flowering	Repair when necessary
Jacaranda	When needed	Repair when necessary
Japanese pagoda tree	**Should not be pruned**	
Laburnum	After flowering	Repair when necessary
Linden	**Should not be pruned**	
Magnolia	After flowering	Prune above outside limbs
Mountain ash	After flowering	Repair when necessary
Myrtle	After flowering	Prune often to control rapid growth
Orchid tree	Late spring	Shape and repair when necessary
Redbud	After flowering	Shape when young
Royal poinciana	After heaviest flowering	Repair when necessary
Serviceberry	After flowering	Repair when necessary
Silk tree	After flowering	Repair when necessary
Silver bell tree	After flowering	Repair when necessary
Smoke tree	Early spring	Cut out second-year wood; thin first-year wood
Snowbell	After flowering	Repair when necessary
Sorrel tree	After flowering	Repair when necessary
Stewartia	While dormant	Repair when necessary
Toyon	After flowering	Repair when necessary
Tree lilac	After flowering	Seldom needed
Tulip tree	**Should not be pruned**	
Whitebud	After flowering	Repair when necessary
Yellowwood	After flowering	Repair when necessary

sap is still running when winter settles in, the tree can freeze, causing irreparable damage. Heavy fertilization in midsummer or later can produce new growth which may not have time to mature before winter frosts. In areas where heavy winter snowfall may be expected, it is important that the trees be pruned so that their branches can withstand the weight of snow and ice. In windswept locations, it may be necessary to protect young trees with guy wires until the roots are firmly established. In some cases the application of an anti-desiccant spray may be needed to protect foliage and wood from drying winter winds.

Herbicide Damage

Herbicide damage to trees and other plant materials is on the increase in my town. The reason behind this is the increased use of herbicides by homeowners to control the weeds in their lawns. This damage can often be identified by the discoloration and premature dropping of foliage and, in many cases, a twisting or curling of the new growth. Wetting the ground with a heavy concentration of weed-killing chemicals may result in their leaching down through the soil to where they can be absorbed by the root systems of the surrounding trees. Herbicides should be used cautiously, applying them only to the foliage of the weeds to be eradicated.

Herbicide injury may also occur from exposure to spray drifts, or excess herbicide mist. To avoid this type of injury, it is important to use low-volatile materials and apply them when there is little or no breeze. A coarse spray applied under low pressure will also limit the amount of spray drift.

Still another way to avoid or minimize damage is to use only the more specific or selective herbicides. Broad spectrum chemicals will eradicate all your weeds, but it will also kill your trees, shrubs, and flowers if the material is not applied carefully.

Spraying for Insect and Disease Infestations

It should always be remembered that the spraying of chemical pesticides is a very dangerous project that could cause serious injury or death. These dangers can be reduced if a few simple rules are followed:

1. Read the package instructions every time you use a pesticide product, no matter how many times you have used the material in the past.
2. Always follow the mixing and application instructions on the package to the letter.
3. Never leave spray materials in your sprayer overnight.
4. Never apply spray material under windy conditions.
5. Never spray around pets or children.
6. Always shower after using chemical pesticides.
7. Never wash the clothes that were used while spraying chemicals with the regular family laundry. You should set aside a special set of clothing for spraying.

The spraying of trees and shrubs is a monthly chore during the growing season, and as a tree grows the chore and the expense grows. When a tree grows to the size where it cannot be sprayed from the ground, it should only be treated when a disease or serious insect problem has been identified. Small trees and shrubs should be sprayed once a month throughout the growing season. By spraying all plant materials once a month, insect and disease problems can be effectively controlled. Any of the all-purpose sprays will do fine, if the soap and tobacco spray, in conjunction with Tomato and Vegetable Dust spray, fails.

Never mix pesticides unless your instructions call for it.

Flowering trees are the anchor in any landscape plan and it does not matter if it is a single flowering tree in the center of the yard with a white petunia collar or a cluster, or a flowering tree in the midst of your flower garden. Everything else added must balance in color, size, and shape.

Add a flowering tree or two to your little corner of the world.

2

❧ ❦

Flowering Shrubs
Blooming Walls

Since the first chapter was on flowering trees, it should come as no surprise that this group of woody, caned plants is included in a book about flowers.

There are three groups of plants in any flower- or land-scape that give you the biggest bang for your buck—evergreens, perennials, and flowering shrubs. Of the three, flowering shrubs are really the best flower investment for your money. In addition to bringing color and drama to your landscape, they can function as noise barriers and windscreens, protecting other plants in the landscape; they can take the place of trees in small yards or patios; and they can direct or discourage traffic. They fill up a great deal of space at very little investment and will live for years and years with very little care and attention.

Flowering shrubs are not only valuable for their spring flowers; in many cases, a planting of a variety of shrubs can provide you with a flowering display throughout the year, depending on where you live. Many of the flowering shrubs—like blueberries, elderberries, and currants—offer the added bonus of bearing fruit. There are over 250 varieties of such fruit- and berry-bearing shrubs, and they are excellent for attracting birds, but keep in mind they will also draw a great number of unwanted guests like mice, rabbits, and porcupines, to name a few. I also want to caution you that not all fruits and berries are safe to eat, so please keep an eye on small children in your garden if you're not sure of the toxicity of the berries on your shrubs.

While we're most interested in the blossoms, berries, and foliage the flowering shrubs provide, let's not forget the visual contribution these same plants can provide in a winter landscape. The texture, shape, and color of a shrub's trunk, branches, and bark can lend interest and beauty to an otherwise drab, flowerless, and leafless outdoors.

YOU'VE GOT TO TAKE THE GOOD WITH THE BAD!

I wouldn't be doing my job if I told you only the good things about flowering shrubs because some of them have a couple of bad habits—like not staying where you plant them.

Most flowering shrubs really want to please you, but like growing teenagers they have a tendency to literally sprout up overnight and become a gangly-looking mess if you don't keep them trimmed. Another bad habit is that they will send out shoots beneath other trees, shrubs, or flowers in an insistent attempt to propagate themselves; this behavior is known as suckering and you must be alert to it, cutting off the suckers at ground level as soon as they develop. When selecting any shrub, especially flowering shrubs, make sure you understand the time and effort needed to keep it in good shape. Read the care and planting instructions that accompany most flowering shrubs, and you and your new plant will both be happy.

SHRUB FORM. Basically you will find the flowering shrub family divided into three forms:

Standard—This means they simply grow very tall and large and generally reach maturity from a cutting in three to five years.

Dwarf—This group is more likely to grow short by virtue of heredity, as opposed to grafting or the use of chemicals that can reduce or inhibit the growth of woody, caned, flowering shrubs. Dwarf shrubs, as a rule, grow under 3 feet; there are over 100 varieties to choose from.

Vine—Honeysuckle and wisteria are two examples of flowering vine, or climber, shrubs. There can be some disadvantages in their use—certain types have been known to tear down a fence or crush an arbor or trellis in one season. However, if they are properly trained and pruned, they can be a pleasant member of the flowerscape.

When you select a flowering shrub, make sure you know what you're getting into—don't be swayed by a pretty face. You must inquire as to the average mature height and width of a plant in order to know how close to cluster or row-plant it. You will also need these facts in order to know how close you may plant it to walls, walks, and drives. It amazes me to hear how many people have to remove trees, shrubs, and evergreens every year because they overgrew the driveway or front door.

You also need to know whether the plant blooms; when, and for how long; the color of the blossoms and foliage; and whether the flowers are fragrant. Finally, make sure the plant you are buying or ordering is hardy in your area—there's nothing more frustrating than buying a plant that doesn't survive its first winter. So, please, before you invite a flowering shrub to live in your garden, make sure the friendship will last.

Buying More Than One

Most landscape architects and designers will combine several different varieties and forms of the same flowering shrub, creating a palette of texture and color. You may want to try the same thing in your own garden, planting several varieties of, say, lilacs or azaleas or clematis, either subtly varying the color (planting, perhaps, only shades of pink) or boldly combining numerous hues. You can also compose a planting of the single- and double-flowered varieties of a particular shrub. There are nearly a hundred, maybe even more, garden catalogs available just for the asking that will show and tell about virtually every variety available in this country. See "Sources" at the back of the book for my list of mail-order nurseries. Send away for a few and enjoy some armchair perusing.

Here are the most popular and widely available flowering shrubs at your garden centers and nurseries. Make sure you check your zone hardiness against their needs.

FLOWERING SHRUBS FOR THE GARDEN

KEY: Zone hardiness indicates the coldest climate area plants can survive
*Shrubs bearing fruit or berries.

COLOR: Y = Yellow R = Red W = White
P = Pink L = Lavender B = Blue
G = Green

HOME GARDEN NAME	ZONE	COLOR FLOWER	FRUIT
Andromeda	5	W	
Azalea	5	Many	
Barberry, standard and dwarf	3	Y	*
Beach plum	4	W	*
Beautybush	5	P	*
Blueberry	4	W	*
Blue spiraea	5	B	*
Bottlebrush buckeye	5	W	
Broom	6	Y,R,B	
Butterfly bush	6	L	
California lilac	4–8	B	
Camellia	7	P,R,W	
Cherry laurel	6	W	
Chinese redbud	6	L	

HOME GARDEN NAME	ZONE	COLOR FLOWER	FRUIT
Cotoneaster	4	P	*
Crape myrtle	7	P,R,L,W	
Daphne	5	R,P,L,W	*
Deutzia	5	W,P	
Firethorn	6	W	*
Flowering almond	5	P,W	
Flowering plum	6	P	
Flowering quince	5	R	
Forsythia	5	Y	
Gardenia	8	W	
Genista	2	Y	
Glossy abelia	5	P	
Hardy orange	6	W	*
Heath	6	R,W,L	
Heather	5	R,L,W	
Holly olive	7	G	*
Honeysuckle	3	P	*
Hydrangea	3	W,P,B	
Japanese snowbell	6	W	
Jetbead	6	W	
Kerria	6	Y	
Korean abelialeaf	5	W	
Kousa dogwood	5	W	
Leatherwood	6	W	
Leucothoe	5	W	
Lilac	3	P,L,W,R	
Mock orange	4	W	
Mohonia	5	Y	*
Mountain laurel	4	P,W	
Ocean spray	5	W	
Parrotia	6	R	
Pearlbush	5	W	

HOME GARDEN NAME	ZONE	COLOR FLOWER	FRUIT
Photinia	7	W	*
Privet	4	W	*
Pussy willow	5	Gray	
Rhododendron	5	R,L,P,Y,W	
Rock rose	8	P	
Rose	5	Y,W,P,R	
Rose acacia	6	P	
St.-John's-wort	6	Y	
Sand myrtle	6	W	
Sapphireberry	6	W	*
Shadblow	4	W	*
Skimmia	7	Y,W	*
Smoke tree	5	G	
Snow wreath	6	W,G	
Spicebush	4	Y	*
Spike heath	6	P,W	
Spiraea	4	W,P,R	
Star magnolia	5	W	*
Stewartia	7	W	
Strawberry shrub	5	Y	*
Summersweet	4	W	
Sun rose	6	Y,R,W	
Sweet spire	6	W	
Tamarisk	5	P,R	
Trailing arbutus	3	W,P	
Tree peony	5	W,P,Y	
Viburnum	5	W,P	*
Vitex	5	L	
Weigela	4	P,R,W	
Winter hazel	6	Y	
Winter jasmine	6	Y	
Witch hazel	4	Y	

By Popular Demand

While I am encouraging you to be creative and try all sorts of flowering plants in your garden, I will give you a list of the flowering shrubs that top the sales lists of nearly every garden department in each of the hardiness zones in the country:

ZONE 3
Bush cherry
Greenweed
Manchu cherry
Tamarisk

ZONE 4
Hardy heather
Lilac

ZONE 5
Azalea
Beautybush
Double kerria
Double-file viburnum
Flowering almond
Flowering quince
Fringe tree
Mock orange
Pussy willow
Rose of Sharon
Spring witch hazel
Wright viburnum

ZONE 6
Butterfly bush
Chaste tree
Chinese Judas tree
Evergreen candytuft
Franklin tree
Hydrangea
Lanceleaf phillyrea
Nippon spiraea
Sargent crab apple
Star magnolia
Weigela hybrids

ZONE 7
Autumn sage
Crape myrtle
Fuchsia
Hebe
Laurel rock rose
Spanish broom

ZONE 8
Broom
Ceanothus
Evergreen mock orange
New Zealand daisybush
Oleander
Pomegranate
Willmott blue leadwort

ZONES 9-10
Bottlebrush
Flame-of-the-woods
Flowering senna
Flowering plumbago

Time to Choose

You have looked at all the pictures in the catalogs and books, you have checked all the lists of suggested flowering shrubs in this and other books, and now it's time to choose. But first you must ask yourself a hard question and answer truthfully—Do you have the time and patience to really prepare your soil before planting? What this means is that you are aware of the basic needs of the shrubs you have selected and willing to dig adequate holes, prepare compost, balance the soil, and improve the drainage when necessary to insure that your new flower addition has the very best start. If your answer is yes, then you can pick any plant on the list for your hardiness zone. But if you must work with the soil and drainage as it is now, your choices will be limited. Check the lists at right for your special situation.

FLOWERING SHRUBS AND BERRIES FOR PROBLEM SPOTS

Flower or Fruit Shrubs for Damp Soil

ZONE 3
Bayberry
Viburnum
Vinebark

ZONE 4
High-bush blueberry
Rosebay rhododendron
Summersweet

ZONE 5
Allspice
Drooping leucothoe
Heather
Mock orange
Mountain laurel
Pussy willow
Red-veined enkianthus
Rhododendron
Shadblow

ZONE 6

American andromeda
American holly
Dahoon holly
Darwin barberry
English holly
Hydrangea
Japanese andromeda
Japanese skimmia
Red chokeberry
Rhododendron
Star magnolia

ZONE 7

Camellia

ZONE 8

Japanese viburnum

ZONES 9-10

Sweet viburnum

Flowering or Berry Shrubs for Dry Poor Soil Conditions

ZONE 3

Bayberry
Bush cinquefoil (Golden drop)
Greenweed
Ninebark

Shrub rose
Siberian pea
Tamarisk

ZONE 4

Dryland blueberry
Lilac
Shrub elaegneus

ZONE 5

Forsythia
Jetbread
Quince

ZONE 6

Broom
Butterfly bush
Lavender
Rose of Sharon
Rosemary
Winter honeysuckle

ZONE 7

Chaste tree
Crape myrtle

ZONE 8

Blue leadwort
Japanese pittosporum
Myrtle
Oleander
Pomegranate

ZONES 9-10
Bottlebrush
Jerusalem thorn
Lantana
Shrub acacia

Other conditions you must consider are how much shade you have and whether your plants will have protection from any continuous prevailing wind. Take the time now to plan, ponder, and procrastinate before you make your selection because once the plant is in the ground, your money, time, effort, and the plant's life could be lost.

THERE IS A SEASON FOR ALL THINGS

Planting time is as important as planting method. With the quality of today's nursery stock and the improved methods of growing and transporting, a whole new world of home landscaping has been opened up for the do-it-yourself gardener. There are corporate giants in the nursery industry just as there are in the auto, apparel, and electronics industries: Select, Greenleaf, Monrovia, Midwest, and Boise Cascade grow and send millions upon millions of healthy, hardy plants to your local garden department every year. It has taken five to seven years to get some of these plants ready for your garden and then as a result of poor planning and planting they pass away in

your garden in less than a month. If you check the section covering planting containers for flowering trees on pages 5 and 6 and use that as a guide for all flowering shrubs, you and your plants can be confident that their life will be a long and healthy one.

Planting Practices

An old friend of mine once said that most new home gardeners get plenty of practice planting because they select the wrong plant and plant it in the wrong spot the wrong way, and then have to replace it. That's an awfully frustrating and expensive way to learn the proper planting practices. Let me give you a leg up with my general guidelines:

1. Dig all holes wider than needed.
2. Dig them twice as deep as needed.
3. Mix 1/4 palm of Epsom salts per 2 bushels of compost before you refill hole.
4. Fill in the hole with a mix of compost and soil, tamping it down as you go.
5. Now dig the proper size hole for the shrub you are planting—twice as wide as the root ball and 2 inches deeper.
6. Water well.
7. Mulch the shrub with shredded wood chips.

Too Big for Its Britches

The size plant you select is dependent on two things:

1. The space you have to work with, and
2. Your pocketbook.

I find that most second and third homeowners lean toward the purchase of larger, more mature flowering shrubs. They often secure —either through the necessity or generosity of friends or neighbors—"move outs," full-grown shrubs that are in the way of new construction or don't fit into a new landscaping plan. These are, as a rule, excellent additions to your garden if you have equipment to move them and the space to accommodate them.

If this opportunity doesn't present itself and you can't afford mature shrubs, I recommend that you wait and save until the fall sales begin to purchase more mature plants. The chances of them surviving into the next year are much better and in the end, though more expensive, they are a better investment.

Easy Does It!

Transplanting can mean trauma and death to a shrub if not done with care. If you must move or remove an established flowering shrub, do it when the plant is dormant—that means without leaves, and preferably in the mid-fall. Take as much soil and as much of the root ball as you can safely handle, and replant, water, and mulch it as quickly as possible.

Pruning

There is a right time, a right way, and a right tool for pruning flowering shrubs and other plants. Why prune your shrubs?—to keep them looking young and fit, not old, sloppy, and out of control.

Annual growth on older stems becomes less every year, which means that new growth will grow out of the center of the crown (the top of the stem or branch) where it won't get enough light, and—in its reach for the sun—it will grow long and skinny with little or no foliage.

In most cases, you need to prune one or two of the older stems to the ground each year; this is best done during the early spring or late fall, while the plant is dormant. After the shrub has flowered, the young wood can be shaped. There are, however, a number of shrubs whose growth should not be pruned back until after flowering. I list them here:

Akebia
Amelanchier (Shadblow)
Azalea (Hardy Ghent, Mollis)
Benzoin (Spicebush)
Calycanthus floridus (Sweet shrub, Strawberry shrub)
Caragana (Siberian pea)
Celastrus (Bittersweet)
Cercis (Judas tree, Redbud)
Chaenomeles (Flowering quince)
Chionanthus (White fringe)
Cornus (Dogwood, without berries)
Crataegus oxyacantha (English hawthorn)
Cydonia (Japanese quince)
Cytisus (Broom)
Daphne (Garland flower)
Deutzia
Exochorda (Pearlbush)
Forsythia (Golden bells)

Hydrangea hortensia
Kalmia (Laurel)
Kolkwitzia amabilis (Beautybush)
Lonicera fragrantissima (Bush honeysuckle)
Magnolia
Philadelphus (Mock orange)
Pieris (Andromeda)
Potentilla (Cinquefoil)
Prunus (Flowering almond, Cherry, Plum)
Rhododendron
Ribes (Flowering currant)
Rosa
Spiraea (spring-flowering)
Spiraea (Prunifolia, Bridal-wreath)
Spiraea thunbergii
Spiraea x vanhouttei
Syringa (Lilac)
Tamarisk (spring-flowering)
Viburnum carlesii
Viburnum lantana
Viburnum opulus (Cranberry bush)
Weigela (formerly *Diervilla*)

Remove dead wood or broken branches whenever they appear and seal all tree wounds with a mixture of 8 ounces of latex paint and 3 drops of liquid Sevin.

They're Not Chow Hounds!

It's almost hard to believe when you consider their rapid and luxuriant growth, but flowering shrubs are not as big eaters as their friends, the flowering trees. As a rule, you can feed your flowering shrubs every other year with a Ross Root Feeder, 3 spikes or 2 or 3

handfuls of any slow-release lawn food sprinkled onto the soil out at the tip of the farthest branch.

I have found, though, that two additional steps will help to insure healthy, robust, flower-producing shrubs.

1. Root prune on the in-between years.
2. Give them liquid fish fertilizer every three weeks along with the rest of your garden. Here's my recipe, which I mix up in my Super K-Gro hose-end lawn sprayer (20-gallon capacity):

> *2 cups of liquid low fertilizer*
> *1 cap of liquid fish emulsion*
> *2 ounces of hydrogen peroxide*
> *½ cup of liquid soap*
> *1 can of beer*
> *1 cup of household ammonia*

and as much water as there is room for. Be sure to place a white golf ball into all sprayer jars that do not contain weed killer; this will keep the solution mixed. You should place an orange golf ball in those containing weed killer.

Root Pruning

This is the equivalent of a pedicure to humans. You simply take a flat-back spade with a razor edge and plunge it into the ground out at the tip of the farthest branch as deep as it will go, in a circle all the way around the shrub. Next, pour one pound of Epsom salts into the cut. Follow this with a mixture of:

1 ounce of liquid soap
1 ounce of household ammonia
1 ounce of hydrogen peroxide
1 ounce of whiskey
1 can of beer
4 tablespoons of instant tea

in 2 gallons of very warm water; pour a quart of this into the cut over the Epsom salts.

Insect and Disease Controls

There are no shrubs I know of that do not have a problem with insects or disease from time to time, so why not take an aggressive approach to these problems in the beginning? To start my program, I dormant-spray all of my woody caned shrubs after they have lost their leaves in the fall with Dexoc's Dormant Spray.

Then, I spray my shrubs in very early spring and repeat at three-week intervals throughout the growing season with a mixture of:

1 cup of liquid soap
1 cup of chewing tobacco
6 teaspoons of Tomato and Vegetable Dust per gallon of water, first made into a paste and then added to the sprayer.

Apply this from a 6-gallon tree and shrub sprayer with a white golf ball in the sprayer jar to keep the solution mixed. Spray after 6:00 P.M. to insure catching the insects off guard.

To destroy problems below ground, such as grubs, apply Diazinon Granules to the soil beneath the plant from its trunk out beyond its weep line as soon as the soil is free of snow. Caterpillars and bagworms can be safely controlled with Bacillus Thuringiensis. And for borers, apply 2 cups of Borer Crystals or paradichlorobenzene moth crystals to the soil beneath the infested shrubs.

If you use the spray above, you will seldom find you have a sick shrub, as it contains a fungicide. As an added protection you can add 3 ounces of Listerine mouthwash to the mix.

EXPANDING YOUR SHRUB FAMILY

This is referred to as propagation. You can grow your own shrubs from what are known as softwood cuttings and hardwood cuttings. It always fascinates my neighbors to watch me take these cuttings from my shrubs and pass them out for free. I can do this because they cost me nothing; so can you and here's how . . .

Softwood cuttings are slips taken from the adult plant's soft growth. Most all of your perennials and your flowering shrubs will yield these cuttings. Take your cuttings in May and early June from new growth after the shrub has flowered. They should be 3 to

6 inches long and the bottom three layers of leaves should be removed. Dip the cutting first into water, then into about a half inch of a root stimulant product called Rootone. Shake off the excess and place the cutting into a pre-poked, pencil-sized hole in your rooting material—sharp sand works best—covering at least one or two of the nodes, or leaf breaks. The best air temperature for rooting is 60°–70°F., while the soil should be 5°

warmer. Keep the soil shaded and always damp, but not soaked, the first few days. Sprinkle the foliage often to encourage humidity.

Move the cuttings into the light as they progress in rooting. When roots are well established, pot them up and move them into the garden. I plant pots and all into soil to protect them. The following is a list of shrubs from which you can take softwood cuttings:

HOMEOWNER NAME	PROFESSIONAL NAME
Azalea	
Barberry	*Berberis*
Beautybush	*Kolkwitzia amabilis*
Bittersweet	*Celastrus*
Boxwood	*Buxus*
Broom	*Cytisus*
Butterfly bush	*Buddleia*
Camellia	
Crape myrtle	*Lagerstroemia indica*
Dogwood	*Cornus*
Firethorn	*Pyracantha*
Fringe tree	*Chionanthus*
Golden bells	*Forsythia*
Heather	*Calluna*
Hemlock	*Tsuga*
Holly	*Ilex*
Honeysuckle	*Lonicera*
Hydrangea	
Jasmine	*Jasminum*
Juniper	*Juniperus*

HOMEOWNER NAME	PROFESSIONAL NAME
Leucothoe	
Lilac	*Syringa*
Mock orange	*Philadelphus*
Oleander	*Nerium*
Oregon laurel	*Arbutus menziesii*
Pachysandra	
Privet	*Ligustrum*
Rhododendron	
Rose	*Rosa*
Rose of Sharon	*Hibiscus syriacus*
Senecio	
Sequoia	
Silver vine	*Actinidia polygama*
Spiraea	
Spruce	*Picea*
Strawberry tree	*Arbutus unedo*
Viburnum	
Weigela	
Winter creeper	*Euonymus radicans*
Yew	*Taxus*

Hardwood cuttings are taken in the late fall or winter. Cut slips 6 to 8 inches long, tie them in bundles, and store them in the basement until spring in a box, covered with peat moss. After any chance of frost has passed, remove the cuttings from the peat moss, dip one end in Rootone, and then plant the slip in your garden, leaving about half of the stem above the ground. Here are the hardwood cuttings that you can take:

HOMEOWNER NAME	PROFESSIONAL NAME
Barberry	*Berberis*
Burning bush	*Euonymus*
Catalpa	
Crape myrtle	*Lagerstroemia indica*
Deutzia	
Dogwood	*Cornus*
Elder	*Sambucus*
Firethorn	*Pyracantha*
Flowering quince	*Chaenomeles*
Golden bells	*Forsythia*
Hazel	*Corylus*
Honeysuckle	*Lonicera*
Lagerstroemia	
Ninebark	*Physocarpus*
Oleander	*Nerium*
Poplar	*Populus*
Privet	*Ligustrum*
Russian olive	*Elaeagnus angustifolia*
Viburnum	
Weigela	
Willow	*Salix*
Wisteria	

LET ME INTRODUCE YOU . . .

⚘ ⚘

What follows are brief descriptions of my all-around favorite flowering shrubs. Not that they are any better than the dozens of others you may have to pick from; it's just that they perform consistently well.

Almond

Flowering almonds (*Prunus triloba plena*) grow into low bushes, though under favorable conditions they may grow as tall as 10 feet or more. They bear a profusion of pink, rosette-shaped flowers that are borne in small clusters densely packed along the branches in early spring before the development of the leaves. The flowering almond makes a good subject for adaptability for espaliering. Trained against a wall in this manner, flowering almonds should be pruned each year after flowering.

Young plants may be easily transplanted in the spring, even if bare-rooted. They prefer light, well-drained soil in full sun. They are grafted on wild stocks, so take care to remove all sprouts which arise from below the point where they were budded. Most tragedies with flowering almonds occur because this task is neglected and the wild stock takes over.

Azalea

(RHODODENDRON)

Azaleas are capable of yielding an extraordinary harvest of beauty, but they do not offer it freely—it must be earned. But to those who fall in love with this lovely flower, no effort is too much.

So that there will be no confusion, let me say that botanists now classify all azaleas as rhododendrons. This includes not only the evergreen kinds, which have large, leathery leaves, but also the deciduous or leaf-losing varieties.

Azaleas, which flower in spring or early summer, may grow only 18 inches tall or attain a height of 15 feet or more, depending on the variety.

The soil for azaleas should resemble, as nearly as possible, that in which they grow naturally—a cushion of acid leaf mold. It should contain a large percentage (60 to 90) of organic matter. This may be leaf mold (especially that of oak leaves), peat moss, decomposed pine, hemlock, or spruce needles, or a mixture of any of these. Good quality soil and a little sand should make up the rest.

Azaleas are "surface-rooters," but you should give them at least 18 inches of this compost and a good surface mulch of partially decayed leaves so their roots will remain cool and moist during the hot summer months. They should also have mulch in winter for protection against severe cold. Most azaleas grow naturally in light, open woodlands or on the fringes of the woods. If shade is too heavy or continuous, they will not flower freely. On the other hand, they do not like the scorching heat of summer. Place them where they will receive some shade or in an area to the north or northeast of the house where they will receive some sunlight for part of the day but shade the rest of the time.

Since azaleas have many feeding roots close to the surface, mulching is preferable to cultivation for keeping down weeds.

Hardy azaleas may be raised from seeds sown in pots or shallow flats in February, March, or April. Fill the flats or pots with good soil covered with a ½-inch layer of sphagnum moss which has been rubbed through a ¼-inch mesh or sieve, and place them in a slightly heated greenhouse or coldframe.

For cuttings, choose half-ripe (new, strong growth) or semi-woody (several weeks older) shoots of the current year's growth in July, taking 2- to 3-inch-long slips, each with a very thin heel or piece of the old branch. Place them in a greenhouse or coldframe in a mixture of sand and peat moss. Keep the frame closed for three to four weeks to encourage the cuttings to form roots, watering them immediately after insertion and keeping them evenly moist, spraying daily, if necessary.

Barberry

(BERBERIS)

There are many good reasons for growing barberries. Some varieties are famous for their beautiful and fragrant flowers, while others are covered with bright-colored fruits later in the year.

The evergreen barberries, which retain their leaves through the winter, are exceedingly handsome. One of the hardiest of these is *B. julianae,* which comes from China.

Among the red-fruited barberries, *B. wilsonae* is a dense shrub about 3 feet high with very spiny branches that bears coral red fruit in autumn. The berries are bundled rather than clustered, and are preceded by yellow flowers. The ripe fruits will yield a good jelly. A choice brandy is also made from the berries, and special, large-fruited types have been developed for this use. The soft, inner bark of the barberries is said to have a healing effect if rubbed on chapped hands or lips.

Barberries will thrive in a wide range of soils, from sandy loam to clayey loam. They are easily transplanted and are tolerant of light shade. They will, however, display more brilliant autumn color if grown in full sun. The evergreen types are best planted in spring; the deciduous, or leaf-losing, types may be either fall- or spring-planted. This shrub will grow into a well-shaped bush naturally, so pruning is rarely required. If cutting back does become necessary, do this as soon as the flowering period is over. Barberries make excellent hedge plants, generally requiring only one annual clipping.

Increase your supply of barberries by sowing seeds as soon as they have ripened or in early spring. Sow them in flats or pots filled with two parts good garden loam, one part leaf mold and one part sand and place them in coldframes. Pick out the young plants and pot them singly in small pots when they are large enough to handle. Later they may be transferred to the nursery border.

All barberries may be increased by cuttings. Take slips 3 to 4 inches long in July or August and place them in a bed of sand or a mixture of sand and peat moss, preferably in a coldframe. Cuttings take about six months to become sufficiently rooted for transplanting. You may also detach suckers from large plants to form new bushes.

Beautybush
(KOLKWITZIA AMABILIS)

Beautybush is a deciduous shrub from China that belongs to the honeysuckle family. The flowers of the beautybush are borne in great profusion in early June and, though smaller and far more abundant, greatly resemble those of weigela. The bell-shaped flowers are a lovely pink with a golden throat. They contrast beautifully with the soft, gray-green foliage that stays on the bush into autumn. The beautybush also has a distinctive bark which peels away from the stems in large flakes.

Beautybush is a vigorous shrub, growing 8 to 9 feet tall, but it can be pruned back to a lower height if desired. Because it can grow quite tall as it matures, it is advisable to place it in the background of the border.

This shrub is perfectly hardy and will thrive in any fair, well-drained garden soil in full sun or very light shade. It may be propagated by either cuttings or seeds, but cuttings are preferable because seedlings will show great variations both in color and flower size.

Blueberry

(VACCINIUM CORYMBOSUM)

This particular variety is known as the high-bush blueberry and is very ornamental because of the brilliant orange-red to scarlet color of its autumn foliage. It has white, pink-touched flowers, cylindrical in shape, which appear in small clusters in May. They are followed by nearly black fruits. Native to eastern North America, it must have an acid, peaty soil and requires abundant moisture at its roots.

Sometimes called the swamp blueberry, this deciduous shrub may grow as tall as 12 feet but is usually much shorter. It has great value for large-scale, naturalistic plantings, but grows rather large for the average lot.

Pruning should be done in late fall or winter or early spring. Up to the age of about three years, the bushes will need comparatively little pruning. Simply remove the small, weak, lateral branches to prevent their fruiting. The long shoots, well covered with fruit buds, may need cutting back so that only 2 or 3 fruit buds remain. Remember that one fruit bud will produce a cluster of flowers, usually followed by a cluster of fruit. If not thinned, too many small, late-maturing berries will be set, weakening the bush.

The best time to make blueberry cuttings is in late winter. Cut 6-inch hardwood cuttings from one-year-old branches, preferably without fruit buds.

Broom

(CYTISUS)

The brooms are delightful plants, bearing pealike flowers of many colors. One of the most effective, the spike-broom, is distinguished by erect, spikelike racemes of honey-scented yellow flowers, at their showy best in July.

Brooms, which reach a height of 4 to 5 feet, have rather dull, 3-fingered, gray-green leaves. They can be used as a light, flowery garden hedge if placed in a sunny location. Prune them back to desired height after the flowering season. Brooms do best in well-drained, rather light soils, but clay can be made more suitable by adding sand and compost.

The wild types may be propagated by seeds sown in pots or flats as soon as they have ripened. Soaking the seeds twenty-four hours before planting aids in germination. Varieties which do not come true from seeds should be increased by means of cuttings. Place them in a bed of sandy soil in a coldframe in August, or in a shaded spot outdoors. Make the cuttings from firm summer shoots. They should be 3 to 4 inches long and have a small piece of the older wood attached.

Brooms do not transplant very successfully, so they should be grown in pots until they are large enough for planting in their permanent location. For the first two or three years, the new shoots on the young plants should be cut back several times during the growing season to ensure the formation of well-branched plants.

Buckeye

Bottlebrush buckeye *(Aesculus parviflora)*, which grows 7 to 10 feet tall, is at home in small gardens and excellent for use as a lawn specimen. The erect, foot-long, candlelike spires of white blossoms produce a striking effect in July and August, especially as they come at a time when few other things are in bloom.

Buckeye matures into a large, billowy shrub, increasing in width by means of suckering roots. Left to itself, it will in time take over a large patch.

Its leaves are 5- to 7-fingered, and are somewhat coarse and plain, but turn an attractive yellow-gold in autumn, again adding color to your garden.

Buckeye is native to the southeastern United States but is reliably hardy further north. This shrub will grow readily in average soils. It is most happy in open situations but will do quite well in light shade.

Butterfly Bush

(BUDDLEIA)

These lovely, colorful, summer- and autumn-flowering shrubs are easy to grow and have great value in the home garden. Many are hardy; others are suitable for outdoor planting only in mild climates. Most are deciduous, or leaf-losing. There is considerable variation in their height, which ranges from 3 to 15 feet at maturity. The blossoms come in many exquisite colors, including deep rose-purple, white, purple, flaming violet, pale lilac, and many shades in between, some of which are made even more striking by orange eyes. A very graceful Chinese type, the weeping willow, or fountain buddleia *(B. alternifolia),* grows 10 feet tall and bears delicate clusters of mauve flowers in June.

Most buddleias will grow in ordinary garden soil to which some organic matter has been added, preferably decayed manure. They may be planted in either spring or fall.

It is important to prune this shrub correctly. The types which flower in late summer and autumn should be pruned each spring by cutting back the shoots of the previous year's growth to within 2 or 3 inches of the older wood. Spring bloomers should be pruned back after they bloom.

In severe climates, the bush may be killed back to the ground during the winter, but as long as the roots survive, new growth will be produced and it will bloom every summer. Mulching the plants during the winter months will be of great benefit, particularly in climates where the ground is subject to hard freezing.

Buddleias are readily propagated by cuttings. These, which may be either half-ripe wood or semi-woody side shoots, should be 5 to 6 inches long. Place them in a coldframe or outdoors in a sheltered, shady location and keep moist.

Buddleias are always happiest and most effective in a sunny location. There they will add to the beauty of the garden by attracting large numbers of butterflies during the day and numerous moths at night.

Chaste Tree

(VITEX)

The attractive heads of small lilac or white flowers borne by the chaste tree from late June on through the close of summer are its chief contribution to the flowering garden. The chaste tree may be either deciduous or evergreen, and though they may be killed back to the ground in the North, they will still bloom that summer on the current season's growth.

This shrub may grow as tall as 10 to 12 feet, but can be pruned back much lower. The leaves are interesting, being divided into 5 to 7 leaflets, gray beneath and dark green above. Chaste trees will thrive in any reasonably good soil, but do like a well-drained location and full sun.

Transplanting should be done with care. Preserve as many of the roots as possible, being careful also to see that they are never exposed to sun and wind. Spring is the best season for transplanting. Keep the plant moist until well established.

Propagate by softwood cuttings.

Cherry Laurel

(PRUNUS LAUROCERASUS)

Cherry laurel is greatly valued as a hedge shrub, as a screen plant, and for its shade. Left unpruned, it will form a large evergreen bush about 15 to 25 feet in height; however, it is most effective as a dense hedge. There are several named varieties which vary in habit of growth and size of leaves. Some have narrow leaves of a rich green, while others have large, glossy leaves.

Cherry laurels are of easy culture in any reasonably fertile, well-drained soil. They will thrive in sun or shade and stand pruning well. Plant them in early spring just before new growth begins, or in early fall after the season's growth is completed. The planting should be done while the soil is still warm enough to encourage the development of new roots, so it may establish itself before cold weather. Newly planted laurels should be watered freely, especially when planted in late summer or fall.

Cotoneaster

The cotoneasters are quite a large genus, and since some members are far more attractive than others, varieties should be chosen with care. Some species are hardy, but most cotoneasters are more vigorous and beautiful when grown in the milder regions of the country.

There are both deciduous and evergreen cotoneasters. They are valued chiefly for their red berries in fall, though some have attractive white flowers in spring that resemble spiraea blossoms. Generally speaking, the deciduous types are hardy in the North, while the evergreen types are more suitable for southern gardens.

Cotoneasters vary in height from a few inches to many feet. For this reason, their uses in the garden are many and varied, some being ideal for the shrubbery border, others for the rock garden, and still others as specimen shrubs. Some work well as hedges and others in an open, naturalized, woodland setting.

Cotoneasters are of very easy culture, thriving in almost any kind of soil, even in poor soil where other shrubs find it difficult to become established. You will, however, be rewarded with better plants if some decayed manure or organic matter is added to the soil. Cotoneasters may be planted in fall or spring. Small potted plants are the most successful.

Pruning is not a great problem, as cotoneasters require very little. With the deciduous varieties, thin out any crowded branches and shorten those that have grown too long. Do this in late fall or during the winter. The evergreen kinds should be pruned about the middle of April.

Cotoneaster may be propagated by seeds or cuttings. The seeds should be sown in late autumn in a coldframe or greenhouse in pots of sandy soil. Cuttings 4 to 6 inches long should be taken from shoots of the current year's growth. They may be grown in the greenhouse or in a sheltered location outdoors if winters are mild.

Crape Myrtle

(LAGERSTROEMIA INDICA)

If "beauty is its own excuse for being," then surely this shrub needs no other. It has long been a southern favorite and is probably more widely planted than any other woody perennial, and with good reason. In regions of little summer rainfall, this stately queen will stand up and bloom when other plants falter and fail.

Standard-size crape myrtle will grow as tall as 25 to 30 feet. Though there are varieties that produce white or light violet flowers, the preferred color seems to be a luscious shade of watermelon pink. And the closely packed clusters of flowers, each individual one about an inch wide, really do resemble fluffed-up crepe paper. Moreover, the season of bloom usually extends from July to September, when few other flowers are seen.

Crape myrtles are by no means confined to the South. In fact, in sheltered places, specimens will survive all but the most severe winters, even as far north as New York City. Should the tops be winter-killed, prune back the dead wood in spring; this will encourage the development of new shoots that will bloom the same season. In milder regions, crape myrtle plants should be shaped each year for balanced growth, pruning away weak and superficial shoots. Do this before spring growth starts, never after.

Those who live in severe climates may still enjoy crape myrtles by setting the dwarf varieties in tubs and boxes and moving them to a frost-free environment in the winter and keeping them very nearly dry.

No shrub is easier to propagate than a crape myrtle. I have started dozens of new plants by simply inserting cuttings in the ground in the fall of the year. These cuttings, 12 to 15 inches long, should be inserted to a depth of about 6 to 8 inches in a shady location and kept fairly moist. They will root readily and may be moved to a permanent location the following spring.

Daphne

Daphnes, both evergreen and deciduous types, are attractive dwarf shrubs, especially valued for their highly fragrant flowers. Some are perfectly hardy, while others are suitable for outdoor cultivation only in the South. The species *D. mezereum* is covered with small, spice-scented, purple flowers in earliest spring. It rarely grows over 3 feet tall and has a stiffly erect habit of growth.

Daphnes, especially the stronger-growing ones, like deep, loamy soil and dislike hot, dry conditions. Some thrive in shade, and many of the dwarf varieties are suitable for rock gardens.

Propagation varies according to the species, but seeds should be sown if possible. Sow them as soon as they are ripe in pots or flats in a compost mix of loam, peat moss, and sand. Some of the very fragrant kinds are best increased by cuttings, which should be inserted in a warm propagation frame in early spring.

Deutzia

Deutzias are splendid for spring and early summer flowering, producing white, pink, rose, or purple flowers. Otherwise they are undistinguished. The majority are of imperfect hardiness in most sections of the country, though easily grown in the South. If you want to grow them, be sure to give them a sheltered location and a good mulch during the winter months.

Deutzias grow about 3 to 5 feet tall on the average, but some species reach a height of 10 feet at maturity. They prefer a sunny location, but will tolerate light shade.

If you want your plants to flower freely every year, encourage them to form well-ripened wood. You can do this by cutting back the old shoots to the point where vigorous young ones are developing as soon as the flowering season is over. The shrub will also benefit from an occasional application of well-rotted manure or other organic matter.

It is easy to increase all of the deutzias by means of cuttings, which should be of soft shoots, about 3 to 4 inches long. Take cuttings in May or early June or take them of firmer wood in July. Place them in a greenhouse or coldframe in a bed of sandy peat. When well rooted, set the young plants in the nursery border, pinching off the ends of the shoots, so the plant will be bushy. They are usually large enough for permanent planting when about two years old.

Dogwood

Kousa, or Japanese, dogwood *(Cornus kousa)* is the Oriental version of our own beloved native species, and a comparison of the two shows that each has much to recommend it. In its native land, the kousa dogwood will make a spreading tree some 20 feet high, but generally it doesn't get nearly so tall in the States.

Our native dogwood blooms in spring, while kousa is at its showy best in late spring or early summer. The flowers are borne over a long period of time and are creamy white in color, often fading to a clear, soft pink. It is worthwhile to grow both species together to prolong the blooming season of this lovely flowering shrub.

The petals of the kousa dogwood blossom are narrow and pointed, whereas those of our native species are rounded and notched. The leaves are smaller and not quite as coarse as those of the American species. They are, however, less brilliant in autumn, turning brownish purple, rather than yellow and red.

The fruits of kousa dogwood also differ. Instead of consisting of individual red berries, they are fleshy, pinkish red "heads," somewhat resembling strawberries in appearance. They usually ripen in August.

If you are using the kousa dogwood in the home landscape, remember that there are subtle differences in appearance according to the angle from which it is seen. Its beauty is shown off to better advantage if it is looked down upon rather than up at.

Dogwoods may be planted in either spring or fall and may be increased by hardwood cuttings taken in October or November. Another easy way to propagate them is by layering; the trees will do this naturally when their branches touch the ground.

Little pruning is needed beyond shaping the trees occasionally or cutting out suckers to prevent the spread of the bushes beyond their allotted area. Pruning should be done after the plant has flowered.

Forsythia

Forsythias are beautiful, hardy, deciduous shrubs. Cherished everywhere as joyful evidence of spring's return, forsythia bear a profusion of golden yellow flowers in March which usually last well into April.

The upright species are very handsome in or out of flower, and have a broad, sweeping growth habit. The leaves, which soon follow the flowers, remain green until late fall. The height varies according to variety, the dwarfs being only 2 feet tall, while others grow as tall as 10 feet.

Forsythias grow easily in any good garden soil, but are more vigorous and flower more freely if you dig in some peat, compost, or well-decayed manure, and mulch them well in late spring or early summer.

All the members of this good-natured family are easily transplanted and grow equally well in full sun or light shade. Planting may be done in spring, but late fall is best. Forsythias are dependable bloomers, rarely injured by severe winters unless they are planted in exposed places or in low-lying frost pockets. If freezing does occur, you may get little more than token blooming that particular spring, but this is rare.

Pruning should be done annually as soon as the flowering season is over. The flower buds for the next year develop on the short side shoots of the old branches. If forsythias are cut back during the dormant season, the greater part of their floral display will be sacrificed.

Forsythia may be propagated by either cuttings or layering. Soft cuttings, which will root readily, may be made in June or July. These cuttings, 3 to 4 inches long, should be inserted in a propagating case in a greenhouse or coldframe. Semi-woody cuttings may be made later in the season and inserted outdoors or in a coldframe. You can even make cuttings of mature wood and insert them in sandy soil as late in the year as October or November, and they will root easily.

Heath

(ERICA)

These are acid-loving plants for sunny locations. They may be either deciduous or evergreen; all have very beautiful, creamy white flowers.

The hardy species are dwarf shrubs, especially valuable for gardens where there is no lime in the soil, particularly on peaty land. The tender heaths grow quite slowly, especially when young, and require careful cultivation. Because they're so finicky, they have declined in popularity in competition with the more quickly grown plants.

There are also tree heaths from the Mediterranean region which grow 12 to 20 feet high and bear fragrant white flowers. Other tree heaths of more dwarf growth bear red or rosy purple flowers.

Both the hardy and tender types can be increased by cuttings of short side shoots that are just starting to get firm. These side shoots should be only about an inch long. Remove the leaves from the lower ⅔ of the stem, taking care that the delicate bark is not torn.

Insert the cuttings in sandy peat which has been made firm and covered with a layer of sand. (They will take root most easily in a propagating frame.) The cuttings will take several weeks to root and should be watered carefully.

Heather

(CALLUNA)

While the common name "heath" is applied to the *Erica* genus, "heather" is reserved for the genus *Calluna*. Heathers are hardy, rather small evergreen shrubs which grow wild in many parts of Europe and in a few places in North America. The name *Calluna* is derived from "kallunein," meaning "to sweep," for the branches were frequently used as brooms.

With their short, spiky leaves and lavender blossoms, heathers look their best when grown in irregular masses, making excellent ground covers where the soil is acid and well drained. Do not try to grow them in wet, poorly drained land.

They should be planted in early fall or spring and set about a foot apart. Each spring, before new growth becomes apparent, the shoots of the previous season should be cut off close to the base of the plants.

Four- to 6-inch cuttings may be taken in July or August and placed in a greenhouse or coldframe in a mixture of sand and peat moss.

Honeysuckle

(LONICERA)

Japanese honeysuckle *(L. japonica)* is the common half-evergreen twining shrub that has become naturalized over a large portion of the United States. Few plants give so much satisfaction for the small amount of care required. Its characteristic fragrance makes honeysuckle perfect for entrance plantings. The flowers open white but change to creamy yellow as they age.

It may also be used as a vine, as a hedge or ground cover, or even as a low bush. It can be propagated by layering or seeds.

Everblooming honeysuckle starts blooming in spring and continues throughout the growing season. The buds and outer parts of the bloom are an attractive purplish red color, and the inner part is yellow. This honeysuckle is slow-growing and not as vigorous as the Japanese type. It may also be used as a ground cover or low hedge but will take longer to cover. It may be propagated by cuttings of young spring growth.

A third type, the trumpet honeysuckle, is native from Connecticut to Florida and Texas. It is a twining vine, and the bloom is an attractive orange-scarlet on the outside and yellow on the inside. It blooms in spring and early summer, with a scattering of blossoms in the fall. It grows best in moist soil.

Hydrangea

This genus of handsome shrubs includes both hardy and tender members and even several woody climbers. A few of the tender types are evergreen, but most are deciduous. When anyone thinks of hydrangeas, they almost invariably picture the blue ones, though the pink color is just as lovely. Remember that pink-flowered hydrangeas will bear blue blossoms where the soil is either naturally acid or treated with one of the chemical bluing powders sold by garden supply centers for this purpose. Other ways of changing the color include mixing iron filings with the soil, or watering it with alum (one teaspoonful dissolved in a gallon of water) or 3 ounces of aluminum sulphate dissolved in a gallon of water. White-flowered types will not turn blue but rather become an unattractive slate color.

Hydrangeas produce their largest flower clusters at the tips of the shoots formed the previous season. If these terminal buds are destroyed by either excessive winter cold or untimely pruning, you will have little bloom. Prune in summer as soon as the flowering season is over. Remove all the old shoots which have flowered down to a point on the stem where the new growth is developing. Also cut out weak and crowded shoots. Leave the strong new shoots at the base of the plant and on the lower parts of the old stems, for they will produce the next season's bloom. Never prune in late fall, winter, or spring if you want flowers.

I have found that tipping a bushel basket over my hydrangea plant and then covering it with leaves affords excellent winter protection. I always uncover it as soon as the weather warms up, and often find that it has made good growth inside the basket.

Cuttings are the easiest way of increasing your stock. Take 4- to 6-inch cuttings from the ends of the nonflowering shoots any time from April to August, being careful to retain 2 or 3 pairs of leaves on each cutting. Remove the bottom pair of leaves and cut the stem across just below a joint. Insert it in a bed of sand in the greenhouse or in a coldframe. Keep it closed until cuttings are well rooted, except to moisten at intervals as needed.

When the cuttings are rooted, gradually admit more air, and when the young plants are hardened off a bit, pot them up separately in small pots. They should be planted in a compost of peat, leaf mold, and sandy, lime-free (if you want blue hydrangeas) loam. If you want pink or white hydrangeas, use fibrous loam, which contains lime.

Kerria

Kerria is a lovable, multipurpose little shrub that seldom grows higher than 4 feet. Its pretty, 5-petaled flowers look somewhat like those of a wild rose and are at their golden best in shade, as they are apt to be rather badly bleached in full sun. They are borne on gracefully arching branches.

Kerria is very useful as an under-planting in lightly shaded locations, where it will provide a pleasing, lacy pattern even in winter after it loses its leaves. The slender, bright green leaves turn a bright, clear yellow in the fall and hold on for a long time before they finally drop.

Like many other obliging shrubs, kerria will grow fairly well in ordinary garden soil but does its best if planted in ground enriched with compost or well-decomposed manure.

Kerria is not completely hardy and may freeze back in severe winter weather, but in a way this is an advantage, for there will be little pruning necessary in the spring. Such winter injury is likely to be less severe in shaded rather than open locations. If your winters are not severe and pruning becomes necessary, do this immediately after the shrub has flowered, generally during the last half of May. Cut back the old branches to where strong new shoots are forming. Also cut off any crowded, weak, or broken branches.

You can easily increase your stock by division of clumps in spring or fall.

Korean Abelialeaf

(ABELIOPHYLLUM DISTICHUM)

Abelialeaf, judged on the merit of foliage alone, is worthy of consideration for the home landscape. A graceful bush of about 2½ feet high at maturity, it is covered with small, shiny, intensely green leaves which turn a rich red touched with bronze in the fall. There is, however, the added attraction of the fragrant, pink-tinted flowers which appear continuously from late June until late fall. These grow in small, loosely branched flower clusters along the side branches and are followed by brown fruits which add a further decorative touch to the little shrub.

Abelialeaf has many practical uses on the home grounds. Place it wherever you need a mass of foliage to serve as an unobtrusive low filler. It also makes a wonderful shrub border or a low hedge.

Abelialeaf will thrive in any good soil that has been enriched with leaf mold, compost, or peat moss. They will stand part-day shade but prefer full sun. Plant in the spring or early fall.

Prune in spring after flowering by cutting out the old shoots or branches which bloomed the previous year, along with any dead branches or weak, spindly growth. Leave the fresh young shoots uncut to blossom that summer. Even if this shrub is winter-killed right down to the ground (but the roots are still alive), flowers will appear on the new shoots the same year they spring from the roots.

If you want to increase your stock, take cuttings, about 3 inches long, of half-ripened or semi-woody shoots of the current year's growth. Cut them in July or August and place in pots or flats of sandy soil in a propagating case or coldframe. Keep them moist until roots are formed, which should take place in about four or five weeks.

Lilac

(SYRINGA)

Lilacs have come a long way and, while the older single varieties still have much to recommend them, I am inclined to cast my vote for the newer, smaller hybrids which seem far better suited to the small home landscape. These are just as fragrant as the older varieties, are available in a number of luscious colors—red, white, purple, blue, and magenta—bear double blossoms, and bloom over a longer period of time, usually half the summer. Though they will grow 8 to 10 feet tall at maturity, judicious pruning can keep them within bounds. If you select "own root" shrubs (many growers graft lilacs for quicker production) your lilacs will be long-lived plants with no wild sucker growth from the understock.

Lilacs are useful as either specimen plants or, planted 5 feet apart, will make a dramatically beautiful flowering hedge. Grow them in single color masses for the most striking effect.

My one minor objection to lilacs is their unsightly seed capsules, particularly noticeable in the double-flowered types. If you find these bothersome, clip them off with a long-handled tree-trimming tool.

The Persian lilac is, in my opinion, the best of the older lilacs and it is singularly beautiful when in flower. Its slender branches form a shapely bush and it grows to a mature height of about 4 to 5 feet. Its flowers, borne in small, sweetly scented clusters, are lavender or white.

Propagate by softwood cuttings.

Mock Orange

(PHILADELPHUS)

I am less fond of mock oranges than other flowering shrubs. They are undeniably fragrant, and their white flowers in May and June are attractive. However, after the blooming period is over, the foliage is not particularly beautiful, and they look somewhat ungainly during the winter months when their leaves have fallen.

To many, their exquisite fragrance is reason enough to plant them. If you want them because of this, choose from the smaller varieties, which range in height from 4 to 7 feet. There are also dwarfs that grow less than 4 feet tall and some lovely double-flowered varieties which are more appropriate to a larger lot. The 'Aureus' variety has golden leaves, its color at its best in spring.

Mock oranges are useful for naturalizing. The smaller ones may be used in the foreground of the border, the taller types in the back. Branches of mock oranges provide ample material for cutting and they do a wonderful job of perfuming the rooms in which they are placed.

Ease of culture is also a recommendation, for all mock oranges may be transplanted bare-rooted in the spring. These shrubs thrive in full sun, but will adapt to light shade. Any garden soil will do for them, but they must be given adequate moisture.

Since blossoming occurs on the branches of the previous year's growth, pruning should take place immediately after flowering so that a good supply of vigorous flowering wood may be produced during the summer growing period.

Propagate by hardwood cuttings.

Mountain Laurel

(KALMIA LATIFOLIA)

The best known and most attractive of the kalmias is the mountain laurel. This native of eastern North America may grow as tall as 20 feet under ideal conditions, but usually forms a shrub 6 to 10 feet high.

When not in flower, mountain laurel bears some resemblance to the rhododendron with its leathery, 3- to 5-inch-long leaves. The blush pink flowers are cup-shaped, often an inch across, and are borne in clusters in late spring. Some of the dwarf varieties have flowers of deeper pink; others have dense clusters of a vivid rose red.

All the kalmias are hardy, deciduous shrubs, and do best in acid or lime-free, loamy soil. If you want to grow them successfully, dig in plenty of peat moss or compost in the soil prior to planting.

Plant mountain laurel in fall or spring; October and April are considered the best months. The roots are apt to be thin and fibrous, so pack the soil firmly about them.

Pruning is seldom necessary and is usually done only for the purpose of training back long shoots to maintain the bush in a more shapely form. Older bushes that have become misshapen may be cut back to the ground, and they will renew themselves by sending up new shoots from the base of the plant. Any necessary pruning should be done after the plant has flowered.

The best means of increasing mountain laurel is through seeds sown in early spring. Place them in shallow flats or pots of sandy, peaty soil in a cool greenhouse and keep moist.

Propagation may be accomplished by cuttings, layering, or grafting. Layering is an easy way to increase your stock. Lay down a low-growing branch and make a slit in the stem just beneath a joint and about 12 inches from the tip. Bury the cut section 2 or 3 inches below the soil and keep it moist. When roots have formed, cut from parent plant and remove to new location.

Pearlbush

(EXOCHORDA)

The pearlbush is valued for its short panicles of large white flowers borne in early June. The pretty green leaves are just developing at this time, so the flowers are prominently displayed.

This shrub will require a little patience on your part, as it may tend to look somewhat untidy and rather leggy in its early stages of growth. It will, however, overcome this adolescent awkwardness as it matures, forming a tall, upright shrub of broad-oval form, 12 or more feet tall. Because of its erect growth it is attractive even during the winter months after its leaves have fallen.

These shrubs are accommodating and will thrive in most good garden soils, preferably enriched with an occasional top dressing of decomposed manure or good compost. Plant them in open spots where they will receive full sun.

Pruning should be done following the flowering period. Cut out any weak or crowded branches and shape the bush to a sturdy, more desirable form.

Three- to 5-inch cuttings of young shoots will root readily if placed in a propagating frame during July or August. Seeds may be sown under glass as soon as they have ripened. It is sometimes possible to detach suckers from older plants in late fall.

Photinia

Photinia, which may grow as tall as 15 feet, is very desirable as a specimen plant and will show itself off to best advantage if permitted ample space and uncrowded development.

Because of its fine, rather thin twigging, photinia presents a shapely outline even in winter and has much to recommend it all year long. Clusters of 1/4-inch white flowers are produced in early spring. These are followed by small, brilliant red berries in the fall.

The leaves, similar in size and shape to pear leaves, are of a good green color but are not glossy and may in some species be somewhat hairy. The leaves usually turn yellow in autumn, though in some areas, they may turn reddish orange. This adds greatly to their beauty at this season, enhancing the clustered fruits which remain on the bush for a long time. Sprays of photinia are excellent for cutting.

Deciduous photinias are generally hardy in the North, but the evergreen types will survive over winter only in climates that are relatively mild. Well-drained, ordinary garden soil is suitable, and spring planting is preferable. Firm the soil well about the roots and soak with water. Plant in a sunny location. Little pruning is necessary other than shortening any extra-long shoots in spring.

Propagate by softwood cuttings.

Plum

Beach plum *(Prunus maritima)*, a native shrub of our eastern coast, is a spreading bush which may be trained into a small tree. It grows naturally near the coast from New Brunswick to Virginia. Its height is variable, ranging from 4 to 10 feet. It is exceedingly attractive in bloom, producing pink blossoms in spring and later edible fruit which may be either dull purple or yellow. It is best used for naturalized plantings.

Privet

(LIGUSTRUM)

Most of us think privet is synonymous with hedge, and it's rather a shame that this excellent shrub has been typecast, for some varieties are beautiful enough to be grown as specimen plants. If given plenty of space to develop, privet will form a handsome bush. It suffers from crowding and hard pruning. Pruning, when it becomes necessary, should be done after its flowers have faded.

Used as a hedge, privet must be kept within bounds by regular trimming. As a hedge plant it is unquestionably king. However, consider using it for untrimmed screens or in a group planting, where its handsome leaves will show up to good advantage. Though trimming is necessary, privet also makes neat, easily kept foundation plantings. I am glad to see that the fad for shaping privet into globes, cubes, or animals has passed.

Privets bear small spikes of white or creamy white flowers in summer which are very dainty in appearance. Their only disadvantage is a disagreeable odor, though this is true of every species of privet. The flowers are followed by large, quite decorative clusters of blue-black berries which birds adore.

All privets are easily transplanted and accommodate themselves to average garden soils. They may be planted in spring or fall.

You may increase your stock by sowing seeds, but since cuttings are so easily rooted this is a more practical method of propagation. Take cuttings 3 to 4 inches long in summer and plant them in a coldframe in Promix. Keep them shaded and moist until roots have formed.

Pussy Willow

(SALIX CAPREA)

Few early spring plants are more charming than pussy willows, especially the newer kinds like the French Pink. Huge, fuzzy catkins of silvery gray gradually turn to a silvery pink, then to a deeper rose pink peppered with hundreds of golden stamens, and finally become solid gold. Pussy willow is highly prized for indoor bouquets—and with good reason. For early indoor bloom, cut branches and place them in a container of water in a sunny, warm window around the middle of January. Children have a lot of fun watching the catkins develop.

The pussy willow has many uses. It may be used as a specimen plant or in the foreground of shrubbery. A pair, used on either side of a doorway, will add a bit of magic in spring. Or use them as a low-growing hedge, clipping them into shape when necessary.

One of the best types of this engaging little shrub grows about 5 feet tall and eventually broadens out to become the "Mr. Five by Five" of the plant world. This rounded, symmetrical bush has numerous slender twigs with narrow, pointed, gray-green leaves.

The pussy willow, like most willows, prefers a wet soil, but will grow reasonably well even in light, sandy soil, provided it is not allowed to completely dry out.

Pussy willows are easily propagated by cuttings of ripened wood, the usual length being 9 to 12 inches. Plant these in nursery rows or where the new plant is to grow in the future. Keep the soil moist until roots have formed.

Quince
(CHAENOMELES)

The Japanese quince has a lot going for it. One of the loveliest of the early-spring-flowering shrubs, it forms a bush 10 to 12 feet high. There are a number of beautiful varieties, and you have a choice of white, pink, or crimson flowers. There is even a lovely semi-double type, rosea-plena. To make things even more interesting, its pretty flowers are followed by aromatic fruits which may be used for making a delicious jelly.

I have grown flowering quince as a hedge shrub and recommend it highly. Little pruning is necessary to keep it compact, and in many situations the spiny branches are an advantage, especially when you're trying to keep kids, cats, dogs, or rabbits out of your yard. When so grown, it will flower well in spring. You can also encourage flowering by pruning the side shoots in early summer to about 5 leaves, and then cutting back to 2 buds in winter. Quinces may be espaliered.

Flowering quince, sometimes called "japonica," belongs to the rose family. It will thrive in ordinary loamy soil and is very showy if grown in a sunny position in the open garden. Flowering quince is hardy but loses its leaves in winter, revealing shapely and attractive branches.

You may easily increase your stock by layering the branches in autumn or by removing the suckers which often appear around the base of established bushes. Cuttings, which may be made in summer of firm shoots, can be rooted in a compost mixture of sandy loam and peat. Seeds may also be sown in the same soil mix in a greenhouse or coldframe in the spring. The named cultivated varieties will not develop true to type from seeds and should be increased by cuttings.

Redbud

The Chinese redbud *(Cercis chinensis)* is a very handsome plant which may be grown as a tree or tall shrub. It will attain a mature height of 50 feet in its native area, but in the region of New York it seldom grows over 3 or 4 feet tall. It is not reliably hardy, except in sheltered locations. It does best in southern climates and in southern Ohio and Indiana. The Chinese redbud has attractive pea-shaped flowers and gray-green leaves. The deep pink flowers, larger than those of the native American species, are borne profusely in early spring when few leaves are apparent. The leaves, though sometimes difficult to distinguish from the native species, are generally of a firmer, somewhat more leathery texture and are usually a deeper green. Its buds are a deeper purple, a darker, richer rose than those of the American redbud.

This shrub thrives well in either full sun or light shade and is attractive when used in the foreground of the border.

Both Chinese redbud and the American species are difficult to transplant, and it is advisable to move them only in the early spring. Always be sure to keep a ball of earth around the roots.

Rhododendron

Let's get something settled right off—all azaleas are classed as rhododendrons, but all rhododendrons are not azaleas. Botanists now include azaleas in the genus *Rhododendron,* but gardeners still regard them as quite distinct from other kinds of rhododendrons and retain their older names.

Rhododendrons come in a surprising number of forms and variations. Some grow into trees, while others are small bushes or low, prostrate shrubs. Other rhododendrons are suitable for rock gardens, and some are even epiphytes (nonparasitic plants which grow on other plants, deriving their moisture chiefly from the air).

Rhododendrons also display many different kinds of flowers and foliage. Some produce leaves as long as 24 inches, while others have tiny leaves barely an inch long. Flower shapes range from the tubular to the saucer-like, and still others are nearly flat.

Rhododendrons are plants of enchanting beauty but, like azaleas, the limiting factor in growing them is climate. They thrive best in a moist, temperate climate where the heat of the sun is often tempered by cloudy skies, such as in the Pacific Northwest. They are of easy culture along seaboard strips, but they are not recommended for amateur gardeners in the central portion of North America. However, there are "mini-climates" in every section of the country, and I have seen rhododendrons growing and doing reasonably well in areas where the textbooks said they would not prosper. If their beauty bedazzles you and you want to try growing them, put them in a sheltered location where they will not be exposed to sweeping winds.

Some garden varieties of rhododendron will thrive in full sun, provided they have sufficient moisture; but shade is better, especially if you live in an area where the summer sun is intense. In the case of the large-leaved kinds, moisture is very necessary. The leaves will burn if exposed to too much light. If possible, naturalize your plants in a woodland. If your home grounds make this impossible, plant them on the north side of a building, or even the northwest or western exposure. A southern location is definitely not satisfactory. Also, remember that exposure to strong light in winter is even more harmful than in summer, for it is then that serious scorching of the leaves occurs.

Rhododendrons must contain an abundance of organic matter in their soil. They dislike lime and will not thrive in soil where it is present in any quantity. If necessary, have a soil test made to determine the soil acidity before you plant. If lime is present, dig out the soil and replace it with soil that is acid or neutral. The addition of rotted compost or well-decayed manure will help, along with acid peat moss.

Rhododendrons are shallow-rooted, so the surface of the ground should not be cultivated once they are planted, as digging among the roots will harm them. Mulch well to keep down weeds, using leaves, peat moss, pine needles, or even sawdust.

In many areas some winter protection is desirable. Do not use tight-fitting barrels or boxes—the plants do not need warmth but require shade and good air circulation.

Water them well—that means at least once a week, especially in the late summer and fall in regions where rainfall is not abundant at those times.

Fertilizing is not necessary as long as the plants maintain good growth, but as they grow older and use up the nutrients of the soil, it is a good idea to add some well-decayed manure or one of the fertilizers recommended for acid-soil plants.

Prune only as necessary after flowering to maintain plants of well-balanced growth. Remove all old flower heads promptly before seeds form.

Rose Acacia
(ROBINIA HISPIDA)

Rose acacia is the "old country" name for the locust, or moss locust, a shrub of the eastern United States that produces numerous suckers. It is a low, shrubby locust with small rose-colored flowers which appear in spring. The flowers are scentless.

Rose acacia forms wide drifts, due to the suckering roots. It is interesting to note that this plant, which grows from 4 to 6 feet high, has come to rely on suckering as a means of reproduction and has almost stopped producing seed pods.

This shrub is very useful in large, naturalistic plantings and where soil is very poor. It is pretty enough for a border in the home landscape, but impractical because of the difficulty of keeping it in bounds.

Sapphire Berry
(SYMPLOCOS PANICULATA)

If you want to grow something both beautiful and unusual, sapphire berry is for you. This rather tall shrub, which occasionally attains a height of 20 feet or more, is well worth planting. It fits nicely into the background of a border and is dramatically outstanding when used as a solitary specimen. In late spring it bears an abundance of fuzzy white flowers which are small but very fragrant. But the pretty flowers are only a preview of the enchantment to come, for they are followed in fall by heavy clusters of beautiful, bright turquoise-blue berries. These berries, unfortunately, are a great favorite of birds, so if you want to enjoy the sight for any length of time, you must find some means of protection. If you don't, the birds will strip the bushes of their fruits soon after they ripen.

Sapphire berries are easy to transplant and thrive in any good garden soil in full to half-shade.

Propagate by cuttings or by seed.

Skimmia

This low-growing, evergreen shrub which comes to us from Japan has many features to recommend it for use in the landscape. It belongs to the rue family, and the name is derived from the Japanese "skimmi," meaning beautiful fruit. Its bright red fruit—borne in fall—is, of course, its most outstanding accomplishment, but the fragrant white flowers it produces in spring are also very attractive. There are several varieties of skimmia, all more or less dwarf, averaging between 3 to 5 feet tall.

You must know your skimmias, for male and female flowers are often produced on different plants and it is necessary to grow bushes of both sexes together to insure fruiting. The gender will be noted on the plant's tag to insure you get what you need.

The best method of propagation is by cuttings, though seeds will grow readily. The reason for propagating from cuttings is that you will be able to grow just the number of plants of either sex that you need, the right proportion being 5 or 6 females to one male.

All the skimmias do well in open places or in partial shade. They like a moist but well-drained soil. They are not reliably hardy in the North, but will grow in sheltered locations if given some winter protection. Skimmias require little or no pruning as they grow naturally into shapely bushes.

Smoke Tree
(COTINUS)

When I was young, I greatly admired a gorgeous smoke tree growing in the garden of a friend. I decided I must possess one for myself. An unscrupulous nursery sold me *C. americanus,* and the amount of smoke produced by this species is exceedingly small. I recommend instead the European smoke tree, which will grow into a large bush 12 feet high with wedge-shaped, bluish green leaves.

Beginning in June and on through the summer, the bush is enveloped in a mist of silky, mauve-purple clusters of flowers and fruit. These feathery plumes give the smokelike effect for which the tree is named. Once you behold a mature tree in its full glory, you will not rest until you have one of your very own.

But this wealth of dainty blossoms is not all that the smoke tree has to offer, for in autumn the foliage takes on striking tints of yellow, orange, and golden red. Add to this the fact that these trees are easily grown in any good garden soil, even succeeding in land that is dry and rocky. As you may have guessed, they prefer a sunny, well-drained location.

Propagate by softwood cuttings.

Snowball

To my way of thinking, the fragrant snowball *(Viburnum x carlcephalum)* is the most attractive member of the snowball family. To enjoy it most, plant it near your doorway or outdoor living area where its fragrance and outstanding beauty will be prominently displayed. Each May this lovely shrub bursts into gorgeous blooms, covering itself from top to bottom with sachet-sweet balls of delicate pink, which gradually turn a waxy white. They are so spicily fragrant that you can smell them several feet away, and the dense heads measure 2 to 3 inches across. This shrub also produces bluish black berries in early summer. In the fall, the leaves turn a lovely wine red. It will grow 3 to 20 feet high and needs a sunny location.

Spicebush

(LINDERA BENZOIN)

The spicebush is a large, aromatic, native shrub of the eastern United States, where it grows in moist soil, sometimes attaining heights of 6 to 12 feet.

The small, yellow flowers, borne in April, are bunched on the naked branches in great profusion, lighting up the hillsides in a shimmer of yellow-green. The leaves, bright green, oval, and slightly pointed, are about 4 inches long and gradually appear as the blossoms fall. There is a good display in autumn of scarlet berries, about half an inch in diameter, but they do not remain on the bush very long before falling.

Spicebush has greater value in the larger landscape than in the smaller home grounds where, in my opinion, it takes up too much room for the rather brief decorative effect it achieves.

If you like the spicy odor, have sufficient room and wish to grow it, spicebush presents few problems. It should be transplanted with a ball of earth, but will flourish in any good garden soil. Give it a sunny or slightly shaded location. You may plant it successfully in either fall or spring.

Spiraea

The spiraeas are a large family, well known, loved, and respected. The name itself refers to the very flexible, graceful branches which at one time were twisted into garlands. This free-flowering shrub is found wild in many parts of the world, including North America, Asia, and Europe.

Bridal wreath *(S. prunifolia)*, a Korean native, is widely grown in American gardens and is one of the most attractive spring-blooming kinds. The double-flowered variety is named 'Plena.' In both, the pure white flowers grow in numerous clusters along stems of the previous year's growth.

S. vanhouttei is a hybrid type which is very vigorous, growing about 6 feet high with long, arching branches that bear clusters of white flowers in June. It is excellent for an informal hedge. *S. henryi* also bears great clusters of exceedingly dainty white flowers, and grows to be 6 to 9 feet tall. *S. douglasii*, native to the Pacific coast, is another beauty that grows to an average of 8 feet, and bears flowers of a deep rose red color. Both blossom in late spring. *S. x billiardii*, another hybrid, grows 5 to 6 feet high and bears abundant bright pink flowers in July and August.

You may plant spiraeas in either fall or spring, grouping them in the open or in semi-shaded locations.

Pruning methods for spiraeas differ according to species. 'Plena' has a rather untidy manner of growth, being rather loose and floppy in appearance. This should be corrected by severe pruning following the flowering season.

Spiraeas which flower from the buds should be pruned just after flowering by thinning out only the older shoots. Those that flower on the ends of the current year's wood should be cut to within a few buds of the base of the flowering shoots in spring.

All the spiraeas are easily increased by inserting cuttings, 4 to 5 inches long, in a coldframe in early summer. They will even root readily outdoors if placed in good soil in a shady location and kept moist.

Stewartia

Stewartia is a beautiful shrub which may reach the noble height of 50 feet when grown as a tree. Most, however, are grown as shrubs and are pruned back to 10 feet or less. While generally considered a bit large for the shrub border, stewartia is very desirable as an individual specimen.

Mountain stewartia *(S. ovata)* bears handsome cup-shaped, white flowers from June through August. These are often 3 inches across and are crowned with golden anthers. Its foliage is very colorful in autumn, changing to golden orange and finally to scarlet. Showy stewartia *(S. ovata grandiflora)*, preferred by many, has dramatically beautiful purple stamens. This variety, however, cannot rival the brilliant autumn color of mountain stewartia, for it assumes a rather drab, purplish look as fall approaches.

Stewartias are well worth growing, but remember, they must have considerable space, should be pruned in early fall, and need a sheltered spot and moist, well-drained soil. They are easily propagated by layering a few of the lowest branches in late summer. Cuttings are slow to take root, but seeds may be sown in a slightly heated greenhouse in spring.

Summersweet

(CLETHRA ALNIFOLIA)

Clethra alnifolia, sometimes called the sweet pepper bush, is native to the Atlantic coastal region and is the best and hardiest type for general cultivation. It prefers low, moist, open woodlands, where it grows 5 to 9 feet tall. Easily established, this shrub produces suckers freely and will soon form a large clump. It is fine for naturalizing in large plantings, and specimen plants are charming even for smaller grounds.

The fragrant white flowers are produced in dense spikes in July and last through August. These spikes are borne on the upper portions of the upright branches in erect, cylindrical clusters at a time when few other shrubs are in bloom. The pointed, rather oval leaves are about 3 inches long and turn a clear light yellow in the fall.

Clethras are surface-rooting shrubs and benefit greatly from a good mulch in early summer. This keeps the ground cool and moist, providing them with conditions similar to their natural environment. They will grow in open locations, but prefer light shade.

The deciduous types may be planted in fall or spring, but the evergreen ones are not hardy and are suitable only for mild sections.

Pruning should be done as soon as the flowers have fallen. The oldest branches should be cut down to the ground, and the oldest parts of other flowering branches should be removed. Vigorous young shoots should be allowed to grow to provide blooms for the next season.

Clethras may be increased by cuttings, but lifting the freely produced suckers is an easier and more popular method.

Tamarisk

(TAMARIX)

Tamarisk is a slender, delicately beautiful tree or shrub whose special attraction is its tiny, ethereal pink flowers. In most kinds, these occur on the upper part of the stems, creating a very showy effect. The leaves are very tiny and in most species a grayish green. They are borne on very slender branchlets, many of which fall in autumn with the leaves.

Tamarisk, while they will thrive in inland gardens, are best suited for coastal areas, where they are very resistant to salt air. They are useful for hedges, either informal or clipped, and will thrive in either light or heavy soil and will even grow in sea sand. Though best suited for mild climates, they may be grown in colder areas. Even if the top foliage may freeze back during the winter, the roots seldom do and new shoots will spring up. They should be grown in full sun.

Tamarisk may be increased by cuttings, generally made 9 to 12 inches long, and inserted in a coldframe in summer or fall.

Weigela

Weigelas are well-formed shrubs, growing 4 to 5 feet tall, which will thrive just about any place. They are deciduous and of erect growth, and are valued for their handsome flowers borne in great profusion in late spring. The blossoms may be white, pink, deep rose, or crimson, with many variations in between. Some are pink with yellow in their throats. The individual blossoms are rather small, but they are borne in such abundance that they more than make up for their size. Weigelas are moderately hardy but may be killed back. If your winters are very severe, plant weigelas in a protected area or give them some type of protection.

Weigelas like full sun but will grow in partial shade, though they will not bloom as abundantly. A good garden soil, neither too wet nor excessively dry, will accommodate them very well. Occasionally some compost or well-decayed stable manure may be dug into the soil. If you have clay soil, lighten it with sand and organic matter.

Since weigelas produce their blossoms on the shoots of the previous year, pruning should not be done until after the flowers have faded. Cut out any crowded older branches and remove any weak or badly placed stems. Weigelas make vigorous growth, so pruning is very necessary from time to time to admit light and air and to give the bush a more attractive shape.

Weigelas are easily increased by making 4- to 6-inch cuttings of half-ripe wood and inserting them in a coldframe in late summer.

Winter Hazel

(CORYLOPSIS)

The graceful, dainty winter hazels are an especially welcome sight in early spring when we have grown weary of winter white. Its delicately fragrant pale yellow flowers are borne in pendant catkins before the appearance of the foliage, and their great profusion makes up for their rather small size.

The best-known varieties of these shrubs come to us from Japan. Spike winter hazel *(C. spicata)* grows 3 to 4 feet tall, its drooping catkinlike clusters often 2 to 3 inches long.

Winter hazels are deciduous shrubs, several of which are hardy in sheltered locations as far north as New York. Others should be grown mostly in mild climates. They prefer a sunny location and will thrive in a light, well-drained soil to which a little peat has been added. Place them where they will be sheltered from cold winds, and give them a good mulch in the autumn.

You may increase your stock by sowing ripe seeds in pots or flats of sandy soil in a cool greenhouse or coldframe. Cuttings of half-ripe or partially woody shoots may also be rooted in a propagating case. Keep the frame closed, opening only to add moisture as needed, until the roots are well formed. They may also be increased by layering.

Take softwood cuttings of new growth in spring. Pot in Pro-mix.

Witch Hazel

(HAMAMELIS)

I've always found the witch hazel truly fascinating. This shrub or small tree may grow as tall as 20 feet. The bark and leaves are used to make a soothing lotion. It grows in the woods of the eastern United States and Canada and, left to its own sweet will, its jointed, curving branches will twist and point in all directions. The forked twigs have been used for divining rods, adding further to the plant's mystique. In fact, the name "witch hazel" refers to this use.

Unlike most of the shrubs we have discussed that bear their flowers in early spring before the leaves appear, witch hazel does just the opposite. After the leaves die, in October or November, the witch hazel puts forth its blossoms. And they are a sight to see, for they grow in dainty, feathery clusters. The fruits do not ripen until the next year. Then, in what seems to be a final burst of mischief, the seeds shoot from their small, woody capsules in spring to a distance of several feet!

The most decorative witch hazel is the Chinese one *(H. mollis)*. It forms a spreading bush or small tree which may eventually grow 18 to 20 feet tall. The leaves are larger than those of other types, being 3 to 5 inches long and 2 to 3 inches wide. It bears very fragrant, golden yellow flowers, which look a lot like primroses.

Plant your witch hazel in well-drained, loamy soil, mixing in some compost and peat. Choose a sheltered location with a southern exposure. If you want a truly dramatic display, plant it where it will show up best—against a dark background. The flowers are not injured by light frosts, and the wood is seldom damaged by cold.

Propagate by softwood cuttings in spring. Pot in Pro-mix.

3

❧ ❧

Perennials
Perennial Favorites

For the life of me, I cannot understand why you younger home gardeners have not discovered the advantages of using perennials in your gardenscape. The initial investment of purchasing a perennial plant is but a few cents more than the cost of a packet of unusual flower seeds and in some cases no more than a single tomato plant.

Perennials can continue as a member of your garden virtually for life—yours. I have mums that are over twenty years old, a nice return from my initial purchase of $1.29—oh, and I almost forgot: I have traded, given away, or sold over 700 daughter plants from this same plant.

Perennials come in every color, shape, and height imaginable and can be used for borders, dividers, backdrops, or solid beds. If you have purchased this book, odds are you know a bit about me, from either my other books, or my TV or radio appearances, so it will come as no shock to you that I speak about plants the way I do about people (in fact, the name of my first book was *Plants Are Like People*). Perennials tend to be rather complacent, and not much shakes them up, whether it be unexpected changes in the weather, a marauding band of bugs, or an overflight of disease spores. It has been said that if perennials were people they would be considered to have low self-esteem, since they're always playing second fiddle to the flashier shrubs. I disagree, however. The perennials in my garden have always known they were tops and that, along with my flowering trees and shrubs, I couldn't get along without them.

WHAT PERENNIALS WILL AND WON'T DO

❧ ❧

If you know what to expect from each other—I mean you and the perennials—your flowering friendship will last for years and years.

1. Perennials are either flowering or foliage plants whose roots live from year to year. Their tops may or may not die back in the winter.
2. Perennials give color to the garden in a shady spot and in front of shrubs. They are colorful in spring and throughout the growing season.
3. Some perennials flower the first year but need protection from drying winter winds. You can grow them as annuals and eliminate the problem of protecting them in the winter.
4. Usually perennials will not flower unless they develop to a certain size and are then exposed to low temperature for a number of weeks, then exposed to increasing day lengths and increasing temperatures. Their flowering time is the result of this sequence of day length and temperature.

Here Is Your Part of the Bargain

Oh, yeah! This is a two-way street and if you expect your perennials to bloom from spring through fall, year after year, you have to perform a chore or two to insure their comfort.

1. Prepare the soil in your flower beds thoroughly.
2. Start with vigorous plants or seeds. The best plan is to buy started plants. Next best is to sow fresh seed where the plants are to grow. Usually, the least satisfactory plan is to start your own plants indoors, as seeds need the outdoor elements to best stimulate growth.
3. Set out plants or sow seed at the recommended times. Plants set out too early may be killed by frost. Seeds will not germinate until the soil warms—and, if sown too early, they may rot. However, early spring growth is important for the survival of many perennials.
4. Provide the recommended distances between plants when thinning seedlings or setting out started plants. Proper spacing is necessary for the fullest development of the plants.
5. Do not grow annuals that grow wildly in the same bed with perennials; they will crowd the perennials.
6. Let the perennials stand out. Give them a background to show themselves off against. Evergreens or wooden fences usually work well.
7. Do not consider perennials no-mainte-

nance plants. Replanting, dividing old plants, and regularly improving their soil are essential for vigorous, flowering plants.

Flower Beds Don't All Have to Be Squares and Circles

In most cases you and other home gardeners have but a limited amount of time to spend in your gardens because of your busy lifestyles. So, before you drop in at the local garden center or nursery, look over the area you plant to landscape thoroughly, very thoroughly. Plan your garden, beds, or borders on paper first; graph paper works well. A rough drawing will do—you don't need to call in a landscape architect. And be very conservative; remember that one tiny little plant can spread out amazingly in a year or so, occupying all its own space and maybe sneaking a little more from somebody else.

If you plan to do most of the gardening chores yourself, you will want the beds arranged conveniently. Don't make them too wide. Six to 8 feet will allow for a wide choice of plants, some to bloom early, others in mid-season, and still others late. Arrange matters so you can have a continuous display of color.

Since most of the tall perennials flower in late summer or early fall, they should form the back of the border, with the smaller ones placed toward the front. Don't exclude the tall plants from the middle—a few placed here and there will help you avoid monotony and make for a more interesting planting. "Tall" plants are those which usually attain a height of 3 feet or more at maturity.

The middle of the bed should consist primarily of plants that range in height from 2 to 3 feet; these, for the most part, flower in midsummer. The shortest plants, the spring-flowering ones which grow 2 feet tall or less, will occupy the front of the bed.

I think curved-line plantings are far more graceful and interesting than long, straight beds. Open areas of lawn provide nice contrast. Make your rough sketch fairly large. You can open up a big, brown paper sack if you have nothing else. Then use something to help you envision what the border will look like when it is planted. An old nursery or seed catalog that shows the various perennials you have in mind may be of help. Cut out the pictures and place them on your diagram.

Move the pictures around until you feel they are pleasingly placed. They will be much easier to move at this time than after the real McCoys have been planted and you decide they should have gone somewhere else. As you clip the pictures, jot down the information on each one—height, color, time of bloom, and growth habits.

Consider all your permanent features, such as outbuildings, the garage, walls, walks, fences, and service yards that you will need to plan around. Some of these may be enhanced by perennial plantings, while you may wish to partially screen others. Select perennials that are native or seem suited to your particular area. Notice what grows well in local gardens, consult nurserymen, check with your state extension bureau, and choose those you

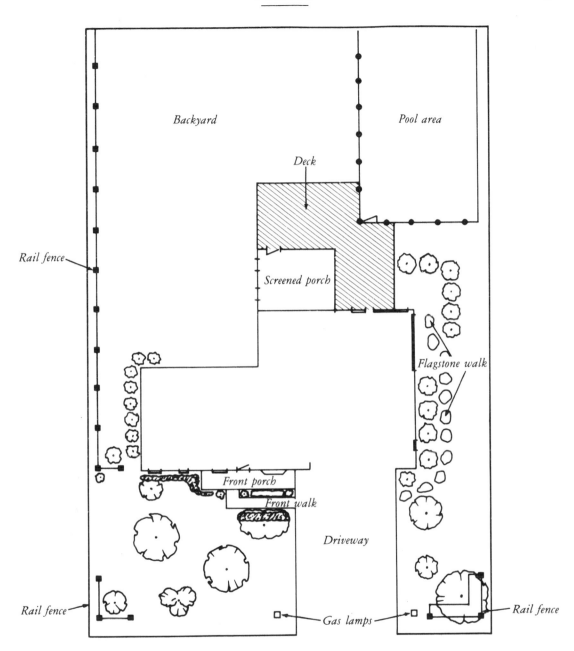

Backyard

Pool area

Deck

Rail fence

Screened porch

Flagstone walk

Front porch

Front walk

Driveway

Rail fence

Gas lamps

Rail fence

SAMPLE YARD SCHEMATIC

find most attractive. The plants discussed in this chapter will do well in most areas of the United States.

Having arrived at some conclusion, you can work toward your goal. Stagger your purchases over a period of time, even a year or two if need be. While you are waiting to buy the more expensive plants, fill in with bulbs and annuals.

Edging Your Beds

Down through the ages gardeners have used various means to establish a line of demarcation between lawn and flower beds, using stone, brick, and wood. The best answer I have found to this problem is a metal strip set flush with the grade; it is neat and unobtrusive. For curved beds, I like the looks of living edges. Daylilies are a wonderful choice, their flexible, arching foliage easy to mow under. Another good edging is liriope, sometimes called lilyturf, an evergreen perennial which grows easily in full sun or deep shade and is not particular about soil requirements. Liriope has flowers similar to those of grape hyacinth, but larger. These are borne abundantly in late summer and are followed by polished black berries. Mature plants grow about one foot tall and have a spread just as wide. Liriope is propagated by division of the clumps immediately after flowering.

Perennial candytuft, which grows only about a foot tall when in bloom, is another excellent plant for edging. As soon as the blooms fade, it can be cut down to a 6-inch

height. While full sun is preferable, it will also grow reasonably well in half shade.

The lovely herbaceous perennial, thrift, or sea pink *(Armeria maritima)* is exceptionally valuable for edging use, especially in sandy soils. An evergreen, it looks attractive all year-round. The foliage is delicate and grass-like in texture, and the deep rose-pink flower heads are borne on 6-inch stalks in the spring.

Hardy Biennials

The biennial always seems like the hidden sister, the Cinderella of the flower family. She's not an annual and as a rule lives for only two years, but when she is in bloom she is the beauty of the flower garden.

The difference between annuals, biennials, and perennials is somewhat relative to climate. Petunias, for instance, may be grown as annuals in the North, but often live over winter in the southern states and may be grown as perennials. A biennial, generally speaking, is a plant which may be expected to grow for two years, producing leaves the first year and flowers or fruit the second.

The hollyhock is one of the garden's most important biennials, though in some climates it's considered a perennial. This tall lady will quite likely perpetuate herself by self-sown seeds. The English daisy is—how confusing can you get?—a perennial which is usually *treated like a biennial.*

Foxgloves, canterbury bells, forget-me-nots, and pansies are also considered biennials.

Perennials Hate a Lumpy Bed

Preparing the soil is extremely important to perennials. Annuals can grow and flower in poor soil, but perennials seldom survive more than one year if their beds are not properly prepared.

Properly prepared beds will have—

- good drainage.
- protection from drying winds.
- adequate water in the summer.

If you prepare beds carefully—by spading deeply, providing adequate drainage, and lightening heavy soil with sand and organic matter—the flowers grown there are almost certain to be outstanding. Water can enter well-prepared soil easily. Seed germinates readily; the plants grow deep, healthy roots, strong stems, and late and abundant flowers. And the benefits of careful soil preparation carry over from season to season.

For new beds, begin preparing the soil in the fall before planting time.

Before preparation, test the soil's capacity for water absorption—your plants should never be under stress, either for lack of water or because of a waterlogged abundance thereof. Dig a hole about 10 inches deep and fill it with water. The next day, fill the hole with water again and see how long the water remains in the hole. If the water drains away within eight to ten hours, the permeability of the soil is sufficient for good growth.

If an appreciable amount of water remains in the hole after ten hours, it will be necessary to improve the drainage of the planting site; otherwise, water will saturate your prepared flower bed and prevent proper development of roots.

To improve drainage, bed up the soil. Dig furrows along the sides of the bed and add the soil from the furrows to the bed. This raises the bed above the general level of the soil. Excess water can then seep from the bed into the furrows.

You may find gullies in raised beds after heavy rains. You can prevent this by supporting the beds with wooden or masonry walls, making, in effect, raised planters of the beds.

Keep in mind that raised beds dry out more quickly than flat ones; little moisture will move up into the bed from the soil below. You must be sure to water beds frequently during the summer.

After you form your beds or determine that the soil's drainage is satisfactory without bedding, spade the soil to a depth of 8 to 10 inches. Turn the soil over completely. In this spading remove any branches, large stones, or trash, but turn under all leaves, grass, stems, roots, and anything else that will decay easily.

Respade 3 or 4 times over the autumn at weekly intervals. If the soil is drying between spadings, water it. If weeds grow, pull them up before they set seed.

In the spring, just before planting, spade again. At this spading, you should work peat moss, sand, fertilizer, and lime into the soil. For ordinary garden soil, incorporate a one-inch layer of peat moss and a one-inch layer of unwashed sand—both are available from building supply stores. If your soil is heavy clay, use twice this amount of peat and sand. By doing this and adding peat and sand to the soil each time you reset the plants, you can eventually transform even poor subsoil into good garden soil. If you prefer, you can use well-rotted compost instead of the peat moss.

In order to determine how much fertilizer and lime you need, have your soil tested. Your state extension bureau will do this and make recommendations. State clearly that you are planning to grow flowers in the soil. Make sure you allow sufficient time to send in your sample and get back the information in time for your planting.

For ordinary soil, add a complete fertilizer such as 5-10-5 at the last spading. Use at a rate of 1½ pounds (3 rounded cups) per 100 square feet. Add ground limestone at a rate of 5 pounds (7 rounded cups) per 100 square feet. Then rake the soil surface smooth.

The Fastest Way—Planting Seedlings

You can buy plants of many perennials from your local nursery or garden shop. These plants usually are in bloom when they are offered for sale, which allows you to select the colors you want for your garden.

Buy perennial plants that are compact and dark green. Plants sold in warm shopping areas are seldom vigorous. You can detect plants held in warm areas too long by their thin, pale yellow stems and leaves. Avoid buying these plants.

Named varieties are most useful in the garden—useful because we know their disease resistance, their heat and cold tolerance, and their plant habit (height, color, and branching), since they are bred to have specific characteristics. They are the backbone of a good perennial garden. Named varieties are available everywhere in the United States.

Don't Delay!

Probably more plants have lost their lives because of delayed planting than because of all the insect infestations and diseases put together. Plants that are mail-ordered, no matter how carefully they are wrapped, most likely have two strikes against them due to the vagaries of mail delivery: their package has probably been crushed or traumatized by other, heavier packages during their journey; and in all likelihood they have been stored in a close, warm room for many hours. Get them into the ground without delay. As a matter of fact, do this regardless of whether a local nursery delivers them to your home or you buy them yourself at a garden center, supermarket, or nursery. Don't let them languish in the back of your car, hot, tired, and thirsty.

Their wrappings differ greatly, some being individually clothed in paper and moss, others in plastic pots or six-packs, and others loose and bare-rooted. Plant the individually wrapped plants first, consulting your garden plan as you go to insure you are planting them where you want them. A cloudy, humid day is always best for planting. Keep this in mind when you go out shopping for plants or are ordering from a local nursery. Always be sure to avoid exposing plants to drying winds when you plant them.

To remove seedlings from flats, slice downward in the soil between the plants. Lift out each plant with a block of soil surrounding its roots and set the soil block in a planting hole.

When setting out plants in peat pots, remove the top edge of the pot to keep rain from collecting around the plant. Thoroughly moisten the pot and its contents to help the roots develop properly. Set the moistened pot in the planting hole and press the soil up around it. The pot will break down in the soil and improve the soil around the plant.

In each case, drench the soil around the planting hole with a liquid fertilizer B-1, mixed with one tablespoon per gallon of water, to stimulate root growth.

When planting most perennials, you should dig a hole a little wider than the plant and only as deep as it stood in its pot. The rhizome-rooted plants, such as irises, should be planted with their roots below the surface of the ground and the rhizome just on the surface. To do this effectively, dig a hole wide enough to accommodate the long rhizome and then build up a little mound in the center. Set the rhizome on this so it will be about even with the surface of the surrounding bed (see figure 1). Let the roots hang downward and cover them with soil, packing it down carefully. The rhizome-rooted plants must feel the kiss of the warm sun or they will not bloom well.

Plants which grow from a central crown should be planted with this crown just at the dirt line—much as you plant strawberries.

Allow plenty of space between plants because perennials need room to develop. Perennials usually show up best when planted in clumps of the same variety.

Starting from Seed

Many perennials do not grow true to type from seed, especially those harvested from cultivated, or named, varieties. You will have much better luck propagating these perennials from leaf cuttings or by clump division.

Certain perennials, however, are best grown from seed each year. Many of the biennials—perennials that flower in their second year of growth—are grown only from seed; these include columbine, foxglove, hol-

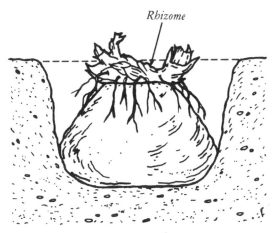

Rhizome

FIGURE 1

lyhocks, canterbury bells, sweet William, and delphinium.

You can sow perennial seeds directly in the beds where the plants are to bloom, or you can start plants indoors early in spring and set them out in beds after the weather warms.

Be sure your seed is fresh. Do not buy it too far in advance of planting time; for the best results, allow no more than a three-month interval. Old seed saved from previous years may lose much of its vitality when stored under fluctuating household temperatures and humidity levels. It tends to germinate slowly and produce poor seedlings. Keep your seed dry and cool until you plant it. Special instructions for storage are printed on some seed packets; make sure you follow them.

When buying seed, look for new varieties listed as F_1 hybrids—they are widely available in annuals and are beginning to show up in perennials. The seed for these hybrids costs more than the seed for the usual inbred varieties, but its superiority makes it worth the extra price. These F_1 hybrids are produced by crossing selected inbred parents. Plants of F_1 varieties are more uniform in size and more vigorous than plants of inbred varieties and they produce more flowers.

Don't be in a rush to start seeds or to set out started plants. As a general rule, delay sowing seed outdoors or setting out plants until after the last frost. Most seeds will not germinate well until the soil warms to about 60°F. If they are sowed in soil that is cooler than this, they will remain dormant until the soil warms and may rot before they get a chance to germinate.

Start seed indoors no sooner than eight weeks before the average date for the last killing frost in your area. If you start seed earlier than this, the plants will be too large to take well when they are transplanted outdoors.

Perennials seeded in the garden frequently fail to germinate properly because the surface of the soil cakes and prevents the entry of water. To avoid this, sow the seed in vermiculite-filled furrows. Make the furrows in the soil about a half inch deep. After filling them with fine vermiculite, sprinkle with water. Then make another shallow furrow in the vermiculite and sow the seed. I usually space them according to the recommended spacing for the mature plant; this avoids my having to thin them later on. However, if you're worried about not all the seed coming up, you may want to sow it more thickly.

Cover the seed with a layer of vermiculite and, using a nozzle adjusted for a fine mist, water the seeded area thoroughly.

To retard water evaporation, cover the seeded area with sheets of newspaper or polyethylene film (plastic garment bags from the dry cleaner are excellent). Support the newspaper or plastic on blocks or sticks 1 or 2 inches above the surface of the bed. Remove the paper or plastic when seedlings appear.

When most outdoor-grown perennials develop two true leaves (see figure 1), they should be thinned to the recommended spacing unless you already did so when you planted the seed. This allows the plants the light, water, nutrients, and space they need to develop fully. If they have been seeded in vermiculite-filled furrows, the excess seed-

FIGURE 1

lings can be transplanted to another spot without injury.

Watering Is a Must

Correct watering can make the difference between a good flower display and a poor one. Don't rely on summer rainfall; water on a regular schedule. Water perennials throughout the growing season, particularly during dry weather. Allow the water to penetrate deeply into the soil; moisten the entire bed thoroughly, but do not water so heavily that the soil becomes soggy. Water again when the soil is dry to the touch and the tips of the plants wilt slightly at midday.

A canvas soaker hose is excellent for watering beds, but it is difficult to maintain because the canvas rots quickly. Water from the soaker hose seeps directly into the soil without waste. The slow-moving water does not disturb the soil or reduce its capacity to absorb water.

If you water with a sprinkler, use an oscillating sprinkler. This type covers a large area and produces rainlike drops of water. Do not use a rotating sprinkler—it tends to tear up the surface of the soil and covers only a small area. Run your sprinkler at least four hours in each place. This deep watering will allow a longer interval between waterings.

The least effective method for watering is with a hand-held nozzle or watering can. Watering with a nozzle has all the disadvantages of watering with a rotating sprinkler. In addition, gardeners seldom are patient enough to do a thorough job of watering with a nozzle; not enough water is applied and the water that is applied is usually poorly distributed over the bed.

Water anytime during the day, even in bright sunlight, but water the soil thoroughly. If possible, however, water in the early part of the day; this will allow plenty of time for the flowers and foliage to dry before night. Night watering increases the chances of disease. Lastly, be careful when watering flowers in bloom; the flowers tend to rot if they catch and hold water. You may want to give such plants a little shake after watering to dislodge some of the drops.

Mulch Is a Must

Mulch gives a nice look to the garden, cuts down on weeds and weeding labor, and adds organic matter to the soil. It will also retard water loss, prevent the soil from baking and cracking, and prevent soil from splashing up on plants when you water.

Trim the plants of low foliage and stems before mulching. Mulch with buckwheat hulls, peat moss, salt hay, pine bark, pine needles, or wood chips. Select an organic material that will decompose slowly, that will allow water to penetrate to the soil below, and that adds a neutral color to the soil.

Spread the mulch over the whole bed, 2 inches deep, and be sure to do it before your plants have made a great deal of growth. Then, water the mulch into place (dry mulches prevent water penetration). Be sure to keep your mulch free of debris—litter is very noticeable.

Winter mulching can be helpful in protecting newly planted or less hardy perennials. But be careful—it can sometimes do more harm than good. Apply mulch around the plants only after the soil temperature has gone down, usually in late fall, after several killing frosts. If the winter mulch is applied too early, the warmth from the soil will cause new growth to start. Severe damage to the plant can result from the new growth being frozen back.

The best winter mulch is snow—if the bed has good drainage. A thin layer of peat moss is sufficient for a winter mulch. Keep winter mulch loose. It must be well drained and have good air circulation to keep the plants from rotting. Winter mulched plants also should be screened from drying southwest winds.

Remove the winter mulch as soon as growth starts in the spring. If you don't, the new growth will develop abnormally as it tries to push through the mulch—your plants will have long, gangly stems due to insufficent chlorophyll.

If you have trouble carrying a particular plant over the winter, a mulch can help. But remember, a mulch is not a substitute for a coldframe. It may be better to grow the plant as a biennial, carrying it over the winter in a coldframe and moving it to the flower bed in the second spring. In many of the colder areas of the United States, spring planting from coldframe-held plants is the only way to have a particular perennial in the garden.

Feed'um or Forget'um

You must feed your perennials regularly. Their extensive growing periods rob the soil of its natural fertility.

Do not fertilize perennials heavily with inorganic fertilizers. A light fertilization program gives a continuous supply of nutrients, producing plants that are easier to train or support on stakes and that do not have foliage so dense it interferes with air circulation and the evaporation of moisture from the leaves. (Air circulation is helped by the proper spacing of plants, also.)

If your soil is highly organic—has lots of peat moss or compost in it—you can fertilize with 5-10-5. Put little rings of fertilizer around each plant. If it lacks organic matter, fertilize with liquid fish emulsion or a sludge-type fertilizer like Milorganite.

Establish a fertilization program, and fertilize all along, a little at a time.

They Need Your Support

Many perennials are top heavy and will need staking. Plants like delphiniums and hollyhocks particularly need staking. If plants fall over, the stem will function poorly where it has been bent. If the stem is cracked, rot organisms can penetrate the break.

Stake plants when you first set them out so that—

- They will grow to cover the stakes.
- They can be gently guided to face the front of the bed.
- They can better withstand hard, driving rain and wind.

FIGURE 1

You can use stakes made of twigs, wood dowels, bamboo, wire, or even plastic. Select stakes that will be 6 to 12 inches shorter than the height of the grown plant. Place them behind the plants and sink them into the ground until they stand firm. Loosely tie the plants to the stakes, using wire covered with a layer of paper or plastic to secure them. Don't use string as it will rot over the course of the summer. Tie the plant, making a double loop of the wire—one loop around the plant and the other around the stake (figure 1). Never loop the wire around both stake and plant—the plant will hang to one side and the wire may girdle the stem.

Divide the Profit

Never leave a perennial planted in the same place for more than three years. The center of the clump will grow poorly, and the flowers will be sparse. The clump will deplete the fertility of the soil in which it is grown and the plant will crowd itself.

Divide mature clumps of perennials into clumps of 3 to 5 shoots each. Select only vigorous side shoots from the outer part of the clump, as they will grow best. Be careful not to overdivide; too small a clump will not give much color the first year after replanting. Discard the center of the clump.

Divide perennials in the fall in southern climates and in the spring in northern areas.

Stagger plant division to avoid digging up your whole garden at the same time; a good rotation will give you a constant display of flowers each year.

Don't put all the divisions back into the same space that the original plant occupied. That would be too many plants in a given area and would result in overcrowding and poor air circulation. Spread them out, move clumps to other parts of the garden, or give them away to friends.

DIVIDING PERENNIALS

Use a spading fork to dig up the clump.

Cuttings Are Part of the Reward

Many plants can be propagated from either tip (or stem) or root cuttings. Generally, tip cuttings are easier to propagate. Select new growth of dianthus, candytuft, and phlox for cuttings.

Make tip cuttings 3 to 6 inches long. Leave all the foliage on the cutting except the part that will be below the soil line. Treat the base of the cutting with a root stimulant and insert it into its own peat pot filled with a soil mix of 2 parts sand, 2 parts soil, and 2 parts peat moss. Water thoroughly.

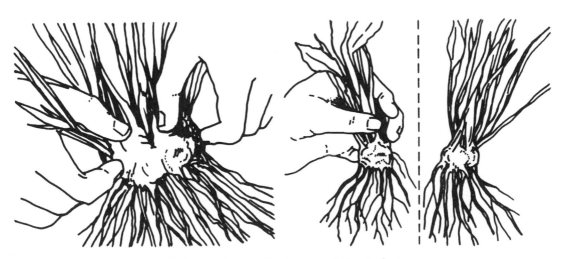

Pull apart into smaller clumps with 3 to 5 shoots.

Place the cuttings in a lightly shaded place. Cover with a sheet of plastic and check regularly to make sure the cuttings do not dry out. When the cuttings do not pull easily out of the soil, they have begun to root. Make holes in the plastic sheet to let in air and to increase the exposure of the cuttings to the air. This will harden the cuttings. Every few days make those holes larger or make new holes.

Finally, remove the cover. Pinch back the tips of the cuttings ten days after the cover is removed—this will promote branching. Transplant the rooted cuttings to a freshly prepared bed in midsummer.

Make root cuttings of phlox, baby's breath, and oriental poppies. To make root cuttings, dig up the plants in late summer, after they have bloomed. Select pencil-size roots and cut them into 4-inch sections. Put each piece in its own peat pot with the same soil mix as for the tip cuttings. Water thoroughly. Place the pots in a coldframe and transplant them the following spring.

Bugs and Blotches Are Facts of Flower Life

If I am in town on Saturday after I complete my broadcast on the Mutual Broadcasting System, a show that lets you and me talk together from coast to coast toll-free, I stop by one of the K-Mart garden shops and say hello. It never fails that someone always wants to know which of the many garden chemicals they should buy for this bug or that.

They are surprised when I tell them that in 9 out of 10 cases, Rose and Flower Dust or Tomato and Vegetable Dust mixed in 6 gallons of water with 1/2 cup liquid soap, at a rate of 6 teaspoons per gallon (make it into a paste first), with a white golf ball added to keep it stirred up, is about all you need to control nearly all bugs or diseases in the garden. Apply after 6:00 P.M. in the evening.

WHO'S WHO IN THE PERENNIAL WORLD

In most cases, the first time you see a perennial is in a picture in a catalog or on the front of a seed packet or box containing the live plant. You probably have little, if any, idea of what to expect, so here is a brief introduction to the tops in flowering perennials.

This list of plants does not include all perennials. It is only a selection of the more commonly available ones. These are the perennials that support and fill out a garden. You can obtain details on particular plants from plant societies and specialty books. Also, consult the many gardening magazines.

I include in each entry the plant's uses, height, and blooming time, to help you plant your garden, in addition to the sowing instructions, if you want to start from seed.

Achillea

Achillea millefolium (Yarrow) grows about 2 feet high. It looks best in borders and blooms from June to September. Achillea is grown also for use as a cut flower. Plant its seed in early spring or late fall in a sunny spot in your garden, spacing them 36 inches apart. The seed will germinate in seven to fourteen days. Because the seed is very small, water it with a mister. Achillea is easy to grow.

Althaea

Alcea rosea or *Althaea rosea* (Hollyhock) grows to 6 feet tall and is used for background screening, blooming from late spring to midsummer. It does best in deep, rich, well-drained soil. Plant seed anytime from spring to September in a sunny spot, spacing them about 3 feet apart. Seed germinates in ten days. You will have to stake the plants to protect them from toppling over in the wind.

Alyssum

Aurinia saxatile (Gold-dust) grows 9 to 12 inches high. It is used in rock gardens, for edging in borders, and as a cut flower. It blooms in early spring and grows well in dry or sandy soil. Plant its seed in early spring in a sunny spot, spacing them 24 inches apart. The seed will germinate in twenty-one to twenty-eight days.

Anchusa

Anchusa azurea (Alkanet) and *A. myosotidiflora* (Perennial forget-me-not—you may also find it listed under its botanical synonym, *Brunnera macrophylla*) grow 4 to 5 feet high. They are used for borders and backgrounds, as well as a source of cut flowers. Anchusa blooms in June and July. Refrigerate its seed for seventy-two hours before sowing it anytime from spring to September in a semi-shaded part of your garden. Space them 24 inches apart and be sure to shade summer plantings. The seed will germinate in twenty-one to twenty-eight days.

Anemone

Anemone pulsatilla (Windflower) grows about 12 inches high. It is grown in borders, rock gardens, and as a container plant. Anemone blooms in May and June, and is an excellent cut flower. Plant its seed in early spring or late fall in a sunny part of your garden. The seed will germinate in four days. Plant tuberous-rooted anemones in well-drained soil in September. Space both 35 to 42 inches apart and cover with straw over the winter. Anemones are not hardy north of Washington, D.C.

Anthemis

Anthemis tinctoria (Golden Marguerite) grows about 2 feet high. It looks best in borders that bloom from midsummer to frost. Anthemis is slightly aromatic and makes a wonderful cut flower. Plants can be started indoors eight weeks before planting outdoors, or you can plant seeds outdoors after the soil has warmed in the spring. Anthemis grows well in dry or sandy soil. Plant in a sunny spot, spacing the seeds 24 inches apart. They will germinate in twenty-one to twenty-eight days.

Aquilegia

Aquilegia hybrid (Columbine) grows 2 ½ to 3 feet high and is used in borders and for cut flowers, blooming in late spring or early summer. It needs fairly rich, well-drained soil. Plant the seeds anytime from spring to September in sun or partial shade, spacing them 12 to 18 inches apart. Seed germinates in about thirty days, though it can be irregular. Grown as a biennial to avoid leaf miner and rotting of the crown.

Arabis

Arabis alpina (Rock cress) grows 8 to 12 inches high. It is used for edging and in rock gardens. Arabis blooms in early spring and grows best in light shade. Plant the seed in well-drained soil anytime from spring to September. Shade summer plantings. Space plants about 12 inches apart. Seed germinates in about five days.

Armeria

Armeria alpina (Sea pink) grows 18 to 24 inches high. It is used in rock gardens, as an edging, and in borders, and the dwarf tufted plants make great cut flowers. Armeria blooms in May and June. Plant the seed in dry, sandy soil in a sunny part of your garden anytime between spring and September, spacing them 12 inches apart. Seed germinates in about ten days. Shade the seedbed until the plants are sturdy.

Artemisia

Artemisia stellerana (Wormwood, Dusty miller) grows about 2 feet high. It is used in flower beds, borders, and rock gardens. Artemisia blooms in late summer. Plant the seed in full sun from late spring to late summer, spacing them 9 to 12 inches apart. It will grow in poor and dry soils.

Aster

Aster alpinus (Hardy aster) grows 1 to 5 feet high. It is used in rock gardens, borders, and for cut flowers. Aster blooms in June. Plant the seed in early spring in a sunny spot in your garden, spacing them about 3 feet apart. Seed germinates in fourteen to twenty-one days.

Astilbe

Astilbe japonica (Spiraea) grows 1 to 3 feet high and is used in borders, blooming in a mass of color in summer. Plant its seed in early spring in rich, loamy soil, spacing them 24 inches apart. Seed germinates in fourteen to twenty-one days.

Aubrieta

Aubrieta deltoidea graeca (Rainbow rock cress), a dwarf, spreading plant that blooms in April and May, grows about 6 inches high. It is grown in borders and rock gardens and along dry walls. Plant its seed anytime from spring to September in light shade, spacing them about 12 inches apart. Seed will germinate in about twenty days. Be sure to shade new-grown plants in the summer. To propagate, divide mature plants in late summer.

Begonia

Begonia evansiana (Hardy begonia) grows 12 inches high and is used in shaded flower beds, providing handsome blooms in late summer. Plant the seed in summer in a shady, moist spot, spacing them 9 to 12 inches apart. Seed germinates in twelve days. You can propagate hardy begonia by planting the bulblets that grow in the axils (where the leaf and stem meet) of the leaves.

Bellis

Bellis perennis (English daisy) grows about 6 inches high and is used in beds, borders, and rock gardens. In cool climates, it blooms all summer; elsewhere, from early spring to late fall. Sow the seed in fall in moist, well-drained soil in partial shade, spacing them about 6 inches apart. Seed germinates in about eight days. English daisy needs plenty of water during the summer and should be protected in winter with cut branches of conifers.

Campanula

Campanula medium (Canterbury bells) grows 2 to 2½ feet high and is used in borders and for cut flowers. Sow the seed thinly, about 15 inches apart, in partial shade anytime between spring and September; do not cover the seed with soil. Seed germinates in about twenty days. Be sure to shade the seedbed in summer. Divide mature plants every other year.

Centaurea

Centaurea cyanus (Cornflower) grows about 2 feet high and is used in borders and for cut flowers, blooming from June to September. Plant the seed in early spring in a sunny spot, spacing them about 12 inches apart. Seed germinates in twenty-one to twenty-eight days. Remove the flowers as they fade (known as deadheading) to prolong the time of display.

Cerastium

Cerastium tomentosum (Snow-in-summer) grows about 6 inches high and is used in rock gardens and for ground cover. The plants form a creeping mat that blooms in May and June. Cerastium does well in dry, sunny spots. Plant the seed in early spring, spacing them about 18 inches apart. Seed germinates in fourteen to twenty-eight days. Cerastium is a hard, tough plant and a rampant grower. Do not allow it to crowd out other plants.

Cheiranthus

Cheiranthus allionii (Siberian wallflower) grows 12 to 18 inches high and is used in rock gardens and for cut flowers. It does very well in cool climates and blooms in May and June. Plant seed in a sunny spot in well-drained soil in early spring while the soil is cool. Space plants about a foot apart. Seed germinates in five days.

Chrysanthemum

Chrysanthemum maximum (Shasta daisy) grows 2 to 2½ feet high and is used in borders and for cut flowers, blooming in June and July. Plant its seed anytime from early spring to September in well-drained soil in a sunny spot, spacing them about 30 inches apart. Seed germinates in about ten days. Shasta daisy is best grown as a biennial. It is winter-killed by a wet location or a heavy winter cover.

Coreopsis

Coreopsis grandiflora (Tickseed), an excellent border plant, grows 2 to 3 feet high, blooming from May through to fall if it is regularly deadheaded. Plant the seed in a light loam in early spring or late fall in a sunny spot in your garden, spacing them about 30 inches apart. Seed takes about five days to germinate. Coreopsis is drought-resistant. Grow it as a biennial.

Delphinium

Delphinium elatum (Larkspur) grows 4 to 5 feet high and is used in borders and for cut flowers, blooming in June; if you deadhead it regularly, it will bloom twice more that season. Plant seed anytime from spring to September in a well-drained, sunny spot, protected from the wind; plants tend to rot in wet, heavy soils. Space the seeds 24 inches apart; they will germinate in about twenty days. Be sure to shade summer plantings and to stake the plants to prevent their falling over when they reach mature height. Foliage tends to mildew.

Dianthus

Dianthus barbatus (Sweet William) grows 12 to 18 inches high; a dwarf form is also available. It is used for borders, edging, and as a cut flower. Sweet William blooms in May and June. It is very hardy, but grows best in well-drained soil. Plant seeds anytime from spring to September in a sunny spot, spacing them about a foot apart. Seed germinates in five days.

D. caryophyllus (Carnation, or Clove pink; Hardy garden carnation) grows 18 to 24 inches high and is used in beds, borders, edging, pots, and rock gardens, blooming in late summer. Plant seed in late spring in a sunny spot, spacing them 12 inches apart. Seed germinates in about twenty days. Cut plants back in late fall, pot them, and hold them over winter in a coldframe.

D. deltoides (Maiden pinks) and *D. plumarius* (Cottage pinks) grow 12 inches high and are used in borders, rock gardens, as edging, and for cut flowers, blooming in May and June. Plant seed anytime from spring to September in a well-drained, sunny spot, spacing them 12 inches apart. Seed germinates in five days. Dianthus is best when grown as a biennial. It is winter-killed in a wet location and very susceptible to rotting at the soil line.

Dicentra

Dicentra spectabilis (Bleeding heart) grows 2 to 4 feet high and *D. cucullaria* (Dutchman's breeches) grows one foot tall. They are used in borders, and as container plants, and are very striking when shown off against an evergreen background. Dicentra blooms in late spring. Plant seeds in late autumn, spacing them 12 to 18 inches apart. Seed takes fifty days or longer to germinate.

Digitalis

Digitalis purpurea (Foxglove) grows 4 to 6 feet high and is used in borders and for cut flowers, blooming in June and July. Plant seed anytime from spring to September in light, well-drained soil in sun or partial shade, spacing them 12 inches apart. Seed germinates in about twenty days. You must shade summer plantings. Select—and propagate—strains that bear flowers at right angles to stem; discard those with drooping flowers.

Echinacea

Echinacea purpurea (Purple coneflower) grows 2½ to 3 feet high and is used in borders and naturalized settings and for cut flowers. It blooms midsummer to fall. Plant seeds anytime from spring to September in well-drained soil in a sunny spot, spacing them about 30 inches apart. Shade summer plantings. Seed germinates in twenty days.

Gaillardia

Gaillardia x grandiflora (Blanket flower) grows 12 to 30 inches high and is used in borders and for cut flowers, blooming from midsummer to frost. Gaillardia is easily grown from seed, which you can plant in early spring or late summer in well-drained soil in a sunny spot in your garden, spacing them 24 inches apart. Seed germinates in about twenty days.

Geum

Geum chiloense (Avens) grows 6 to 24 inches high and is used in borders and rock gardens and for cut flowers. Most geum plants bloom in June and July; some, however, bloom from May to October. Geum will grow in most types of soil and will take up to medium shade. You can plant seed in spring or summer in a sunny spot. Space plants about 18 inches apart. Seed germinates in twenty-five days. Geum is winter hardy if you give it some protection.

Gypsophila

Gypsophila paniculata (Baby's breath) grows 2 to 4 feet high and is used in borders and for cut and dried flowers. Gypsophila blooms from early summer to early autumn and does best in a deeply prepared soil that is high in lime content (alkaline). Plant seeds anytime from early spring to September in a sunny spot, spacing them about 4 feet apart. Seed germinates in about ten days.

Helianthemum

Helianthemum nummularium (Sun rose) grows about 12 inches high. Used in borders, they are evergreen, and bloom from June to September. Helianthemum will grow in dry soil. Plant seed anytime from spring to September in a spot that gets full sun all day, spacing them 12 inches apart. Seed germinates in

about fifteen days. Shade the seed bed until you're ready to transplant the seedlings.

Helleborus

Helleborus niger (Christmas rose) grows about 15 inches high and is used in borders and as a specimen plant, blooming in early spring. Plant seed in late fall or early winter in well-drained, organic soil in a sunny spot, spacing them about 24 inches apart. For spring planting, refrigerate the seeds two months before sowing. Germination can be very slow, but usually takes about thirty days. Do not disturb after planting, as helleborus does not transplant well at all. The plant will require three to four years to bloom.

Hemerocallis

Hemerocallis (Daylily) grows 1 to 4 feet high and is used in great masses in borders or placed in smaller groupings among shrubbery. To have flowering daylilies throughout the growing season, plant various species of this perennial. Plant seed in late fall or early spring in well-drained soil in full sunlight or partial shade, spacing them 24 to 30 inches apart. Seed germinates in fifteen days.

Heuchera

Heuchera sanguinea (Coralbells) grows up to 2 feet high and is used in rock gardens, borders, and as a cut flower, blooming from June to September. It grows best in soil with a high lime (alkaline) content. Plant seed in early spring or late fall in partial shade, spacing them about 18 inches apart. Seed germinates in about ten days. Propagate by division in spring.

Hibiscus

Hibiscus moscheutos and *H. oculiroseus* (Mallow rose) grow 3 to 8 feet high and are used in flower beds or as background plants, blooming from July to September. Plant seed in spring or summer, in full sun or partial shade, and in moist or dry soil. Space the seeds at least 2 feet apart; they will usually germinate in fifteen days, but may take much longer.

Iberis

Iberis (Candytuft) grows about 10 inches high and is used in rock gardens and for edging and ground cover, blooming in late spring. Candytuft does well in dry places. Plant seed in early spring or late fall in a sunny spot, spacing them about a foot apart. Seed germinates in twenty days. Deadhead (snip off) the flowers as they fade to promote fullness.

Iris

German, Japanese, Siberian, and dwarf iris are the most commonly grown types. They grow from 3 inches to 2½ feet high and are used in borders and as cut flowers. Planting a variety of iris will insure you flowers throughout spring and summer. Plant their bulbs or rhizomes in well-drained soil in a spot that gets full sun in late fall, spacing them 18 to 24 inches apart. They germinate the following spring.

Kniphofia

Kniphofia (Tritoma) and *K. uvaria* (Red-hot poker) grow 3 to 4 feet high. They are used in borders and as a cut flower, blooming from August to October. Plant seeds in early spring or late fall in well-drained soil in a sunny spot, spacing them about 18 inches apart. Seed germinates in twenty days. In northern climates, dig and store roots over the winter.

Lathyrus

Lathyrus odoratus (Sweet pea) grows 5 to 6 feet high. It is used as a background vine, trained onto a fence or trellis, or used as a cut flower. Sweet pea blooms June to September and will succeed almost anywhere without care. Plant seeds in early spring in a sunny spot, spacing them about 2 feet apart. Seed germinates in twenty days.

Liatris

Liatris pycnostachya (Gayfeather) grows 2 to 6 feet high and is used in borders and for cut flowers, blooming from summer to early autumn. Liatris is easily started from seed; plant its seed in well-drained soil in early spring or late fall in a sunny spot, spacing them about 18 inches apart. They will germinate in twenty days. You can propagate new plants by cutting its thick, fleshy roots into pieces and planting them.

Limonium

Limonium latifolium (Sea lavender, Perennial blue statice) grows 2 to 3 feet high and is used for bedding and as a cut and dried flower. Sea lavender blooms in July and August. Plant seed in a sunny spot in well-drained soil in early spring while the soil is cool. Space them about 30 inches apart. Seed germinates in fifteen days.

Linum

Linum perenne (Flax) grows about 2 feet high. It is used for bedding and in rock gardens. Linum blooms through the summer. You can plant seeds anytime from spring to September in a sunny spot, spacing them 18 inches apart. You will need to shade summer plantings. Seed germinates in about twenty-five days.

Lunaria

Lunaria annua (Money plant or Honesty) grows about 4 feet high and is used in cutting gardens as a source of seedpods for use in everlasting bouquets. Lunaria blooms in summer and is easy to grow. Plant seeds in early spring in a sunny spot, spacing them about 2 feet apart. Seed germinates in ten days.

Lupinus

Lupinus polyphyllus (Lupine) grows about 3 feet high and is used in borders and for cut flowers, blooming in summer. Soak its seeds in water for twenty-four hours in the refrigerator before planting and inoculate them with legume aid. Plant them in early spring or late fall in a sunny spot that has perfect drainage, spacing them about 36 inches apart. Plant the seed where the lupines are to flower, as they do not transplant well. Seed germinates in about twenty days.

Lythrum

Lythrum (Loosestrife) grows 4 to 6 feet high, blooming in July and August. Use lythrum scattered in gardens and yards or among trees and shrubs. Plant seed in late fall or early spring in a moist, lightly shaded area, spacing them 18 to 24 inches apart. Seed germinates in fifteen days.

Monarda

Monarda didyma and *M. fistulosa* (Bergamot, Bee balm, Horsemint) grow 2 to 3 feet high. They are used in borders and massed for color. Monarda blooms all summer. Plant its seeds in spring or summer in a spot that gets full sun to medium shade, spacing them 12 to 18 inches apart. Seed germinates in fifteen days. If you cut the plants back after flowering, they will bloom again the same season.

Paeonia

Paeonia (Peony) grow 2 to 4 feet tall. They are used in borders and for cut flowers, blooming in late spring and early summer. They are difficult to grow from seed; plant tubers in late fall at least 3 feet apart and 2 to 3 inches deep.

Papaver

Papaver nudicaule (Iceland poppy) grows 15 to 18 inches high, while the *P. orientale* (Oriental poppy) grows 3 feet high. Both are used in borders and for cut flowers, blooming in the summer. Plant seeds in early spring in their permanent location; poppies do not transplant well. Choose a sunny spot and space the seeds 2 feet apart. Seed germinates in about ten days.

Penstemon

Penstemon Murrayanus (Beard-tongue) grows 1½ to 2 feet high and is used in borders and for cut flowers. If planted as soon as the soil is workable, penstemon will bloom all summer long. It grows best in well-drained soil and does well in rather dry soil. Plant seeds in early spring or late fall in a sunny spot that is sheltered in winter, spacing them 18 inches apart. Seed germinates in about ten days.

Phlox

Phlox paniculata (Summer, or garden, phlox) grows to about 3 feet high and is used in borders and for cut flowers, blooming in early summer. Plant seeds in late fall or early winter in a sunny spot, spacing them about 2 feet apart. The seed must be kept in the refrigerator for one month before sowing. Keep soil moist. Germination takes about twenty-five days but can be very irregular. Plants grown from seed will vary greatly in color and form.

Phlox subulata (Moss, or mountain, phlox) grows 4 to 5 inches high, is drought-resistant, and is used in borders and as edging, blooming in the spring. *P. subulata* is normally grown from stolons, planted in a sunny spot and spaced about 8 inches apart.

Physalis

Physalis alkekengi (Chinese lantern) grows about 2 feet high and is used in borders and as a specimen plant. The "lantern" is borne the second year, in September and October; it dries well and will keep nicely for several weeks in a winter bouquet. Plant seed in late fall or early winter in a sunny spot, spacing them about 3 feet apart. You can plant Chinese lanterns in the spring if you keep the seed in the refrigerator over the winter (the seeds need the cold to germinate). Seed germinates in about fifteen days.

Platycodon

Platycodon grandiflorus (Balloon flower) grows about 2 feet high and is used in borders and for cut flowers, blooming from spring until frost. Plant seeds anytime between spring and September in a sunny spot, spacing them about 12 inches apart. Seed germinates in ten days. In the fall, dig up the roots and store in moist sand in a cool (but frost-free) cold-frame. Replant them in early spring.

Primula

Primula x polyantha (Primrose) grows 6 to 9 inches high, while *P. veris* (Cowslip) grows 6 inches high; both are used in rock gardens and bloom in April and May. In early spring pot up some soil and sow its seeds on the soil's surface. Then, water it with a mister, cover the pot with glass, and place it outside to freeze; once it has done so, bring it inside to germinate. Seeds also can be planted outside in the spring if they are first frozen in ice cubes. Usually the seeds are planted in late autumn or early winter. Choose a spot in partial shade and plant the seeds about a foot apart. They will germinate in about twenty-five days, but can be very irregular.

Pyrethrum

Pyrethrum roseum, also known by its botanical synonym, *Chrysanthemum coccineum* (Painted daisy), grows about 2 feet high and is used in borders and for cut flowers, blooming in May and June. Plant seeds anytime from spring to September in a sunny spot, spacing them about 18 inches apart. Seed germinates in twenty days. If grown in wet soil, pyrethrum will be winter-killed.

Salvia

Salvia azurea grandiflora (Blue salvia) and *S. farinacea* (Mealy cup) grow 3 to 4 feet tall, blooming from August until frost. Use salvia in borders. Plant seeds in spring in a sunny spot, spacing them 18 to 24 inches apart. Seed germinates in fifteen days.

Stokesia

Stokesia laevis (Stokes' aster) grows 15 inches high and is used for borders and cut flowers. If planted as soon as the soil is workable, it will bloom its first season—in September. Plant seeds in a sunny spot anytime from spring to September, spacing them 18 inches apart. Be sure to shade summer plantings. Seed germinates in about twenty days.

Trollius

Used in borders, *Trollius ledebourii* (Globe-flower) grows about 20 inches high and blooms from May to July. Trollius requires a lot of moisture, so water regularly. Plant seeds in late fall in well-drained soil. If you want to plant in early spring, you must soak the seeds in hot water for thirty minutes before sowing. Sow the seeds about a foot apart. They will germinate in fifty or more days.

Veronica

Veronica spicata (Speedwell) grows about 18 inches high and is used in borders and rock gardens and as a cut flower, blooming in June and July. Veronica grows easily. Plant seeds anytime from spring to September in well-drained soil in a sunny spot, spacing them 18 inches apart. Seed germinates in about fifteen days.

Viola

Viola cornuta (Tufted, or horned, violet) grows about 6 inches high and is used for bedding, edging, and in window boxes, blooming all summer if you deadhead it regularly. *V. cornuta* is easily grown from seed and is very hardy. Plant seeds anytime from spring to September in well-drained soil in partial shade, spacing them about 12 inches apart. Seed germinates in ten days.

Viola x wittrockiana

I always think of pansies as the little old men of the garden. They remind me of Snow White's seven friendly dwarfs. They often seem to have angry little faces, grimacing in disapproval at the rest of the flowers. But these grumpy little men are just hiding their soft hearts and waiting for a friendly word. Tell them how nice they are, and just watch what brilliant colors they will display for you!

Pansies do best in rich, well-drained soil. So, before you plant the seeds, add manure, peat moss, or a 5-10-5 commercial fertilizer to the soil. If the soil is exceptionally heavy, dig in some sand. Spade the soil to a depth of 6 to 8 inches. Make sure it is fine and free of lumps, stones, and other coarse materials.

If you plant seed in containers, select boxes 9 to 12 inches deep, and fill them with rich, sandy, loamy soil. Broadcast the seed or sow them in rows.

If you plant in open beds, sow seeds in rows about 4 to 6 inches apart in a spot that gets full sun to light shade. This will make it easier for you to identify the seedlings when they emerge, and it permits you to cultivate and weed more readily.

Whether you plant indoors or out, in frames or in open beds, water the seedbed first. Then, when the water has drained away, sow the seeds thinly. Cover the seeds with only ⅛ inch of soil or coarse washed sand, and press down with a flat board. Water the bed again, but don't wash the seeds away. If possible, use the mister. Pansy seeds are very tiny.

Plastic film, aluminum foil, or a piece of

moist burlap placed on the seedbed will help keep moisture in. Remove this as soon as the seeds begin to sprout (in about five to eight days). Shade the seedlings with a canopy for a few days until they develop their first true leaves. The canopy (an inexpensive, make-shift one will do) should be arranged a foot or two above the bed to let the air circulate.

Water lightly every morning. Seedlings should be neither too dry nor too wet. If the seed dries out after it begins to sprout, it will die; but if you keep it too moist, it may rot.

After the seedlings have emerged, thin them to an inch or more apart. Use care in removing the extras so that you will disturb the roots of those that remain as little as possi-ble. Replant the seedlings you remove in an-other prepared bed.

The planting procedure for seedlings you buy is about the same as for seedlings you have grown yourself. When you bring them home, sprinkle them with water and let them stand a little while to restore lost moisture before planting. When planting, carefully separate and spread the roots. Press the soil firmly around the plants so that good contact will be made with the roots, but don't press the soil so tightly that it will harden and cake when dry.

Where summers are hot and dry, it is best to start with new seedlings each year. In fa-vorable climates, zones 6 to 8, you may prop-agate your own pansies by dividing old plants.

THE FOLIAGE PERENNIALS ARE PERSISTENT AND ACCOUNTED FOR

Having introduced you to the flowering perennials, now let me tell you about the best of the bunch. Even though it flowers and in the early days of popular home gardening it was called the shade lilies, the hosta is known for its size, shape, and the luxuriant color and growth of its foliage; it can make a complete garden by itself. Here is what my favorite supplier of hostas, Wayside Gardens, says: "Hostas, sometimes called shade lilies, are the most important and versatile of all foliage perennials." Long favorites of the Japanese, who have bred them for centuries, hostas are now taking their rightful place in America's better gardens. And American breeding leads the world—connoisseurs in England and Europe would give their eyeteeth for some of these varieties!

"For sun, partial shade, or full shade; for ground cover, edging, mid-border, back-ground or specimen planting, you'll find a variety of hostas to suit your needs. Hostas provide long-season landscape interest; their foliage delights flower arrangers.

"Hostas will flourish under a wide range of light conditions, with those on the blue side coloring best in deeper shade, while the yel-lows prefer more sun ($\frac{1}{4}$ shade). Their main requirements are ample moisture and a soil well fortified with organic matter. They are virtually free of insect pests and disease. Hostas may require a couple of years to establish themselves before they show their beauty to the fullest; after that, they get better and better with the years.''

Listed below are the top hostas offered today in the United States. All of them are hardy in zones 3–10.

'GOLD MEDALLION.' A selected clone of H. tokudama 'Golden', with round, cupped, puckered golden leaves that hold their brilliant color all season. An exceptionally heavy producer of white flowers in early summer. Grow in ¼ to ¾ sun.

'INVINCIBLE.' A fine Paul Aden introduction, with exceptionally shiny bright green, light-tolerant foliage. Grows less than 10 inches tall—a fine ground cover, with light lavender fragrant flowers in midsummer. Grow in shade to ¾ sun.

'HALCYON.' This is considered by many to be the best of all the introductions by the late Eric Smith of England, famed for his blue hostas. Its chalky blue leaves form a medium-sized clump. Abundant soft blue flowers in June. Shade to ½ sun.

H. VENTRICOSA 'AUREA-MARGINATA.' Its large, heart-shaped, green leaves are accentuated by broad, irregular margins of yellow to white. A splendid ground cover, it produces mauve flowers in midsummer. Best in full shade to ¾ sun.

'TRUE BLUE.' Many experts consider this the best of all blue hostas. It is a large plant, excellent in the back of a border where it will form a large, flaring mound. The leaves are heavily textured and will readily withstand sun. Its flowers are orchid, edged in white, a very unusual combination, and are produced in June. Best in ¼ to ¾ sun.

'BIG DADDY.' Deep blue puckered leaves on fast-growing plants, perfect for the back of the border or for architectural use in the landscape. It produces white flowers in early summer. Grows well in shade to half-shade.

'CELEBRATION.' A rapid grower, with lance-shaped leaves of cream with striking green margins, this is among the earliest hostas to leaf out. It produces late summer flowers of delicate lavender. Good for rock gardens or as a ground cover. Full shade to ¾ sun.

'SHOGUN.' This vigorous grower matures to a height of 18 inches and a width of 30 inches. Its bold, wide, white-leaf margins provide outstanding contrast—a very choice and much-sought-after variety.

'SEA SPRITE.' Excellent for the front of the border, this rapid grower has wavy yellow to cream leaves outlined in green. It bears pale orchid flowers in midsummer. Shade to ¾ sun.

'JANET.' This chameleonlike plant often varies from chartreuse to yellow to white, offset with green margins. In our shady garden, it remained a striking combination of yellow and white all summer—a truly magnificent sight! It produces delicate lavender flowers in June. Shade to ¾ sun.

'WIDE BRIM.' Truly a magnificent specimen plant, with blue-green leaves with very wide, irregular margins of cream tinted with gold at maturity. This is a fast grower that is a favorite with flower arrangers. It produces soft lavender flowers in midsummer. Best in full shade to ¾ sun.

'SEA DRIFT.' Truly different and delightful, this variety has leaves so ruffled they give a piecrust effect. It produces lavender-pink flowers in June. Grow in shade to ¾ sun.

'ON STAGE.' An extremely rare and choice introduction from Japan by Paul Aden, who managed to secure one of the only two existing plants from a temple garden, this rapidly growing variety has large yellow leaves with attractive irregular green margins. Soft lavender blooms appear early in the season. A truly imposing collector's gem, virtually impossible to obtain, but well worth the effort.

'SAMURAI.' A handsome plant with blue-green leaves with wide, irregular yellow margins. White flowers adorn it early in the summer. Excellent for background plantings; does best in full shade to ¾ sun.

'SHINING TOT.' A lovely dwarf, mound-shaped plant with lustrous deep green leaves and lilac flowers in midsummer. Very vigorous; thrives in shade to ¾ sun.

'FRAGRANT GOLD.' A new introduction from Paul Aden that produces extremely fragrant lavender flowers in mid-August. The foliage is golden with prominent ribs; it flourishes in shade to ¾ sun.

'DAYBREAK.' An impressive specimen type from Paul Aden, with deep gold leaves emphasized by prominent textured veins. The leaves are extremely heavy to withstand adverse weather. Shade to ½ sun.

4

The Bulb Group
Dutch Dandies

When you say "bulbs" to a knowledgeable gardener, it's like opening Pandora's box because we lump the corms, tubers, true bulbs, and bulblike plants all together.

As I begin this chapter, I wonder to myself if this just might be the biggest and most important one of the book. And where do I begin? Most of you are familiar with the spring-flowering bulbs from Holland, and many of you receive at least one catalog from one of the main sources that offer them by mail. If you don't, check the appendix for addresses and send away for a few. These catalogs will give you an idea of the wide range of colors, shapes, heights, and bloom times that are available to you. You can plan a bulb garden that will bloom from the late days of winter in the north, when the snow is still on the ground, throughout the summer, fall and, in some instances, into the early winter. In the warmer climates you can have flowers virtually all year round. Don't ever get the idea that flower gardening is limited to the lazy, hazy days of summer—not when there are bulbs to be had.

ALL BULBS AREN'T BULBS

My first step to a lifelong love affair with bulbs was discovering that everything that looks like a bulb and acts like a bulb isn't necessarily one. Only about half the 3,000 types of plants ordinarily called bulbs are true bulbs. The others are corms, tubers, tuberous roots, or rhizomes.

All 3,000 types are alike in one way, though. During the growing season, they all gather food from their foliage and store it in their built-in underground pantry for future use when it's once again time to wake up and grow.

Only an awfully mean person would risk putting his plants to sleep permanently by treating every type alike. Go ahead and call all of them "bulbs" until you're alone with them. Then let your hair down and call each by its own first name. Think about your own family. There's moody Aunt Molly, sensitive Uncle Arthur, and good-time Cousin Charlie.

The hardy bulbs, like daffodils and crocuses, can remain in the ground many years with a minimum of care. Half-hardy bulbs, including the summer hyacinth and bulbous irises, make excellent cut flowers, but they insist on protective winter mulching and a little extra attention. The tender bulbs, like dahlias and cannas, enjoy the outdoor life only until cold weather sets in, when, like the birds, they need to head for other winter quarters. Since they can't go south, you'll have to take them indoors.

What's in this for you? You'll be tickled pink and red and orange and white and a lot of other colors when your plants start blooming. You'll be glad you didn't spare the TLC when you're rewarded with an array of colorful smiles.

When you realize that a small but perfect plant is inside each dead-looking bulb, you'll understand why you can't treat your bulbs roughly. Never carelessly drop a bulb into the bottom of a shopping bag—bruised bulbs seldom recover. Neither will bulbs with mushy, gray spots on them. They're not worth carting home, so if you find some at your local garden center, just let them die in peace where they are, not in your plant bed. If you buy pre-packaged bulbs and find some of them mushy, take them back and demand a refund or exchange.

It's while the bulb is dried out, in its dormant stage, that bulb dealers ship them all over the world. The bulbs might look dead, but they're very much alive and living off their built-in food supply.

No healthy bulb can go to sleep on an empty stomach and not wake up several months later feeling anemic. If you want your bulbs to wake up feeling lively and ready to grow, you'll have to make sure they're well fed and healthy before they settle down for their long winter's nap. You must take proper care of the foliage. No bulb can develop normally or produce beautiful flowers unless the foliage is protected and allowed to die a natural death. A natural death, according to all the bulb coroners I've ever known, does not mean chopping off the leaves as soon as the flowers die. If you are ungrateful enough to murder a bulb's foliage (which I admit is not very attractive) after it's gone all-out to produce a beautiful display of flowers for you, then you deserve what you're going to get—and that's no flowers at all the next year! By destroying the bulb's foliage, you're destroying its only source of food and literally starving it to death.

Here is a brief description of the make-up of each group.

True Bulbs

In each true bulb, there is a perfect miniature of the mature plant that will ultimately blossom. At the bottom of each, you'll find a basal plate which really holds the bud and the storage tissue (layers or scales) together. It's from this plate that new roots develop. If you'll inspect the inside of a cut-open tulip bulb carefully, you'll see a dark spot near the bottom. That's the new bulb, or offset, already forming.

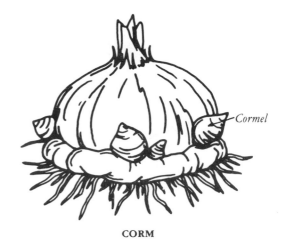

Cormel

CORM

Offset

BULB

Corms

The solid, starchy corm does not have layered scales like the true bulb, but it does have a basal plate from which roots develop. At the risk of hurting its feelings, I must point out that the corm is a greedy little fellow who eats himself up every growing season. What starts

out as a swollen, firm stem is only a shriveled shadow of its former self by the end of the growing season. Unlike the true bulb, the corm doesn't have an embryonic flower in its center, but it does have one or more growing points from which the plant develops.

As the plant grows, the corm shrivels—but don't think it's done for! After the plant blooms, it gets busy building a new corm on top of the old basal plate. Baby corms, called cormels, grow around or on top of the old corm, too. The cormels will take two or three years to bloom, but the new corm will produce for you the following season.

Corms come in all different shapes and sizes. Some are rounded like the crocus, but others are flat at the top like the gladiolus.

Tubers

A tuber is a rough hombre, partner! It's different from the true bulb and corm in that it has no dry outer leaves and no basal plate. If you're judging a beauty contest, a tuber is not your number, at least not in the bulb stage—but it makes up for lost time when it blooms. Few flowers can equal the tuberous begonia for beauty and grace, and it has very humble origins. The begonia tuber looks like a miniature version of the Creature That Ate Chicago.

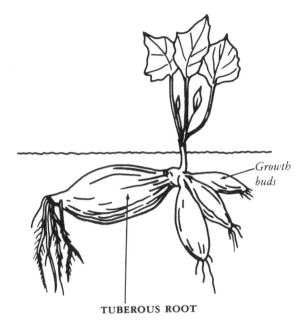

TUBEROUS ROOT

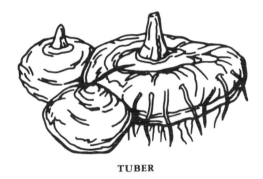

TUBER

The tuber has a tough, lumpy skin. The lumps are actually buds, or "eyes," from which roots and shoots will develop. Tubers are usually fat. Some, like the potato, lose weight as the plant grows; others, like the tuberous begonia, get even fatter. More new tubers are produced every year, and if you're feeling greedy, you can cut a tuber into pieces (just make sure each piece contains at least one eye), and plant each one.

Tuberous Roots

Will the real root please stand up? To tell the truth, tuberous roots are the only true root in the bulb family. Growth buds don't form on the tuberous root itself, as they do on the tubers, but grow on the root's neck or crown. It depends on its fingery root system to draw food from the surrounding soil.

The dahlia is the most famous member of the tuberous root family, and rightly so. It comes in every hue except blue and will grow anywhere in the United States and Canada—as long as its toes don't get frostbitten.

The glory lily, another tuberous root that, like the dahlia, has to be taken indoors for the winter, makes an excellent potted plant. The glory lily's outrageously beautiful blooms will brighten up anybody's patio or front porch.

Rhizomes

The rhizome is an underground stem that creeps along just beneath the surface of the soil. Every now and then, it sends up a stem. I think it does so for the same reasons submarines send up periscopes, to take a look around. There are little buds on the sides and tops of the rhizomes, and it's from these that the plants grow. The roots grow from the bottom of the rhizome.

Pip

RHIZOME

The lily of the valley and some of the other rhizomes send up very small stems with their own roots—these are called pips.

THE BLOOM CALENDAR

If you ever wonder where the flowers "is," you'll find the bulb bunch up long before the grass has "riz." I just cannot say enough in praise of the whole bulb group, and their ability to blend into any gardenscape, from late winter in the North and early winter in the South and West well into the fall, with their blooms of beauty.

No matter what your preference is, every season is bound to offer something that's just your cup of tea. Take a good look at a listing of available bulbs and you'll discover colors that you never dreamed of finding in the flower world. And range of sizes, too. Just take the versatile dahlia, for example—its blooms, depending on the variety, vary from less than an inch across to more than a foot wide.

Every season has its special treats to offer, and if you look through a few catalogs, you'll have to admit that there's something in the bulb world for everybody. Even when the outdoor bulbous plants stop blooming, you can cultivate bulbs indoors and replace winter's dullness with a splash of color.

Maybe, just maybe, I can show you skeptics who have always thought bulbs were for parks and pictures that they will fit into your little corner of the world. Here is a preview, season by season.

Spring Bulb Festival

The snowdrop, winter aconite, and crocus all try to beat the groundhog up every spring. Soon afterwards, you can look for daffodils, chionodoxa, grape hyacinths, early tulips, and narcissus. As these begin to fade, the late tulips, including the show-off parrot tulips and quaint cottage tulips, will start brightening your landscape, along with hyacinths, anemones, and still more daffodils.

You'll have to start to work in autumn and winter to prepare for your spring festival. From the Atlantic to the Pacific, spring-flowering bulbs will grow if planted at the proper time. The crocus, scilla, and snowdrop—the little bulbs—should be planted as soon as they are available from suppliers in snow country. Early December is a good time to plant in the South and West. Tulips, however, are ready for bed when they feel the first chilly breezes of fall. Rome wasn't built in a day, and neither will you grow a tulip in a day. Plant early in the fall to be sure of strong root growth. I always try to have all my fall-planted bulbs in the ground a month before the ground freezes.

As soon as you drop them into well-prepared soil, true bulbs and corms begin to release their pent-up energy. Roots and stems start to develop from the embryonic flower inside the bulb. Then, just out of sight beneath the surface of the soil, the bulb waits like a lunar rocket ready for lift-off. The moment the temperature starts to climb upward, the bulb begins its countdown. When all systems are "go," it blasts its way through the ground and continues its upward thrust. In a few days it will accomplish its primary mission. A bud will explode into bloom for you to enjoy.

Choosing bulbs to celebrate spring with you is no easy task. Daffodils come in eleven categories alone! Crocuses, hyacinths, and tulips can't be neglected. I always grow lots of these old favorites—they're dependable and colorful.

But don't limit yourself to the old favorites. Why not surprise your neighbor next spring by including some of the lesser-known bulbs such as chionodoxa or snowdrop? If you really want to make his eyes pop out with envy, plant some anemones and ranunculuses.

If you want to spice up your spring bouquets, try allium, a beautiful and sophisticated member of the onion family. When you first cut the stem of the allium, hold your nose. It smells like its humble relatives (onions and garlic), but this odor will disappear once the stem is in water. In spite of the scent, alliums make excellent cut flowers—they come in many colors and last a surprisingly long time. They're also lovely in a planting of other bulbs. A friend once said they looked like balloons floating above the rest of the flowers.

There are lots of other guests you can invite to your spring festival, including dwarf irises, ixias, stars-of-Bethlehem, and fawn lilies. But if you really want something different, let me give you a tip. The checkered fritillary is the court jester of the bulb kingdom, and he'll really put on a show in your garden. The small, bell-shaped blossoms are purple and white checked.

Summer Flowering Carnival

Spring can't last forever, and neither can your spring bulbs. You won't have much time to mourn their demise, though. Your summer will burst into bloom before you've had time to shed a tear if you've planned your garden wisely.

Like your mother-in-law's annual visit, you can expect your hardy lilies back summer after summer. Most of them are hybrids, bred to withstand extreme weather conditions. For June through August blooms, choose the varieties carefully and plant in the fall or early spring. For example, you might choose coral lilies and star lilies for an early-summer show; meadow lilies for midsummer; and Japanese goldband lilies for the last days of summer. Other groupings work just as well, of course.

Dahlias, long the darlings of summer-flower lovers, will stay in bloom from July until Jack Frost nips at your windowpane. And keep on cutting those blooms the whole time! You can't overcut dahlias. One plant is capable of bearing between fifty and one hundred blossoms a season. That's a lot of bouquets! The dahlias you grow today aren't like your grandmother's—they've been improved, thanks to the horticulturists, so the stems are stronger. You're less apt to have your dahlias act tipsy because their weight is too much for their stems.

I want to introduce you to another fine summer porch plant—the caladium. You've probably met him already. This is a fancy-leaved plant that seems determined to shame the rainbow with its display of colors. You can pot the tubers or start them inside about March, then plant them outdoors when it warms up. I have experimented with leaving the tubers in the ground after the weather turned cold, but they rotted. I haven't made that mistake twice, and you shouldn't make it at all. Let your caladiums spend their winters indoors.

While you're planning for summer, don't neglect some of the other sun lovers, such as gloriosa lilies, cannas, hardy amaryllises, calla lilies, and tuberoses.

Gladioluses are one of the hardiest summer-flowering bulbs and one of the most popular. If you're growing them to exhibit—either in a show or in your home—you want straight flower stems with no spaces between the individual blossoms. My judge friends also tell me that they look for flowers with uniform color and no faulty streaks or thinned out spots. You should hope for an equal number of open flowers, buds, and closed flowers on each stalk. Look at your glads and you might have some winners.

In general, you should plant gladiolus corms as soon as all danger of late spring frosts is over. Cormels (small, developing corms) may be planted earlier. In any climate, the planting ought to be staggered so that all the flowers don't bloom at once. Wherever you live, you will have a tremendous range of colors and sizes to choose from in the glad world. If you can't find room for all you want in your yard, plant a row for cutting in your vegetable garden.

Do you have a front porch, a patio, or a deck? If you're like most of us, you probably don't use it very often. Tuberous begonias may help you with that problem. Plant some in pots or hanging baskets and arrange them attractively on your porch. You might add a few ferns, too. If all those beautiful, lush blossoms and the cool, green foliage don't lure your family away from the television set on a warm summer evening, nothing will!

Fall Bulbs

The last rays of summer don't have to leave you flowerless. Dahlias bloom until frost, remember, and some bulbous flowers hold their flowering display until fall.

Fall-blooming crocuses will brighten up your rock garden until the last leaf falls. When the crocuses stop blooming, you can leave them in their warm bed and cover them with a warm blanket of mulch. In spite of their small size and fragile-looking flowers, they're really tough little guys that don't bat an eye at icy winds and freezing temperatures.

Dahlias, however, don't dally in the frost. They want to be out of the elements before old Jack's premier performance.

The colchicum, alias the meadow saffron, can be planted in August to bloom in late fall. The pale lilac blooms are always a surprise when they pop up from the ground with scarcely a leaf to protect them from the cold.

Cannas are good choices for the canny garden planner. They keep blooming all through the summer and don't slow down for fall.

Cyclamens are a lot like the proverbial bad penny that keeps turning up, but you'll be glad that they do. You can find some in bloom in almost every month of the year. Indoors, the florists' cyclamen thrives in the coldest months. The fall-flowering cyclamens include the Neapolitan and European species. The former is known for its white or rose-colored blooms and unusual silvery leaves, while the latter has fragrant, crimson blossoms. These plants always remind me of a cloud of butterflies hovering over the grass when they flower. I wouldn't be a bit surprised to see a near-sighted collector sneaking up on them with a butterfly net one bright autumn day.

If you really want to work a little autumn magic, plant one or more bulbs from the *Lycoris* family. The foliage appears in spring, then dies down—but don't turn up your nose yet. In the last sweltering days of summer, a bud will stick its nose above the ground. You probably won't notice it. Then one day when you come home from another day at the office and are all ready to snarl at your family about the traffic, you'll see it—a 2-foot-tall stalk topped with gorgeous blossoms. And that, my friend, is why they call one species of *Lycoris* the "magic lily." The blossoms can be red, yellow or pink, depending on the species you choose, and most are trumpet-shaped. The spider lily (*Hymenocallis*), however, has a delicate, graceful blossom surrounded by long curving stamens.

Winter Bulb Parade

If you live in a frost-free climate, you can enjoy the amaryllis outdoors all year long, as well as the white-cupped tarzetta narcissus. If you're not so lucky, you can still enjoy them—both can be forced in any climate.

Don't be greedy, though, and bring all your spring-flowering bulbs indoors at once. Space them out so you can enjoy a succession of blooms.

If you, like me, can't stand to be shut up all

winter, you'd better think about some plants to enjoy outdoors, too, unless you don't mind carrying a potted tulip with you on your walks. Snowdrops will bloom before winter is over. I've often seen them nodding their pretty little heads over a blanket of snow. If the snow is very deep, you may not see these early birds at all.

YOU CAN FOOL BULBS INTO BLOOM

You don't have to be a Houdini to force spring bulbs to grow indoors, but you do have to be pretty good at faking. Bulbs have to think it's time to go to sleep, so you'll need to regulate the inside temperature just as Mother Nature does outdoors. Cold is essential to bulb development; bulbs need a resting, or "dormant," period. Afterward, you can give them an artificial "wake-up" call by putting them in sunlight or artificial fluorescent light.

I try to be the first one in line in the late summer and early fall to buy my bulbs for indoor planting. That way I'm sure to get the healthiest, largest bulbs available, even if it means bribing my garden dealer with a slice or two of homemade cake. I rush home and plant my bulbs as soon as possible, but if something prevents immediate planting, I store them at 60°F. until I can put them to bed in their pots.

I use a good house plant potting soil mixed with perlite or vermiculite. Some people add a bit of garden loam to the soil.

Plug up the drain hole in the pot (plastic or clay, whichever you prefer) before adding the soil. Half fill the pot, then gently place the bulb on top of the soil. Continue filling the pot and firming the soil in place. Leave about an inch between the soil and the top of the pot to make watering easier. Hyacinths grow best alone, but several daffodils can live very comfortably together in one large pot. You can even put two layers of daffodils in the same pot if it's deep enough and if you arrange the bulbs so they won't get in one another's way when they're growing. The reason for double layering is obvious—you'll get a fuller pot of blossoms the next spring.

Always make sure your bulbs have breathing room. Leave from one-half to one-fourth of each bulb out of the soil.

Drench the soil thoroughly after you're through planting. You know how thirsty you are after a day's hard work. Well, bulbs undergo a tremendous upheaval at planting time, so they need a long, cool drink. Besides that, their hardest work is just ahead.

Gather up some of those old newspapers you've been saving and wrap the whole pot in newsprint. I bury mine six to eight inches deep in my garden and mark the spot with bamboo shoots, but some of my friends store their pots in their garage; if you park your pots there, keep them in the dark, damp, and between 40° and 50°F. for ten weeks.

Your wife (or husband) will thank you profusely when you dig up your planted pots after ten weeks because you'll be able to discard the dirty newspaper and reveal clean pots. Put the pots in your basement or in a dimly lighted room that's not warmer than 65°. When the foliage is about 3 inches high, place the plants in direct sunlight and keep them moist. The blossoms should appear soon.

As soon as they do, take the plant out of direct sunlight, as the blossoms will last longer. Keep them in a cool place; turning back the thermostat at night suits the plants fine. With proper care, you can expect your blooms to last about ten days. When the last blooms shrivel, cut back the flower stem and set the plants in a cool, sunny place. Do not cut back the foliage. Gradually water the plant less and less. When the leaves finally wither, let the soil dry completely. I then store my pot, bulb and all, in a dry, airy place until the next time around.

Amaryllis the Queen

If you're easily addicted to things, you'd better not start growing amaryllises *(Hippeastrum)* indoors. They'll grow on you, and before you know it, you'll have pots and pots of them all over your house. No flower surpasses the amaryllis in beauty, and what house couldn't use a little cheer when the kids have been snowed in from school for a week and the television set is on the blink?

Use a good potting soil for amaryllises, as well as for most other spring-flowering bulbs. If you begin with a good, rich soil you can expect to have a healthy plant for several years. You can buy packaged potting soil or you can mix garden loam, peat moss, and perlite or vermiculite in equal parts to make your own. (I usually use the packaged soil because it's convenient and disease-free.) If you have any fertilizer (preferably 5-10-5) left over from your garden, stir a little into the potting soil before planting but don't go overboard—a teaspoonful to a 6-inch pot is plenty. I would suggest that further fertilizing be done with a liquid brand but don't use it more than once a month and then sparingly, 10 percent of the recommended amount.

For amaryllis you can use a plastic or a clay pot. I like some of the new bright-colored plastic ones and, of course, you can still buy beautiful ceramic pots and jardinieres as well as the old standbys—unglazed red clay pots. Unglazed pots ought to be soaked overnight or they will deprive your plants of much-needed water by drinking it themselves. If you use hand-me-down pots, clean them thoroughly with soap and hot water so your amaryllis bulbs won't catch any leftover germs.

I like to pot my amaryllis around September or October, but I've known people who potted them right on up to spring with success. They like to crowd a pot with their large bulbs and roots, so don't give them too much extra room. Set the bulb in place, spreading the roots carefully. Then add a little potting mix and gently pack it around the bulb, making sure the bulb is centered in the pot. Keep filling and firming until one-third of the bulb is above the soil. (Amaryllises like to keep their noses clean and well above the soil level.) Pat down the soil around the bulb and water generously. Don't water again until growth begins.

I like to place my amaryllis in a warm, visible place so I can watch its progress. It shouldn't be placed in bright sun, though, until growth begins. I imagine you'll have at least a month's wait from planting time to blossoming time, but you'll think it's worth it when you see the glorious blooms.

Don't plant your amaryllis in a pot that drains too freely. If you can't beg, borrow, or buy a pot without a drainage hole, plug the hole up with a piece of broken pottery or a bottle cap. If you're used to watering your house plants and letting the excess water drain into the bottom dish and onto your coffee table, you'll have to learn some self-control. Overwatering is one of the fatal mistakes of amaryllis growers, as too much water will cause the plant to fail to bloom.

The other mistake that Amy Amaryllis won't forgive you for is exposing her bulb to the cold. Temperatures below freezing are enough to make her give you a cold shoulder—and she'll certainly refuse to bloom. Here again, you've got to have heart and consider the feelings of your plants. I'm sure, though, that once you're in love with Amy, you'll always be in love with Amy—Amaryllis, that is.

After the flowers die, cut the stems down to 2 inches, leave the pot in direct sunlight, and continue to water and feed the plant. You need to allow it to build up an adequate food supply for next year's bloom. When summer comes, you can set it outside, pot and all. Feed it regularly until August or September, then stop feeding but keep on watering moderately. When the leaves have dried out, stop watering the plant altogether. Let the soil dry out thoroughly and just before frost, move it, pot and all, to a dry, well-ventilated place kept at 60°-70°F., like your garage or basement, and leave it there until new growth starts. It'll need a dormancy period of about ten weeks.

Although I have cut an amaryllis bulb and successfully grown a plant from each segment, you'll get blooms sooner if you don't cut them. Since the amaryllis is a true bulb, you can collect the bulblets that develop beside the bulbs and grow new plants from them if you have the patience to wait until they reach flowering size each season.

The Magic Achimenes

African violet growers will appreciate achimenes, for the two plants are similar in their growing habits. The long, trailing achimenes make ideal basket or potted plants, especially on sun porches or semi-shaded patios. (Night temperatures shouldn't fall below 60°F.) Some varieties have stems that trail up to 18 inches.

Wherever you decide to plant your achimenes, use a good potting soil. A sand- and peat-moss mixture will suit them fine. I start my rhizomes soon after the first of the year, but you can start them any time if you plan to keep them indoors. Don't bury the tiny rhizomes deeper than an inch. Keep them moist, but don't overwater, as this will rot the rhizome, just as too much direct sun will wilt the plant. Indirect light, filtered through shade, suits achimenes best. They'll also flourish under fluorescent lights. You might want to hang a basket near the office water cooler so everyone can enjoy the beautiful blooms all day long.

Colors abound in the achimenes' family, as do its poetic common names, like magic flowers, nut orchid, and widow's tears. You can choose among white, yellow, purple, pink, lavender, and red achimenes, and some of the newer varieties have veined or bicolored blossoms. You can pick one or two favorite colors, or you can plant several colors in the same pot for a real summer carnival of color.

The Pebble Beach Bunch

Tazetta narcissuses grow exceptionally well in water and pebbles. Most women appreciate this method of indoor forcing because the dish used for growing doesn't have to be a plain-Jane clay or plastic pot. You can use your best china or that lovely vase Aunt Matilda brought you from Sweden. No drainage hole is necessary. Actually, the slightest crack would be disastrous as these plants live by water alone.

After choosing your planter, fill it almost to the top with pebbles or gravel. I like to buy the colored gravel made for aquariums and fish bowls. In the sunlight the tiny stones actually sparkle and the colors make both the container and the blossoms look even prettier. If you prefer, of course, you can use plain perlite or vermiculite.

Leave three-fourths of the narcissus bulb above the water and allow at least an inch of breathing room between the bulbs. Do not submerge the whole bulb unless you're growing water lilies. Paper-whites or any other bulb grown in water will rot if water-soaked for long. It's the roots that are avid swimmers, not the bulb itself. Keep the bulbs in dim light.

Whoever has the job of watering your plants—I'm the official rainmaker at my house—should know to keep the water level just even with the bottom of the bulb. The roots have to be covered with water at all times, so if you go on vacation, ask your next-door neighbor to baby-sit. Leave written instructions, as any good parent would, telling exactly how to care for your bright-eyed darlings. And be sure to tell the baby-sitter their names.

When the stems are about 3 inches tall, move the container into curtain-filtered sunlight. Wait until the flowers are ready to appear before you give the plant full sunlight. Move the plant to a shadier area when it does blossom. I know you'll want to put it in the brightest, cheeriest spot in the house, but don't. Direct sunlight shortens the life of blooms.

The tazetta narcissuses give you a lot for your money because each stem bears from 4 to 8 blossoms. The paper-whites are the most popular, but two other varieties—Soleil d'Or and the Chinese sacred lily—are also excellent for forcing in water.

By the way, you don't have to add pebbles or shells to the water when forcing these indoor plants. They can live in water alone but the pebbles make it easier to maintain the proper water level and add to the attractive-

FORCING PAPER-WHITES

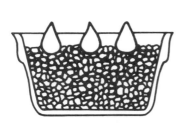

Set bulbs on gravel.

Fill pot with water so that three-fourths of the bulb is above water. Roots will grow down into the gravel.

In a few weeks you'll have a fragrant pot full of paper-whites!

ness of the plant. They also keep roly-poly bulbs from toppling over.

Although I try to look on the cheerful side and remember all the happy memories the water-grown bulbs bring, they do have sad endings. By the time these bulbs stop bloom-ing, their lives are finished. They use up all their stored energy producing blossoms for us. As I throw away the spent bulb, I just tell myself and the bulb that it isn't the length of

a life that counts but what it has accomplished in its living. I certainly think the water-grown bulbs are well worth the investment.

Plain Water Hyacinths

Gardeners of all ages enjoy watching plants grow in plain water. Besides enjoying the sel-dom-seen beauty of root formations floating in water, you'll be the hit of the garden club meeting when you show off a lovely hyacinth or other bulbous plant grown in a hyacinth glass. This vase looks like an hourglass and works just as you think it would. Set your bulb, nose upward, in the top of the glass. The bottom part of the glass should contain plain water or water and pebbles. I don't use pebbles in my hyacinth glass because I like to see the intertwined roots and because I think the whole arrangement looks more delicate without pebbles.

Once you've bought a hyacinth glass and top-quality bulb, you're ready to begin. First, clean up the bulb. Remove any soil, dead skin and shriveled roots that you see on the bottom of the bulb. If you don't, this debris will rot and cause the water to look and smell foul. Fill the glass with water up to the base of the bulb and set it in a cool, dark place until roots reach the bottom of the glass and the top starts to grow. Then move the glass into a cool, bright room until the plant blooms. Hyacinths are my favorites for this type of forcing and I guess the crocus would be my second choice. Started in late fall, either makes a worthwhile contribution to my Christmas blessings.

HYACINTH GLASS

THE OUTDOOR FACTS OF BULB LIFE

If you buy a good-quality bulb, you are almost assured of a healthy plant and blooms in the first season. What happens after that depends on the attention you give to your plants.

How you treat your plants, however, will

matter little if you're going to stick them into soil that is sick itself. Wouldn't it be foolish to buy a bulb, plant it, and then leave it to fight the world of insects, rodents, malnutrition, and poor drainage alone? As your personal friends, your bulbs deserve the best lodgings you can give them. And I don't mean the guest room. They want a bed of well-prepared garden soil.

If in Doubt, Test Your Soil

In the interest of healthy bulbs, I wouldn't take Uncle Joe's word about the acidity of your soil, nor your mother-in-law's. Both are probably wrong and your bulbs would suffer. So would you when you thought of your investments dying in the ground.

Bulbs do best in slightly acid soil; the pH should be between 6.0 and 6.8. Only a soil test can measure the acidity of your soil. You can have your soil tested by the nearest extension service laboratory for a small fee or you can do it yourself with one of the many kits available. Take samples from several different locations, always digging down to a depth of at least 4 inches.

When you receive the results of the acid test in the mail or when you complete your own testing, you ought to be prepared for the next step.

Let's suppose you discover that your soil is too acid and you need to reduce the acidity so that the pH registers 6.0 to 6.8. Your soil needs to be sweetened, and lime is generally

the first remedy that comes to mind. As I'm sure you know, lime is strongly alkaline and quickly neutralizes acids, thus lowering the pH rating of overacid soil. (It's a lot like taking an antacid for heartburn.)

I've known people who thought lime was a plant food and that their bulbs needed no other food. This is not true.

You can use calcite or dolomite, the two kinds of ground limestones, in the amount suggested on the package directions. The smart gardener will work this into his soil well before bulb-planting time so that the soil can prepare itself. I always try to lime my soil at least two weeks before planting time.

You'll discover, possibly through trial and error, that heavy, clayey soil will require a little extra lime.

Humus Your Bulbs

Organic material comes from decaying vegetable and animal remains. If your garden spot happens to be in a wooded area, you'll have plenty of rich organic materials in your soil. Dear old Mom Nature will provide fallen leaves, twigs, and branches to keep the soil rich and fertile with decomposing organic matter, known as humus.

Out of the woods, it's sometimes a different story. Your garden spot might be in a beautiful location but sadly deficient in organic materials. Maybe you don't care about the organic materials in that lovely setting, but your bulbs do. Consider those little darlings and you'll immediately perk up your ears at the mention of organic materials.

Humus holds water in the soil so the root system can use it. It also keeps water from running off and taking your soil with it. I had a friend who stood at his picture window and watched the first real gullywasher run off his lawn after a long, dry spell. He said his "sense of humus" left him right then, but I don't think any humus had ever been applied to his soil or the water would have soaked in well. Humus acts like a sponge, gulping up moisture when too much is present and releasing it a little at a time when the soil is dry.

After breaking up my soil and removing the rubble, I spread a 3-inch layer of humus over the soil and work it in thoroughly. I usually use peat moss, but if you're lucky enough to have enough compost or manure, you can use that. Be sure to work the humus in deeply. A tiller will save you a lot of work and probably a Monday morning backache, but a spade and a little elbow grease will work just as well.

After planting my bulbs, I put a blanket of leaves or light bark chips over the ground for looks and to keep the soil moist.

If you have a shredder, you'll enjoy munching up a mulch. I ask my neighbors to rake their fall leaves into my yard, then I shred them up into a lovely leafy salad for my flowers. I'm not above asking them for their leaves if I see them bundled in plastic bags beside the garbage dump. When I have enough on my flower beds, I put the rest in my compost heap. Pride doesn't stand in the way of providing for the needs of my flower children!

Compost Is Gourmet Dirt

I know people who have used compost for years without really knowing why. I suppose if you asked them they could give you one of the basic reasons for using compost—to make the soil more manageable.

Have you ever seen the washing powder commercial that shows all those greedy, hard-working critters that devour all the dirt in clothes? The bacteria in compost do about the same thing—they go to work the instant the compost is introduced to the soil, gradually breaking it down and making it easier to till. Good tilth is impossible without bulk material, and compost is your best bet for providing it.

Some soil has enough organic matter in it without additional compost. If yours does, then pat yourself on the back and go out and buy a new dahlia bulb to celebrate. Unfortunately, a lot of you will have soil that is nutrition-poor. Remember that our soil has been tilled for many years in America and even longer in the rest of the world.

Composting is tied in with humus and mulch. Compost is actually a homemade fertilizer made of rotten vegetable matter and animal manures. Not many years ago, you would have been laughed out of the Bridge Club if you had suggested reading *The Farmer's Almanac.* Today, however, the educated and the uneducated alike devour its pages for the technical information it contains. By the same token, compost heaps weren't exactly considered a proper topic for cocktail-party conversations a few years back. Now, if you make a compost heap you're a practicing ecologist, and the bigger your heap the better your standing in the social pasture of life.

One of the first steps to becoming a practical, practicing ecologist is to save your grass cuttings and other organic refuse. Put them in your compost heap or spread them directly on your garden. (Tuck them under a straw mulch if you like.) Save your newspapers to add to the pile, too, as well as leaves, twigs, wood bark and chips, and chunky peat. For bulbs, oak-leaf compost seems to be ideal (oak leaves produce an acid compost and bulbs are acid lovers), so I hoard oak leaves like a miser. If you have an oak tree in your yard, save those leaves for your bulbs. You might even make a separate compost heap exclusively for oak leaves.

If you've never attempted to use compost before, I'd better warn you about the mistake beginning composters often make. You cannot use fresh, raw manure on your bulbs—or anything else, for that matter. Harsh, raw manure will burn your plants. It is also full of weed seed and damaging salts. So leave manure in your compost pile for six months to a year before using it in your bulb beds. While the heap is waiting patiently for its turn in the garden, be sure it gets a drink of water now and then. Make the top of your pile concave in the middle so that water can collect there. To make sure the heap is getting enough air, turn it periodically with a fork. If this sounds like too much work, drive a stake into the center of the heap. This is an excellent way for it to blow off steam—just pretend the heap is a vampire.

Bulbs Can't Swim

James Russell Lowell said, "One thorn of experience is worth a whole wilderness of warning." I've been pricked with more than enough thorns in the bulb business, so maybe my advice can save you from wandering in the woods. One of the things I've learned beyond the shadow of a doubt is that bulbs demand good drainage. A few are real daredevils who'll plunge right into the water, root, bulb and all, like the calla lily, but most of them are real dry-weather friends.

I believe you can get by with poor soil easier than poor drainage when you're dealing with bulbs. Just keep in mind that it's the roots of the bulbs that need water and not the bulbs themselves, which rot easily when kept wet. Remember the hyacinth glass and the paper-whites grown in water? Their roots needed water, but the bulbs themselves were kept high and dry.

There are several types of soil, as you probably have realized just from poking around your backyard. Some soils are sandy: these are made up of coarse mineral particles. These soils are usually low in nutrients and organic matter and must be fortified with humus or compost.

Clay soils hold water too well. Bulbs are apt to rot in clay soils. You can pick up a dab of clay soil between your fingers and it will almost certainly feel damp, even in relatively dry weather. Clay soil packs down hard, too, and makes it difficult for tender roots to stretch and grow. The addition of sand will make clay soil workable and improve the drainage, too. Your old standby—compost or other organic material—is good for clay too. In fact, it's an excellent spring tonic for almost any soil.

So how can the amateur gardener decide whether or not his soil drains properly for bulb growing? You won't believe how difficult this experiment is! The next time it rains, have the good sense to go out into the rain; then stand there and observe your soil. Move around and check several places, as drainage will differ according to the lay of the land and types of soil. If you have a lawn plugger, take a few samples and inspect them. You can't tell anything about drainage by looking only at the top of the soil. Drainage is not determined by how fast the water runs off your ground, but by how well the water seeps into your soil. To be fair to you, I guess I should tell you that you could try this experiment on a fair day, too, by soaking several areas of your yard with a hose laid on the ground.

You Can't Dampen Some Bulbs' Spirit

Some bulbs will thrive in moist soil; this does not mean, however, that you can plant them in an area that is a miniature version of Dismal Swamp. If you do own some marshy, mucky ground, you can set out calla lilies. They will grow well in very damp soil with partial shade. Planted in the spring, they can even remain in the ground through the winter if you mulch them and if the climate isn't extremely cold.

If you have moist places that present problems even after you've treated them for drainage problems, don't despair. Experts have come up with several varieties of bulbs which may turn your eyesore into a beauty spot. Many crocuses thrive in moist soil. Clivias enjoy a moist soil and produce lovely orange or scarlet blossoms with a delightful fragrance. Numerous types of iris will grow in moist spots, as well as caladiums, cannas, and white fawn lilies.

I told a cousin once that schizostylis grew well in damp soil so she ought to plant some down by the stream in back of her house. She later informed me that that particular plant couldn't be found anywhere in her little town, but that she did set some crimson flags out and they were flourishing. I'm still hoping to get up the nerve to tell her that they are one and the same!

You also might try the wild hyacinth, which is available in blue, white, or cream. This easy-to-please plant will grow in shade or full sunlight where the ground is wet. The sweet-smelling lily-of-the-valley likes moist soil and full to partial shade—no garden is quite complete without this fragrant old favorite.

If you have small children in your family, I suggest that you plant an elephant's ear. No—it will not grow an elephant. Elephant's ear is the very appropriate common name for *colocasia,* which is also known as taro. The leaves of this plant reach giant proportions.

Sunshine Is Their Life

Bulbs nap when it's dark and cold and grow when it's light and warm, so sunlight is essential to their development. If some of your tulips always bloom earlier than the rest, you can bet they're the one smiled upon by the sun. So don't scold the later bloomers—they're not being lazy.

You can tamper with Mother Nature by planting your spring-flowering bulbs in a warm, sunny spot, perhaps against a wall; you'll get blooms a week or so earlier than usual. Later in the season the same spot might be too hot for growing anything else, so spring is the best time to make use of it.

If you want to risk fooling Mother Nature again, you can delay the blooming time of some bulbs by planting them in a cooler spot—a northern hillside perhaps.

The Shady Characters

I've told you several times that bulbs are an eager-to-please lot. So it shouldn't surprise you to learn that there are quite a few bulbs that will be very happy in shady locations. I guess you could call them shady, underground characters.

By shade, I don't mean a total eclipse. If you plant a caladium under your evergreen trees where no sun has shone for fifty years, you won't be very happy with the results. Partial shade means just what it says. Bulbs do need some sun, filtered through tree foliage or from the early morning or late evening sun, if they are to develop properly.

Keep a Weatherly Eye on Your Bulbs

Remember Dorothy in *The Wizard of Oz*? She was uprooted and blown away by a Kansas tornado. Even if you don't live in Kansas, the same thing can happen to your tall plants if you don't provide them with some protection—and I don't mean a pair of ruby slippers, Glinda!

The early flowers, such as daffodils, snowdrops, and crocus, seldom suffer much serious wind damage, but any flowers that come along in March and April risk their lives. That old saying that March comes in like a lion and goes out like a lamb still often proves itself to be true. While you're quoting things, you can also recall that those April showers that bring May flowers often ruin tulips, daffodils, hyacinths, and other plants with mud damage. Did you ever try to set up clumps of daffodils, sturdy though they be, after a hard rain? It's tougher than putting Humpty Dumpty together again.

Windbreaks are exactly what their name implies—structures that break the force of the wind and keep your plants from losing their heads on the first gusty day. You should always try to place tall, top-heavy plants near the house, the garage, a wall, a hedge, or anything else that will provide protection.

Our old pal Mother Nature provides her own windbreaks, and since she is the one who sends the rain and wind, she ought to know how to protect her children from them. The next time you go for a walk in the woods, look around at her handiwork. Small, fragile plants nestle up against their larger, stronger cousins, and against boulders and hillsides. When you go home, look around your yard for similar windbreaks. You can safely plant even bulbs that thrive in hot, dry areas under tall, high-branched trees. The shade they provide is light and they will protect the flowers when winds or storms come.

When I was riding through the countryside not long ago, I saw a truly lovely sight. Someone had found the time to plant a large clump of tulips against an old stone wall. They were nodding happily at me so I had to slow down and pay my respects. I felt glad that my new friends had such a safe, snug home. Those tulips won't be ruined in a storm. That charming old wall serves as a windbreak against rain and wind and hail, in addition to being a good background for my show-off friends.

Once again, you can combine beauty and practicality, and achieve similar results at your home. Surely you have an empty-looking wall or fence somewhere on your land. I like to see tall glads growing beside a garage or in a border that curves against the wall of a house. If you have a mailbox on a large post you can plant tall glads or dahlias or tulips at the base of the post and thrill the postman daily with the blossoms which will greet him. At the same time, the post will protect the flowers in a storm. If you really want your plants to feel secure, you can tie them loosely to the pole.

I also like to see daffodils and other spring bulbs naturalized on gentle slopes. This sort of arrangement has a casual, "drifting" look that's hard to beat. And I'm sure the plants are happy with so many friends to wave at and talk to. If the ground slopes away from the direction of the prevailing wind, the hillside will provide quite a bit of protection.

BULB MARRIAGES ARE NOT MADE IN HEAVEN

Selecting just the right bulbs for you and your garden can be a puzzlement, but with a little knowledge and luck you can choose the right ones for you.

Bulbs are big business, and if you fall in love with bulbs, you're messing around with a million-dollar baby. Over $300 million is spent throughout the world on bulbs every year. The United States buys more glads than any other kind, perhaps because these flowers are so popular in cut bouquets.

You may feel pretty small in the world of big bulb business, but you can get as good a bargain as the biggest bulb tycoon on Wall Street if you learn something about when to buy, what kind of bulbs to buy, and where to buy.

The Catalog Concept

Many bulb growers buy only from catalogs because they feel they get a greater variety and better quality bulbs. That may be true, since few nursery facilities are equipped to keep unusual, seldom-bought bulbs on hand during the purchasing season. Catalogs offer varieties seldom seen in your local bulb market and the photographs (which can be deceiving as to color and size) may stimulate your thinking and inspire you to buy new exotic varieties.

Once you buy from a reputable catalog dealer, he'll keep you on his mailing list, hoping that you won't be able to resist that new species of tulip or that dazzling new dahlia he's planning to offer next year. If you're not receiving catalogs regularly, write to several dealers in early summer and ask for their newest catalog. You have to plan ahead of time to receive your bulbs in time for fall planting. If you wait too long, all the other bulb lovers will have beaten you to the punch and there won't be any catalogs left. If you're going to plant in the spring, you should plan on getting your catalogs early in the fall so you'll have all winter to decide.

reject back in the proper bin—which brings me to one of the disadvantages of local bulb buying. Not all bulb browsers are as considerate as you and I. I've seen people take bulbs out of one bin, inspect them, then put them down—in the wrong bin. The next unsuspecting bulb buyer who comes along to buy a batch of tulip bulbs will have an unpleasant surprise a few months later. He'll discover that his all-yellow tulip bed looks as if it's got a case of measles.

Bulb buying is a lot like playing the stock market. It's better to invest in a few dependable blue-chip bulbs than in lots of cheaper bulbs that may or may not give you a good return on your investment.

So how do you pick a blue-chip bulb without a broker? Just look at it and feel it. Does it feel fat and firm, as it should? Look for mold and other signs of disease. Small cracks, dents, or other broken places in the skin can

Home-Known Bulbs

Your local garden centers usually know their business. Now, I'm a great believer in word-of-mouth advertising, so if you're new in town and don't know which bulb dealer can order that new hybrid tulip you want, find somebody who plants a lot of bulbs.

The best reason for buying your bulbs locally is that you get to see and feel what you're buying. You can pick the fat, healthy-looking bulbs out from the shriveled, anemic ones. Pick them up, one at a time, and inspect them carefully. Do be sure to put any you

The bulb on the left will always be a good buy; avoid bulbs, like that on the right, with cracks, dents, or broken places in the skin where diseases and pests can get in.

let diseases and pests into the bulb, so discard any bulbs with bruised or scratched complexions. Check to see how many "noses" each bulb has—the more the better. Each nose will grow into a flower stalk.

Dutch Treat

Windmills, wooden shoes, and tulips usually pop into my mind when I think of the Netherlands. Nowadays, though, more and more bulbs have Made in Japan tags, but I still prefer the Dutch bulbs, partly because of the fascinating history behind them and because I honestly believe Dutch bulbs produce stronger plants with larger, longer-lasting blooms.

When I mention Dutch bulbs, I mean the tulips, hyacinths, crocuses, narcissuses, grape-hyacinths, snowdrops, and wood hyacinths for the most part. All of them provide an abundance of beauty without an abundance of work, indoors or out.

The Japanese are number two in the bulb export business, so I suppose they do try harder. Even though I prefer to go Dutch, I must tell you that Japanese bulbs have been greatly improved in the last few years. And Japanese bulbs tend to be cheaper than Dutch bulbs.

Not all the bulbs you buy are from faraway lands. Lots of them are born and raised right here in the good old U.S.A. Holland, Michigan, produces a good many tulip bulbs. Washington State, Oregon, and northern California specialize in lily and daffodil bulbs. Florida is a leading producer of the world's caladiums, and California is a leader in begonia bulbs.

Bulbs Don't Grow in Bags

No matter where your bulbs come from or what their background, they'll do you no good until you plant them. So with bulbs in hand, you must now decide if you want to set them in beds or naturalize them. That is entirely a matter of personal preference.

Where and how you plant bulbs, like everything else, follows certain trends and styles. Years ago, Grandpa planted his bulbs in strict, symmetrical designs. Hardly anybody does that now unless he owns a castle, a huge estate, a park, or perhaps a hotel. A strictly formal bed would look as out of place in most yards as a hoop skirt in a shop window full of minis. I have, however, stopped at some service stations that laid out their bulb beds as if they dug graves after hours. Perfect rectangles encircled shrubs and multicolored flags waved overhead. I assume that this is not the decor you'd choose for your yard.

Most people prefer informal designs in their gardens as this fits in with today's fast-paced but casual lifestyle. Nevertheless, a clump of daffodils beside an oak tree may not suit your personality or fit in with the rest of your landscaping. You may be more comfortable walking in gardens almost as formal as the very beautiful Biltmore Gardens in Asheville, North Carolina. If so, plant your bulbs according to your heart's desire with my full blessing. The most important consideration is your happiness and the pleasure your planting gives you.

If you prefer to naturalize your bulbs, simply follow the lay of your land. If you have sloping hillsides, you can set clumps of crocuses, daffodils, tulips, or anything else you happen to like up and down the sides of the hills. Perhaps you have a rock garden laid out by yourself or Mother Nature. In either case, you have an ideal location for naturalizing small, strategically placed clumps of bulbs. The key to successful naturalizing is planting everything so that it seems to have grown wild. What you're really doing is fooling around with Mother Nature again—and enjoying every minute of it.

The natural lay of your land will influence your choices in making bulb beds as it does in naturalizing, but there is no limit to the patterns and designs you can enjoy if you use a little imagination and plant wisely. If a corner of your garden spot is very sunny, you'll want to plant your first-blooming spring flowers there as well as some of the heat-tolerant summer bulbs. Shady areas call for some of the more delicate beauties that are susceptible to sunburn. Just remember not to force your bulbs to live in conditions they can't tolerate. If you do, your beds will never look as attractive as they might, no matter how much hard work you put into them.

I like to mix ferns with bulbs whenever possible, so it's difficult for me to think of laying out bulb beds without sketching in some ferns, too. The ferns serve a double purpose—they make a perfect backdrop for bright blossoms and they do an admirable job of hiding the bulbs' unattractive foliage until it dies away. I use them as a sort of all-purpose gardening cosmetic to highlight beauty spots and hide bad features.

If Andrew Jackson's wife could shape her front lawn like a guitar, I have the right to design my bulb beds to suit my own tastes. So do you, but being on the lazy side, I avoid laying out any flower beds that have sharp corners or 360° circles and I suggest that you do likewise. I'd much rather mow around flower beds than get down on my knees and clip their sideburns by hand. Hard-to-mow areas might result in plant damage, too, so lay out your beds in gently curving lines. One of the best ways to do this is to lay a garden hose in the line you want your bed to follow. Stand back and look at it, then test it with your mower, experimenting until it works.

If your yard is small and flat with no distinctive features, you'll have to create your own beauty spots from scratch. Try a mixed border along your sidewalk or driveway. This is a conglomeration of annuals, biennials, perennials, and bulbs. Stick to tall, bright-colored bulbous flowers, like crown imperials and dahlias, so they'll stand out from the rest. Scatter your bulbs here, there, everywhere, among the border plants. Lump only a few bulbs together in each spot for the best effect.

But what if you live in a house with almost no garden area? Don't throw in the trowel. Plant some moderately tall bulbs in front of your foundation. Hang baskets of tuberous begonias from the eaves of your house or plant tulips and hyacinths in pots and window boxes. Just use your imagination and your life can be filled with flowers no matter where you live!

You can create your own mixtures of plants but I'll share some of my own recipes for garden beauty. Tulips, spaced farther apart than usual, are gorgeous with pansies tucked between them. The color patterns are unusual, and you'll be surprised every time you look out your garden window and see the two together.

In the early spring you can sow California poppies between your bulbs. Other annuals that fit nicely among your spring-flowering bulbs include clarkia, annual larkspur, phlox, and portulaca. Later in the spring you can set out sweet alyssum, pansies, daisies, or wall-flowers between your flowering bulbs. And if you like anemones as well as I do, you'll have to include some in your bulb bed. Their jewel-like colors look especially beautiful with tulips.

If you're tired of staring at that redwood fence you built, get out your palette of bulb colors and make it the frame for a summer masterpiece. Plant cannas, tigridias, daylilies, dahlias, glads, and lilies, all in shades of red, orange, and yellow. For still more zing, throw in some zinnias and plant a row of yellow marigolds and red geraniums along the front of the arrangement. But be careful—the exuberance of this arrangement is catching. If you don't exercise some self-restraint you may find yourself obsessed with a mad desire to fill your whole yard with red, yellow, and orange flowers. And there are plenty to choose from.

If your tastes are more sedate, you might like a fence planting in the pink, lavender, and purple color range, accented occasionally with white and crimson. You might train a crimson or white climbing rose to grow up the fence and serve as a backdrop for dahlias, glads, Japanese iris, and lilies, all in pink, purple, or lavender shades. Add some of the new double-flowered hollyhocks and foxgloves to fill in the background. In the front of the planting you could use pansies, violas, violets, sweet alyssum, phlox, or even carpet bugle.

There is no "right" planting for a particular spot. Instead, you have to choose among a multitude of possibilities according to your own likes and dislikes. The first time you plan a flower bed and plant it accordingly, don't be surprised if you're not entirely satisfied with the results. Planning attractive gardens, like any other creative endeavor, takes a lot of practice. You can't pick up a paintbrush and create a masterpiece on your first attempt.

A Bath Before Bed

Bulbs have rough, unappealing faces, but inside they're very sensitive. After all, they have a flower for a heart. Bulbs can be severely damaged or destroyed by insects and burrowing animals, though they usually suffer fewer problems than other flowers. To be sure that they are pest-free, I treat my bulbs before planting them. There's nothing a bulb loves more than a warm bubble bath before bed.

I mix a tablespoon of 44 percent chlordane into a mild solution of two gallons of soap and water. I carefully drop the bulbs into the water, stir them gently, then remove and plant them. Quick and painless, this preventive medicine is just what the doctor ordered to keep insects away from your bulbs.

Planting Is a One-at-a-Time Job

When it comes to planting your bulbs, give each the individual attention it deserves, whether you plant it in a clump or in a bed individually. Make sure you know when to plant it and how deep to plant it and which end is up. Being dropped in a hole and covered with dirt is traumatic enough without having to stand on your head at the same time.

Bulbs will grow if you chuck them into the ground upside down, but they'll grow in spite of your treatment, not because of it. Learn what each kind of bulb looks like and how to tell the nose from the basal plate. Then plant it nose up so that the roots will grow downward and the foliage and plant will grow up and out as they should. Plants will develop and grow the long way around if you plant the bulb upside down, but this wastes energy that could better be spent on flower production.

A step-on bulb planter would make a great Christmas present for an avid bulb fan. This little tool lifts out a 6-inch cylinder of soil and is ideal for making individual plantings. After you've removed the soil, you can easily break it up and work in a handful of compost and a teaspoon of bone meal. Replace enough soil to make the bulb sit at the proper depth, set it in the hole, and cover it. What could be easier?

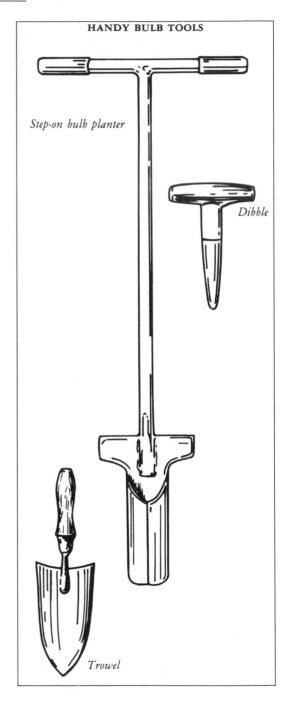

HANDY BULB TOOLS

Step-on bulb planter

Dibble

Trowel

For larger clumps of bulbs, lift out a section of soil with a shovel. Make the hole wide enough to house all the bulbs and at least 6 inches deep. Break up the soil, add compost, and ¼ cup of bone meal, mixing it into the soil thoroughly.

For your birthday, you could suggest that someone get you a dibble. Some folks call it a dibber. Whatever you call it, it's a tool that punches holes of whatever depth you want for bulb planting. However, a dibble has a rather pointed end so most bulbs don't fit exactly into the hole. Therefore, you have a worrisome space between the bottom of the bulb and the bottom of the hole. When the roots start growing, they'll be reaching out into nothing if you leave that air space there. Some people carry a pail of sand around with them and drop a little into the point of the hole before placing the bulb in it. Watering the bulbs immediately after planting will accomplish the same thing.

You probably own several trowels already. I have one that is notched, not to show how many bulbs I've planted, but to indicate the proper planting depth for several kinds of bulbs. This little trick has saved me many trips back to the garage to pick up the ruler I forgot to take with me. This leads me to an important point in planting bulbs. I have already told you any old hole in the ground won't do, and that goes for the depth at which you set your bulbs in their holes. At right is a general guideline for how deep to dig them.

The Dutch Bulb Institute produces some of the best color booklets and instructions I have ever seen, and they are free at your garden center.

SPECIAL ATTENTION, PLEASE

Webster must have been a gardener because his dictionary says that the word "cultivate" means "to give special attention to." When you cultivate your plants, that's exactly what you do—you give special attention to them once they're established in the homes you've chosen for them. You make sure they're well fed and healthy. You keep their greedy neighbors, the weeds, out of their front yard and you make sure they're snug and cozy in the winter. Basically, you treat them like very welcome guests who will provide you with a great deal of pleasure in return for a little hospitality.

	DEPTH
Amaryllis	5"
Anemones	2"
Begonias (tuberous rooted)	1½"
Calla lilies	2"
Crocuses	4"
Daffodils	8"
Dahlias	7"
Gladioluses	5½"
Hyacinths	4"
Hyacinths (Grape)	3"
Lilies	10"
Tulips	9"

Bulbs are among the easiest guests to entertain. They're not as susceptible to attack from insects and diseases as most other flowering plants, and they require no pruning to keep them trim and fit. Some bulbs, such as crocuses and narcissuses, will be very happy if you just treat them like family. Others, including dahlias and tuberous begonias, need a little extra care if they're to be happy and productive.

Don't become overconfident and lazy if your bulbs produce gloriously beautiful blossoms during their first blooming season. You can take credit for buying fat, healthy bulbs and planting them correctly, but the first blooms are really courtesy of the grower who produced the bulbs and gave them the grow-power that produced the blossoms. After the first season, however, it's all up to you. You have to make sure the bulbs stay strong and healthy so they'll continue to produce those glorious blossoms. If you take care of the foliage and allow it to mature properly, the blossoms will take care of themselves.

Weed Weapons

Have you ever grown onions from sets? If you've done any vegetable gardening at all, you probably have. This humble but delicious bulb is one of the easiest and most surefire crops in the vegetable garden—if, that is, you keep the rows free of weeds. If you don't, the onions you pull will be so scrawny and anemic that you'll end up running to the grocery store to buy some decent ones.

Glamorous flowering bulbs are no different from their humble cousins when it comes to weeds. They don't like to compete with weeds for the soil nutrients they need to produce strong foliage, fat bulbs, and lots of blossoms. Since bulbs can't defend themselves, you'll have to do it for them. So check your arsenal of anti-weed weapons, then get out there and fight!

There are three weapons available to you in your war on weeds. You can knock out weeds by hand with a hoe or other tool, or with pre-emergence weed killers. Whichever you choose, the key to success is getting an early start. If you wait until the weedy intruders have completely surrounded your bulbs, the battle will be twice as hard as if you'd begun your attack early in the season. Never let weeds get a foothold in your bulb beds! They grow faster than other plants (or seem to anyway) and they're real robbers and scoundrels. You can't afford to leave them in your bulb beds out of pity or laziness.

There are many different kinds of hoes and hand-weeding tools on the market, but my favorites are the Warren hoe and the hand cultivator. The Warren hoe has a pointed, triangular blade which makes it easy to work between plants without injuring them. A hand cultivator is simply a three-pronged claw.

Actually, when I find a stubborn weed growing very close to a bulb, I usually engage in a little hand-to-hand combat. That way I don't have to worry about cutting up the bulb or its delicate roots. Hand weeding is also the best way to clear weeds out of a naturalized planting where you don't want a lot of bare soil showing.

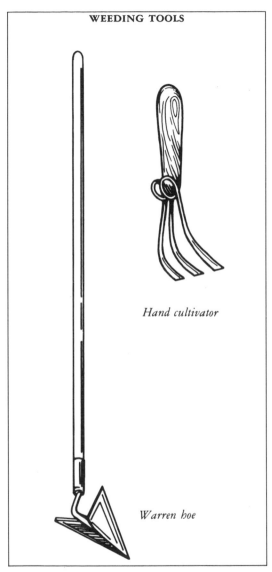

WEEDING TOOLS

Hand cultivator

Warren hoe

chop a weed, thanks to some relatively new discoveries. I'm talking about pre-emergence weed killers—I call them kneeless weeders.

These chemical wonders will protect your flowers from weeds for months, and they're not as dangerous to non-target plants as other types of weed killers. In the spring, after you've planted your bulbs or after you've stirred up the soil in an already-established bed, just spread your pre-emergence chemical over the soil. It will prevent the weeds from sprouting. It will not kill any plants which are already aboveground, so you must remove all existing weeds before applying the chemical.

As with any other potentially dangerous chemical, you must take certain precautions to avoid harming non-target plants, animals, children, or adults. So be sure to read every word of the small print in the manufacturer's directions. This should tell you how much to apply and when to do so as well as which plants you can safely use the product with. Don't neglect to read the cautions either, even if you think you know exactly what they say.

A good mulch is a lot like a Swiss army knife—both will take care of a lot of different jobs. First and foremost, a good thick layer of mulch will keep weeds from rearing their ugly heads in your bulb bed. Once you've spread on a mulch, you can forget about hand weeding, hoeing, and pre-emergence weed killers. You'll have to add a little more mulch now and then, and you might have to pull out an occasional weed that's slipped through your defenses, but that's all!

As if a weed-free bed weren't enough, a

If all this talk about weeding has just strengthened your desire to avoid the task altogether, don't despair. You don't have to resort to plastic tulips and daffodils planted in asphalt. There is now a way to have lovely flower beds without ever having to pull or mulch also protects your bulbs from winter frosts and freezes, enriches the soil with organic matter as it decomposes, keeps the soil cool and moist in summer, and makes your beds look neat and well groomed all the time. What more could you ask?

Lilies are especially fond of having their feet covered in mulch. If you're planting them late, just before frost, use a mulch to keep the ground frost-free as long as possible. Then, once the surface soil has frozen, pile on more mulch to make sure the ground stays frozen. In the spring and summer a mulch will keep your lilies' feet moist, cool, and comfortable.

Many materials are available for mulching. Perhaps you'd like to try a live mulch in the form of low-growing ground covers, such as ivy or vinca. I like to use ground covers around short plants, like crocuses and grape hyacinths, to keep their little faces from becoming mud splattered. Ground covers also protect the bulbs against alternate freezing and thawing in winter, which can cause heaving of the soil and root injury. Actually, such heaving is the only thing the spring bulbs need to be protected from. If you've naturalized your spring bulbs in grassy areas, you don't have to worry about a mulch. Mother Nature has provided one for you in the form of grass. To protect spring bulbs in beds, spread on a blanket of mulch after the ground has frozen to a depth of about 2 inches. You can use salt hay, pine needles, wood shavings, bark, or evergreen boughs. Remove the mulch in spring before the bulbs sprout.

If you prefer a more attractive mulch that you won't have to remove, spread on a layer of buckwheat hulls, chopped bark, or similar material in spring after the foliage appears. You can also use small, polished stones, but I don't really think these are as attractive around bulbs as more natural-looking materials.

If you and I have been garden friends for long, it should come as no surprise when I say mulch is still the easiest way to beat the weeds.

Your Turn to Buy the Drinks

You've seen photographs of Holland bulb fields, I'm sure, but have you ever stopped to wonder why bulbs do so well there? Well, one reason is that they get plenty of water. The water table is constant and not far below the surface—which is just a fancy way of saying that you can dig down a few feet and hit water or water-saturated soil just about anyplace in the Netherlands.

You don't have to pack up your bulbs and move to the Netherlands, though. You just have to make sure they get enough water when they need it most. Have you ever been so thirsty you felt as if you could drain the city reservoir in five minutes? Chances are you'd been working hard on a hot day. And that's when bulbs need extra water too—when they're working hard to produce foliage and blossoms in spring and summer.

There's usually enough rain in the spring to provide spring-flowering bulbs with the water they need to produce blossoms. However, if Mother Nature is stingy with the April showers or if she's feeling sulky and cooks up a prolonged dry spell, you'll have to give your bulbs a drink yourself. Even after the spring bulbs have stopped blooming, they're still producing foliage, and if it dries out and dies before it matures properly, your bulbs will put on a poor show the next spring. So don't be a fair-weather friend, and neglect your bulbs after they've stopped blooming for you.

A soaker hose is best for watering bulbous plants. You can use a sprinkler, but you run the risk of burning foliage if you water on a sunny day. Sprinkling is especially hazardous for tuberous begonias and tulips.

Whichever method you use, be sure you water deep. A shallow watering does more harm than good. When you're watering your bulbs, get to the root of the matter, don't just sprinkle their uniforms. Shallow watering will cause a shallow root system.

Lunch Time

Having house guests wouldn't be much of a problem if you didn't have to feed them. I'm sure you ladies will agree with this since you're the ones who often do the extra cooking and dishwashing. And it's not just a matter of quantity, is it? You don't want your in-laws or your son's girlfriend to think you're the original burger queen, so you have to prepare something a little special 3 times a day. And that's a lot of trouble!

Well, ladies—and gentlemen—let me reassure you! Bulbs are perfect house guests. I've already said you can treat them like family, and that goes for feeding too. Bulbs don't need a lot of fancy feeding and they don't demand, or even particularly like, hard-to-get gourmet food.

When I plant my bulbs, I pack an organic lunch for them just to keep them from getting hungry. For bed plantings I spread at least 10 or 15 pounds of well-rotted manure or compost and 5 pounds of steamed bone meal over every 200 square feet of soil. If you have a fireplace in your home and have been wondering what to do with the ashes in the bin, put those on your bulb bed—up to 15 pounds per 100 square feet. They supply potassium, which helps your bulbs develop good, strong stems and flowers and fat, firm bulbs. If you're fresh out of wood ashes, you can buy muriate of potash, but use it sparingly—no more than one pound per 100 square feet. Unless you have very poor soil, your bulbs could probably do without this initial feeding, but I like to make sure they're off to a good start—particularly the fall-planted bulbs that have a long, cold winter ahead of them. You mothers know how good it makes you feel to give your children a good hot breakfast before sending them off to school on a cold winter day, don't you? You'll feel the same way when you give your fall-planted bulbs a good feeding.

Don't neglect to feed individually planted bulbs, either. Work a handful of compost and a teaspoonful of bone meal into the soil in each hole before setting in the bulb.

The only other feeding I give my bulbs is a light snack in early spring. When I notice that they have begun to stick their noses out of the soil, I go outside to admire their progress and spread half a handful of garden food, 4-12-4 or 5-10-5, over the soil at the same time. Of course, I also tell them how glad I am to see them again and encourage them to do their best for me.

Something to Lean On

I've already told you that bulbous plants, especially tall ones, can suffer a lot of damage if they have to stand unprotected in storms and high winds, and that planting them near a windbreak is one way to keep them from getting battered by rain and wind. If you've already planted your bulbs in the open or if you're planning to because you happen to like the sight of plants growing in solitary splendor, then you'd better plan on staking your regally tall beauties.

Any plants over 2 feet tall ought to be staked or protected by a windbreak. Dahlias, irises, lilies, glads, and a few others fall into this category. For prize seekers, staking is not a suggestion, it is a command. Don't expect your deeply beloved, much-nurtured glads to bring home any blue ribbons after they've weathered a couple of Mother Nature's temper tantrums.

A lot of folks use bamboo shoots for plants, but I've found that they don't sway with the wind as they should. I prefer 8- or 9-gauge galvanized wire stakes because I think they're easier to use and less conspicuous. They're also good in extremely heavy winds because

they sway a little and aren't as likely to cause the plant's stem to snap.

Plant your stakes when you plant your bulbs. Count Dracula may deserve a stake through the heart, but not your bulbs—and that's what you risk if you wait to stake the plant until it's tall. One small miscalculation can damage the bulb and allow disease or insects to enter it. Planting the stake with the bulb will also help you remember where your bulbs are. The stakes aren't going to interfere with mowing if you've been smart enough to leave mowing lanes between them and your lawn. If you don't want a lot of tall stakes in your landscape, use short ones at first and replace when necessary.

For actually tying the plants to the stakes, nothing works as well as those wire twists you've been stuffing in a drawer every time you open a bread sack. They're more durable than garden twine—and cheaper.

WHAT'S BUGGIN' YOUR BULBS?

Make it plain right away to all insects that you mean business. Shower your young plants with soap and water before they flower. Dust the soil with Diazinon granules if there are any signs of insect damage.

For disease control, keep your bulbs free from weeds and litter. Both carry diseases. Observe your plants, too. Learn to spot the first signs of insect or disease damage. Then immediately tackle the problem with a 50 percent solution of Malathion, a dusting of 6 or 10 percent chlordane, or something similar suggested by your garden dealer.

Mice eat any bulbs except daffodils, which contain a slightly poisonous sap. Mice, chipmunks, and moles will eat your bulbs right out of the garden if you don't do something to curb their appetites. Since traps give only partial control and various poisons will pollute the soil, try planting your bulbs in mesh baskets set into the ground. You also can surround your bulb beds with ½-inch wire mesh, buried a foot deep. I guarantee this will drive the rodents nuts!

To heat up the action, mix a little cayenne pepper with crushed paradichlorobenzene crystals (moth crystals) and spread it about your bulb beds—it'll keep out dogs, moles, and surface insects.

Aphids

Aphids are very small, soft-bodied insects that come in many species and colors. They suck the plant's juices, reducing its vigor. Aphids cause various deformations, spread virus diseases, and secrete honeydew, a sticky substance which attracts ants. Sometimes they hide away with stored bulbs.

Malathion is usually recommended for a severe infestation, but you should try spraying them off with water from a garden hose first, paying special attention to the undersides of the leaves. For house plants, a spray made of Pyrethrum (a natural insecticide) works well, as does washing the aphids off

with soap and water. Flea and tick shampoo, 6 drops per quart of water, also does the job.

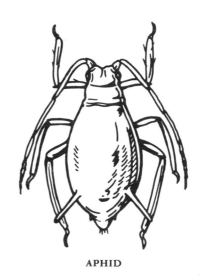

APHID

Bulb Mites

Minute, white, spiderlike creatures, bulb mites infest the rotting bulbs of many plants. They also eat cavities into healthy bulbs, transmitting the organisms that produce bulb rot, a soft mushy condition.

Amaryllises, crocuses, daffodils, freesias, gladioluses, hyacinths, lilies, and tulips are among those bulbs damaged by this pest.

Infested bulbs should be discarded. Healthy bulbs may be sprayed or dusted with Diazinon. Care should be taken to store the healthy bulbs in air-tight containers until you're sure they've beaten the bulb rot.

Gladiolus Thrips

These tiny insects are, at maturity, about the size and color of a lettuce seed. Host plants show silvered leaves and/or streaked flowers. Sometimes they attack stored bulbs.

Thrips favor gladioluses, but they also go for freesias, irises, and lilies.

Diazinon or Sevin spray or dust are effective against thrips. Dusting bulbs with Malathion before storing them is good added protection.

Japanese Beetles

Japanese beetles are about ½ inch long and metallic bronze in color. Although they feed on the foliage, stems, and flowers of many plants, cannas and dahlias are among their favorites.

Sevin seems particularly effective against adult beetles on flowers. You can also fight heavy infestations with sprays of Carbaryl, Malathion, or Methoxychlor. A sure cure is hand-picking or knocking them into a can of water covered with a film of anti-freeze (I use WD-40).

Narcissus Bulb Fly Larvae

These are fat, yellow maggots which eat into bulbs and encourage decay. The narcissus, tulip, and Easter lily all are susceptible to this pest. Successful control is difficult to accomplish; however, a good preventive measure is to dust the trench and bulbs with Diazinon granules before planting. Soft bulbs should be discarded. After the plants are finished blooming you can sprinkle naphthalene flakes around them to keep the flies from laying eggs.

JAPANESE BEETLE

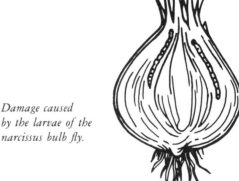

Damage caused by the larvae of the narcissus bulb fly.

Slugs

Slugs are fat, legless mollusks, 4 to 5 inches long. They mostly feed at night, leaving a slimy trail behind them. Dahlias and lilies are among their prime targets.

SLUG

Leaving out shallow containers of beer or grape juice will lure these pests to an untimely death. A border of coarse sand or cinders around your bulb bed is another good protection from slugs. For heavy infestations, metaldehyde bait is standard control. Dusting or spraying the soil with metaldehyde is also recommended.

Stem and Bulb Nematodes

These transparent, microscopic worms leave the tissue they inhabit scarred, stunted, or distorted. Their pattern is to enter new shoots and feed upward, then return to infest the bulb, leaving rings of brown damaged tissue in their wake.

Plants affected include daffodils, dahlias, gladioluses, hyacinths, irises, lycorises, snowdrops, and tulips.

Dig up and burn all infested plants. Prac-tice clean cultivation and dip your tools in alcohol to avoid spreading the infestation. Treat the soil before planting with Vapam.

Wireworms

Wireworms grow up to ¾-inch long. Their segmented bodies are yellowish brown in color. They are the larvae of click beetles and develop from eggs laid in the soil. After they tunnel into bulbs they hollow out the plant's stem, causing it to fall over.

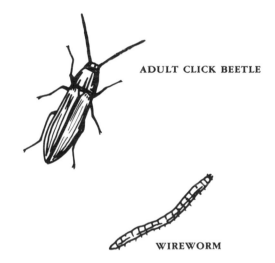

ADULT CLICK BEETLE

WIREWORM

Dahlias, gladioluses, and tuberous begonias are most susceptible to this pest.

In order to eliminate wireworms, it is best to pre-treat the bulb bed before planting. Apply Diazinon and work it into the top 6 or 8 inches of soil. After the bulbs are set in place you may spray or dust them as well with Diazinon before covering them with soil.

ALL GOOD-BYES AIN'T GONE

Who gives a hoot about a plant after it has stopped blooming? People who love the total plant, not just its beauty when in bloom, that's who. And what happens to your spring-flowering bulbs next season depends on the care they get this season.

Care should be taken that dead blooms aren't left on your plants, except the ones with lovely seed pods, like the Jack-in-the-pulpit or the blood-lily. Dead blooms can rob your plant of much-needed nutrition.

As I've told you, the foliage is the bulb's food-manufacturing factory, busy at work trying to build up a food supply to be stored in the bulb during the dormant season. If you have deficient foliage, you'll have an unhealthy bulb. Water the foliage if it begins to dry out, gradually decreasing the amount as the foliage reaches maturity. You can even feed anemic-looking foliage a little plant food now and then, up until you stop the watering.

Foliage sometimes gets messy toward the end, but don't get impatient with it or hostile toward it. It's just doing what comes naturally. Some people plait or braid the long leaves of daffodils and similar plants after the blooms are gone. I personally like the ponytail look—on the plants, not myself—so I turn the fading foliage down and make little ponytails. I tie the little bunches together with rubber bands saved from my daily newspaper. This prevents the foliage from sprawling all over my bulb bed.

Years ago when more formal bed designs were the rage, foliage could not be left to die a natural death. The foliage of tulips, hyacinths, and other bulbs used in formal settings was ruthlessly chopped back after the blooms withered. If you use a formal design in your garden today, take up your bulbs as soon as they stop blooming and immediately replant them elsewhere. I can't guarantee you that the bulbs will develop normally, but they stand a better chance. If you merely take them up and let the foliage die, next season you'll have to buy new bulbs or do without flowers. So replant immediately in a shaded area, preferably in a trench lined with peat moss. Water thoroughly and cross your fingers. An apology might help too.

Although those bulbs may not be the healthiest ones on the block next season, they should produce blooms that won't disgrace you. And maybe by the next season you will have learned to like more casual planting patterns.

You've Got to Dig for Surprises

Bulbs will multiply as surely as children will grow. Look at your daffodils. You'll probably notice that their blooms aren't as large and pretty as they were a few years ago. Chances are, the bulbs are overpopulated and need dividing. The longer you wait to replant the bulbs, the harder the job will be and the smaller your bulbs will be. Bulbs can't grow large if they've got no place to go.

Some people keep daffodils for ten or more years without ever seeing their bulbs, but yours may need to be divided sooner. The best way to tell is to look at the size of the blossoms.

It's best to dig up your bulbs for dividing at the beginning of the dormant period just after the foliage dies back. Some bulbs, like the colchicum, have very short dormant periods, much like my vacations have always been. The colchicum is dormant from about the Fourth of July to the middle of August, which means you have to make hay while the sun shines to divide these cookies. As soon as the foliage is dried up, go to work moving them.

The best tool for dividing bulbs is the spading fork. I like one with large tines so that I

DIVIDING BULBS

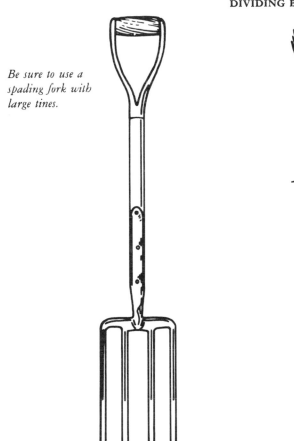

Be sure to use a spading fork with large tines.

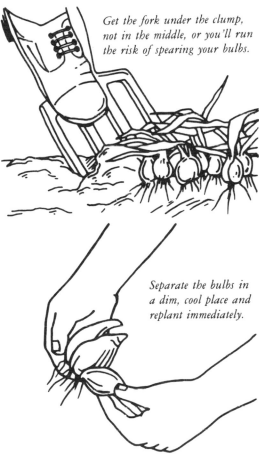

Get the fork under the clump, not in the middle, or you'll run the risk of spearing your bulbs.

Separate the bulbs in a dim, cool place and replant immediately.

can get the fork under a clump of bulbs and not in the middle of it. I don't want to lie down at night with speared bulbs on my conscience and I wouldn't wish that fate on you.

Try to lift out the whole clump at once. Then find a cool, dim place for separating the bulbs—don't let them dry out any more than necessary. Replant them immediately. I put my larger parent bulbs in the most conspicuous place with their smaller offspring behind them. If you prefer, you can put the babies in a nursery bed until they reach adulthood and begin to blossom heavily. Then they can be moved into the limelight with Mama and Papa.

Store Them Cozy, Clean, and Cool

The bulbs of gladioluses, dahlias, and tuberous begonias, and often cannas, must be dug up and stored during the freezing months. I like to wait until the foliage has been blackened by the first frost. If you want to jump the gun, go ahead and dig a little early. Tag the bulbs and temporarily put them in glassed-in coldframes or a ventilated shed for a few weeks. The idea is to keep them out of the frost. When the bulbs are dry, shake them in a bag of fungicide powder to prevent storage rot. Then place them in their winter home. Few modern cellars have ideal temperatures for bulb storage anymore (55°–60°F.), so look around for a place where the bulbs will be safe and comfortable.

You'll notice that bulbs in storage separate by themselves, so you won't have to pry them apart. If you have a small number of bulbs, you can store them in plastic bags filled with peat moss, perlite, or vermiculite. Once you've packed your bulbs up, don't worry about them. If they're stored properly, they'll keep until it's time to replant them again.

Dry tender dahlia roots for a couple of hours before storing them in plastic-lined shallow boxes. Blanket them with perlite, vermiculite, or peat moss. Store at about 45°F. A higher temperature might cause sprouting.

Tuberous begonias should be dug up and given a bath. Dust the begonia bulbs in sulfur and store in shallow, open trays. If all in the family agree, tuck the tuberous begonias away in the vegetable bin of your refrigerator. Just don't eat them by mistake! They don't make good sandwiches, believe me!

In all cases, cover the sorted bulbs with fine mesh wire or plastic to keep out mice and other rodents.

GROWING YOUR OWN . . .

Propagation of the new babies that you helped bring into the garden world is the greatest satisfaction of any gardener. Why not give it a try? I don't suggest growing bulbs from seed unless you don't mind waiting a long time—up to six years for daffodils—to see the results of your effort. However, there are several easier and faster ways to propagate bulbs.

Even though I own more bulbs than I can possibly keep an accurate account of, I am always trying to procure more. Sometimes friends give me new bulbs, especially if I've hinted enough. My family sneaks bulbs into the house and makes a big to-do about surprising me with a new hybrid. Mostly, though, I collect my bulbs from offsets (smaller bulbs) that form on true bulbs or from sections that I've cut up.

Sometimes a well-meaning acquaintance who hasn't had his hands in the dirt since he left the farm will say, "Do you know you're a nut—a real, first-class nut? You've already got acres of bulbs. I think you've got way too many already. Let's go play eighteen holes of golf instead of dropping more bulbs into holes you have to make yourself!"

What my friend doesn't realize is that propagating and planting bulbs is fun. If it weren't, I would be playing golf instead. I suppose I'll just have to content myself with the thought that my friend will lose more often at golf than I will with my bulbs.

Aside from being just plain fun, plant propagation can become a fascinating educational hobby. The first thought a beginning propagator usually has is that he might become the next great hybridizer! So he plans and works and prays and devotes his energies to developing a new strain of tulip. Tireless effort may finally pay off for him, as it has for others.

We are, however, concerned more with the bulbs, corms, tubers, tuberous roots, and rhizomes that are propagated in more ordinary ways. Ask the average daffodil grower how he propagates new plants and he'll say he collects the offsets at the daffodil bulb's side. Talk to the dahlia enthusiast and he'll show you how to cut the dahlia root to grow new ones.

If you are interested in increasing your bulb crop, the ways to do it are easy to understand and easy to put into practice. No hocus-pocus or magic tools are needed, just know-how and a little bit of work. The offspring of spring-planted bulbs can either be set outdoors when the soil temperature is above 50°F. or started earlier indoors in peat pots filled with Pro-mix. Fall-planted baby bulbs should be set into the soil after the first heavy frost.

Bulbs

The most common method of propagating true bulbs is by the removal of offsets, which are small bulbs that develop within the parent bulb and then split from it. Bulbs which produce offsets can simply be dug up and divided every few years.

Daffodils, which should be left alone unless overpopulating an area, probably won't need to be dug up more than once in five years. Dig only if the blooms decrease in size or if you absolutely have to move them. I told you how to dig and divide bulbs in the Culture section of this book, so I won't repeat the instructions. Lilies are more complex than daffodils—they can be propagated in three different ways besides growing them from seed. Since lily bulbs are usually pretty expensive, I am very glad that they are so willing to produce offspring.

Propagating Lilies

OFFSETS. The easiest way to propagate lilies is to lift the bulbs and pick off the bulblets, or offsets. These should produce flowering plants in about two years. Some experts debud their lily plants, which simply means they strip the plants of their buds before they open. That sounds cruel, but it apparently increases the number of bulblets that form on the parent bulb.

After picking the offsets off your lily bulbs, clean, dry, and store them for the winter and plant them at the proper time.

SCALES. You know that fish must be scaled before cooking and that mountains are scaled by adventurers. Singers sing scales and you weigh on scales. But did you know that scaling is a good way to grow more lilies?

Look at your lilies in the spring and you'll see the thick fleshy scales that wrap around the center of the true bulb (see figure 1). Carefully break off the outer, strong scales, but don't be greedy. Take only 5 or 6 scales to be sure your bulb will have all the food it needs in spite of the scaling. Dust the scales and bulb with fungicide. Then place all the scales in a plastic bag of damp peat moss, sphagnum, or vermiculite. Fasten the bag and store at about 70°F. for a few days (seven to ten). Peek in on your babies every now and then. After the bulblets form roots, put the

FIGURE 1

Scales

bag into the refrigerator until early fall and then plant. Place them in your nursery bed and in a couple of years you'll have several new flowering-size lilies.

Amateurs and pros alike get excellent results with this method, so don't be afraid to try it.

BULBILS. Some lilies, such as tiger lilies, can be propagated from the tiny bulbils that develop at the joints between their leaves and stem (see Figure 2). Pick these bulbils off the plant when they are ripe, which is always some time after the plant has flowered. When ripe, the bulbils will snap off easily. Don't rush them.

Plant the bulbils about an inch deep in a mixture of equal parts loam, coarse sand, and peat moss. Store them in a coldframe over the winter. When they sprout in the spring, move them to a new home, either in your garden or in a nursery bed.

FIGURE 2

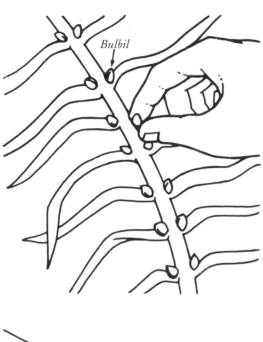

Bulbil

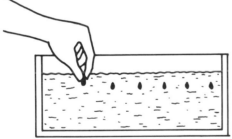

Corms

Unlike bulbs, corms don't fatten up during the growing season. When you gently tug the plant out of the ground in the fall, you'll see that the original corm is dead. It has dried up, having gobbled up all its energy. In its place, however, is a nice new corm, surrounded by smaller corms, or cormels.

After you've dug your corms, let them dry for two or three weeks in a shady place before you start picking off the cormels. (Women, save those snagged nylon stockings you usually throw out. They're perfect for storing corms and cormels. The open-mesh bags that potatoes, onions, and citrus fruits come in are good too.) Keep the corms cool—no warmer than 50°F. but not in danger of freezing. When they're dry, carefully clean off any soil that's sticking to the bulb and remove the cormels, which will be clustered around the basal plate of the old, dead corm. I know this sounds heartless, but there's nothing you can do to save the old corm. You can, of course, say a few kind words over it before you throw it in the wastebasket.

I always separate my corms and cormels according to size just after I divide them. This makes it easy to decide where to plant them the following spring. I put the fattest corms in the spotlight and the cormels in my nursery beds. When they reach blooming size in two or three years, I'll give them their chance to show off.

Corms multiply rapidly. One gladiolus corm will produce 25 cormels. Crocus corms multiply even more rapidly than glads if the soil is rich and cared for. I don't recommend digging them up more than once every three years, however.

Tubers

Tubers, tuberous roots, and rhizomes, unlike true bulbs and corms, do not form small "off-spring." Neither do potatoes, the most beloved of all tubers.

Propagating tubers, such as gloxinias, gloriosa lilies, and caladiums, is simple. Just cut them up the same way you would a seed potato. Make sure each piece has at least one eye. Dust all cut surfaces with a good all-purpose fungicide powder and let the pieces dry for two or three days before you plant them. Set them in the ground with the eyes looking upward, 3 to 4 inches deep for the small bulbs, 4 to 6 inches deep for the larger bulbs.

Tuberous Roots

Tuberous rooted plants, such as dahlias, are also propagated by cutting, but with them the operation is a little more difficult. All the eyes on tuberous roots are in the same place, at the base of the original stem, so you'll have to include a piece of this stem in every section you cut. Cutting the sections apart is a little tricky, but with a little practice, you'll be able to do it like a professional horticulturist. Just remember that no horticulturist would use a dull knife for anything but spreading butter. Dip each piece in medicated baby powder and plant them 4 inches deep with the eye looking up. If spring planted, they'll bloom the same year.

Rhizomes

Rhizomes are propagated by cutting too. As I told you, rhizomes are really fat, underground stems that creep along just below the surface of the soil and send down long, branching roots. All the eyes are on top of the rhizome. When you cut them up, make sure there is at least one eye per section. (I usually include 2 or 3 just for good measure.) Dust each piece in medicated baby powder. If you live in the colder northern half of the country, you'll want to start your lilies of the valley and other rhizomes indoors in damp sand or peat moss. If you live in one of the warmer parts of the country, you can set them outdoors, 4 inches deep with the eye looking upward, immediately after dividing them. Wherever you plant them, rhizomes will usually produce a flowering plant in their first full growing season, unlike their slow-poke cousins who may loaf around for five years before producing one bloom.

SOME OF MY BEST FRIENDS ARE BULBS

Don't get all excited, I'm not going to introduce you to all 3,000 bulb varieties, just a couple of dozen you can easily find and count on. I again want to remind you to secure as many catalogs as you can so that you can better understand—and take advantage of—the vastness of the bulb family.

Achimenes

(MAGIC FLOWER, WIDOW'S TEARS)

Achimenes are hanging-basket and straw-berry-jar favorites. From spring until fall they bear small, colorful, trumpet-shaped blossoms on graceful, trailing stems. They are available in many colors, including purple, pink, yellow, blue, and red; some of the newer varieties have contrasting veining or bright-colored throats.

Achimenes require warm temperatures throughout their growing period. They are very susceptible to cold; even one light frost can kill the rhizomes for good. For these reasons, they are usually grown in containers or as house plants.

Achimenes rhizomes look like tiny pine cones and are very fragile. Handle them with great care. In late winter or early spring, pot them in a mixture of 2 parts peat moss, one part purchased potting soil, and one part clean sand. Cover the rhizomes with 1/2 to 1 inch of soil and water from below. Set them in bright indirect sunlight and keep moist. After they've sprouted, you can move the container outdoors to a spot in light shade.

When the plants stop flowering, let them die back. The rhizomes can be stored in the pot or sifted out and stored in dry peat moss or vermiculite. Keep them at about 60°F. until February, when you should move them to a window and start watering again.

Agapanthus

In warm climates, agapanthuses can be grown outdoors with no winter protection. In moderate climates, they require winter mulching; in cold climates they must be grown as house plants or in tubs that are taken in during the winter. All agapanthuses produce abundant straplike foliage and clusters of blue or white flowers for several weeks in summer. They vary in height from 18 inches to nearly 5 feet.

Plant agapanthuses any time in a spot that receives full sun. The tuber should be set just below the soil surface, and the plants should be placed at least 24 inches apart.

Wood tubs make the best containers for agapanthuses. They do best in tubs if their roots are severely crowded and left undisturbed. Clay pots are frequently broken by the pressure of the growing roots. Pot them in a mixture of equal parts purchased potting soil, clean sand or perlite, and coarse peat moss.

Keep outdoor or container plants moist throughout the growing season, but somewhat dry the rest of the year. Feed container plants with a standard house plant fertilizer every month or two. Propagate them in spring.

Amaryllis

(BELLADONNA LILY, NAKED LADY)

The true amaryllis, or belladonna lily, is often confused with the amaryllis *(Hippeastrum)* grown as a house plant and with the hardy amaryllises of the *Lycoris* genus. It differs from both. This unusual lily grows long, flat leaves in early spring. These die back and are followed by a leafless flower stalk in early summer. A month or more later clusters of fragrant, trumpet-shaped blossoms unfold on the 2-foot-tall stalks. The flowers, which bloom for six to eight weeks, may be mauve, white, pink, or rosy red.

Belladonna lilies can be grown in all but the northernmost states. Plant in well-drained soil enriched with compost or well-rotted manure. In the Deep South, cover the bulbs with 1 or 2 inches of soil; elsewhere cover with 5 to 8 inches of soil, depending on winter temperatures. Apply 5-10-5 fertilizer when the foliage appears.

Leave the bulbs undisturbed until you're ready to propagate from offsets. This should be done in the spring.

Anemone

There are several species of anemones, some of which are daisy-flowered, while others are poppy-flowered. Colors include white, pink, red, blue, and purple; and they attain heights that vary from 3 to 18 inches. Anemones, which bloom in the spring, make lovely and long-lasting cut flowers. Just remember to cut the stems with a sharp knife or pair of scissors, as pulling them by hand can injure the tuber.

Apennina and Greek anemones (the daisy-flowered ones) do best in the southern half of the country, but may be grown in protected places or with a good winter mulch in the rest of the country. They should be set out in spring.

All other anemones should be planted in early spring and dug out in late summer in the northern half of the country. Elsewhere they may be set out in fall and left undisturbed for years.

All anemones thrive in light shade or full sun and in well-drained, enriched soil. Soak the tubers (or seeds) of all anemones in lukewarm water for forty-eight hours before planting.

Propagate them by dividing the tubers after the foliage matures, or by seed, which will take eighteen months to produce a flowering plant.

Begonia

There are two species of begonias in the bulb category, the hardy begonia and the spectacular tuberous begonia. Both species bloom in summer, require shade, and grow from tuberous roots.

The hardy begonia produces clusters of tiny pink flowers on 2-foot-tall plants. Plant the small tubers 1 to 2 inches deep. In the South they may remain in the ground unprotected; in the middle states, they require a winter mulch; and in the North they should be taken indoors in winter.

The tuberous begonia produces blossoms from 2 to 10 inches in diameter and in every color except blue and green. Both upright and trailing varieties are available. The tubers may be started indoors or outdoors, but in all parts of the country they must be taken indoors for the winter. To start them indoors, set the tubers in flats or boxes of damp peat moss; press them down firmly but don't cover them. After the tubers sprout, transplant them to 6-inch pots; move them outdoors when the night temperatures stay above 50°. Outdoors, set the tubers in soil to which manure and peat moss have been added. Apply a mild fertilizer every two or three weeks throughout the growing season.

Propagate begonias from seed in midwinter for blooms the following summer or from stem or root cuttings in spring.

Bessera

(CORALDROPS)

Coraldrops provide two months of midsummer color. Their clusters of small, bell-shaped, orange-red blossoms are borne on 2- to 3-foot tall stalks. The foliage, which consists of 2 or 3 narrow, spindly leaves, is not noticeable.

In the southern half of the country, plant them in clusters in fall in a spot that gets full sun to light shade, 2½ to 3 inches deep, and leave undisturbed. In the middle states, apply a winter mulch; in the North, plant in spring and dig up the corms after the foliage dies back.

Propagate from cormels that develop around the parent corm. The cormels should be harvested in the fall and planted in spring.

Canna

Cannas are becoming popular as bedding plants again. The modern hybrids range in height from 1½ to 5 feet and send up spikes of large blossoms from early summer until frost. The color range covers white, yellow, and pink to scarlet. The handsome, broad leaves may be green, bronze, or blue-green.

All cannas prefer moist, rich soil, full sun, and high temperatures. In the southern half of the country, cannas can remain in the ground all year; elsewhere they must be dug up in fall after frost blackens the foliage. In the North, start cannas indoors in Pro-mix in late February; elsewhere set them 15 to 18 inches apart in the garden after all threat of frost has passed and cover with 1 or 2 inches of soil.

Propagate by dividing the rhizomes in spring.

Chionodoxa

(GLORY-OF-THE-SNOW)

As its popular name implies, the tiny chionodoxa is one of the first bulbs to bloom in the spring. The most common species bears small, star-shaped, violet-blue flowers with white centers, 8 to 10 per stem. Other species bear lilac, white, pink, and porcelain blue blossoms.

Plant the bulbs 2 inches deep in fertile, well-drained soil in early autumn. They do best in full sun or light shade. No further care is necessary.

Clivia

(KAFFIR LILY)

The most popular species of clivia is the scarlet kaffir lily, which is commonly grown as a winter-blooming house plant. Kaffir lilies have fragrant orange to scarlet blossoms with yellow throats. Other clivia species come in salmon, yellow, and white.

Although kaffir lilies can be grown outdoors in the Deep South, they are usually grown in containers there because they do best when their roots are crowded. They will bloom in summer outdoors.

Pot them in a mix of equal parts potting soil, peat moss, and clean sand, just barely covering the bulbs. Keep the pots in a place receiving bright indirect sunlight. Apply a house-plant fertilizer once a month until fall. In fall stop fertilizing and water very sparingly until the plant blooms.

Propagate from offsets in fall.

Colchicum

(AUTUMN CROCUS)

Colchicum blossoms spring out of the ground in fall, long after their foliage has died. The flowers look like crocus and occur in shades of pink and lavender as well as white.

Plant colchicums in late summer, covering them with 3 to 4 inches of soil. They prefer full sun or light shade and should be situated so they can remain undisturbed for many years.

Propagate from cormels after the foliage dies back in early summer.

Colocasia

(ELEPHANT'S EAR)

Elephant's ears are grown for their large, spear-shaped leaves which often grow to 2 feet in length. The plants often reach 6 feet tall.

Only in the Deep South can elephant's ears remain outdoors over the winter. Elsewhere they must be dug up after the first fall frost.

Plant them in a sunny or lightly shaded spot in moist soil that's been worked with peat moss, sand, and rotted manure. For a container planting, use a mixture of 2 parts potting soil, 2 parts peat moss, one part rotted manure, and one part sand. Move indoors before frost and place in bright indirect sunlight.

Propagate by cutting the tubers into pieces in spring. Dust with fungicide and allow to dry for two or three days before planting.

Convallaria

(LILY-OF-THE-VALLEY)

Delicate, fragrant lilies of the valley are indoor and outdoor favorites, blooming all summer. They are good for indoor forcing and for creating a neglectable ground cover in shady areas.

Lilies of the valley do not do well in warm

climates. Elsewhere, in fall or spring plant the pips one inch deep in moist, acid soil.

Propagate in fall by dividing the pips after the foliage yellows.

Crocus

Crocuses are among the most popular of the spring-flowering bulbs. Less widely known species also bloom in fall and even in winter in mild climates. The small, cup-shaped blossoms are available in a wide range of colors, including lavender and purple, yellow, white, or striped.

Crocuses are hardy throughout the country and do best in areas with low winter temperatures. Plant crocus corms 2 to 4 inches deep as early in the fall as they are available. Every fall, sprinkle a little bone meal or 5-10-5 fertilizer on the soil covering them. No other care is necessary.

For indoor forcing, plant corms in October in a mixture of equal parts potting soil, peat moss, and clean sand. Place the pots in a cold-frame until February, then take them indoors to sprout.

Cyclamen

There are two types of cyclamen—the large-flowered florists' cyclamen (*C. persicum*) and the smaller but more hardy species cyclamens. Florists' cyclamens are usually bought as pot plants and may be grown outdoors in the far South. Species cyclamen can be grown outdoors in all but the Deep South and far North. The butterfly-shaped flowers of cyclamen may be pink, red, or white, and may appear at various times in the spring, summer, and fall, according to the species. The attractive heart-shaped foliage may be either marbled or solid green.

Plant the tubers of the small-flowered species cyclamens 1 or 2 inches deep in midsummer in a lightly shaded location in soil that has been worked with compost. Compost also should be applied as a mulch every spring.

Propagate cyclamen from seed. Blooming plants can be expected in about eighteen months.

Dahlia

Dahlias will provide blossoms in every color but blue from midsummer until frost in all areas of this country. The flowers range in diameter from 1 inch to 1 foot, and the plants vary in height from 1 to 7 feet. Dahlias come in a wide variety of shapes, including ball-shaped, cactus-flowered, pompom, anemone-flowered, and single-flowered.

Dahlias may be bought in three forms—root divisions, plants grown from cuttings, and pot roots. In all but the Deep South, dahlias should be planted in spring and dug up in the fall. They prefer full sun, but will tolerate light shade. Before planting, work compost, peat moss, and 5 pounds of 0-20-20 fertilizer per 100 square feet into the soil. Plant pot roots and plants the same as you would any seedling. Lay root divisions on their sides in 7-inch-deep holes and cover with 2 inches of soil; add more soil as the plants grow. When the plants are growing well, water with a light application of complete fertilizer. Tall plants may need to be pinched back to encourage bushiness or staked to prevent them from toppling.

In the fall, after the plants have stopped flowering, dig up the roots and place them in plastic-lined boxes of dry peat moss or vermiculite. Keep in a very cool place to prevent premature sprouting.

Dahlias may be propagated from root divisions, stem cuttings, or seeds, which will produce flowering plants the first year.

Eranthis

(WINTER ACONITE)

The honey-scented, yellow flowers of winter aconite are among the first to appear in spring. Winter aconites are hardy in all but the far North and will flourish in virtually any soil. They do best in full sun or light shade and should be planted in a location protected from the wind.

Plant the tubers as early as possible in late summer or fall. Soak them in water for twenty-four hours, then plant them 3 inches deep.

Propagate winter aconite by cutting the tubers. They also grow readily from seed, but will take two to three years to flower.

Eremurus

(FOXTAIL LILY)

The flower stalks of foxtail lilies may reach 9 feet in height. When the plants blossom in early summer, the top 3 to 4 feet of each stalk is covered with hundreds of small flowers, which may be white, yellow, orange, pink, or rose. Foxtail lilies make excellent and long-lasting cut flowers.

Foxtail lilies can be grown in all areas, except the Deep South and the far North, if they are given good winter mulch. In the fall, plant the tubers 6 inches deep in compost or manure-enriched soil. Once planted, leave foxtail lilies undisturbed. They should do well for ten to fifteen years.

Freesia

Freesias are popular as winter-blooming house plants because of their bright blossoms and intense fragrance. They can be grown outdoors only in the Deep South (with the exception of corms specially treated to bloom in summer). Freesias come in pink, white, yellow, lilac, blue, purple, orange, and vermilion.

To grow as house plants, set the corms in a mix of equal parts peat moss, potting soil, and clean sand. Cover the corms very lightly. In the summer, set the pots outdoors in a cool, shaded place. Move them indoors to a sunny window before the first frost. Keep the soil moist, and apply a house-plant fertilizer once a month until the buds begin to color.

Propagate from cormels after the foliage

dies back. Store both corms and cormels in a dry place until June, when they should be repotted. Plants grown from seed will flower in six months to a year.

Fritillaria

(CROWN IMPERIAL, CHECKERED FRITILLARY)

The striking flower clusters of crown imperials *(F. imperialis)* appear atop 2- to 4-feet-tall stalks in early spring. The cluster of large, bell-shaped blossoms, which may be red, bronze, yellow, or orange, are crowned with a mass of narrow, pointed leaves. The smaller checkered fritillary *(F. meleagris),* also known as the guinea-hen flower, grows to one hundred thirty-two inches tall and bears pendant, bell-shaped flowers which may be purple- and white-checkered or all white.

The checkered fritillary is hardy throughout the country, and the crown imperial is hardy in all but the northernmost states. Plant the bulbs of both in summer in a lightly shaded location. Plant crown imperials 6 inches deep and checkered fritillaries 4 inches deep. When the plants appear in spring, make a light application of 5-10-5 fertilizer.

Propagate them from offsets in early summer after the foliage has died back.

Galanthus

(SNOWDROP)

Snowdrops are among the first flowers to bloom in spring. Their delicate blossoms are white, tipped with green, and the leaves are slender.

Snowdrops can be grown in all parts of the country except the Deep South. They do best, however, in cool climates.

Plant the bulbs 2 or 3 inches deep in early fall, preferably in a shady location. No further care is necessary.

To grow snowdrops indoors, plant the bulbs in fall in a mixture of equal parts potting soil, peat moss, and sand. Leave the pots in a coldframe until after the first of the year, then place them in indirect sunlight in the coolest room in your house.

Snowdrops can be propagated from offsets after the first frost.

Gladiolus

The gladiolus is the bestselling bulb in the United States, primarily because of its popularity as a cut flower. Gladioluses are available in many sizes (ranging from 1 to 5 feet in height) and in 28 different colors. A gladiolus plant has a bloom period lasting only a week to ten days, but staggered plantings can provide blooms over a period of three months. Because its tall, stiff foliage is not very attractive, gladioluses are usually restricted to a special cutting garden.

In the South, gladiolus corms may remain

in the garden all year; elsewhere, they must be dug in the fall and replanted in spring. Regardless of climate, gladioluses do best when dug and replanted annually.

Prepare the gladiolus bed, which should be in full sun, by working compost, peat moss, and 5-10-5 fertilizer (at a rate of one cup per 25-foot row) into the soil. Plant the corms 5 inches deep in spring after the last frost. New plantings should be made every week to ten days up until two months before the first fall frost; this will insure a prolonged period of continuous bloom.

When the spikes appear, apply 5-10-5 fertilizer at the same rate as above, watering it into the soil. When the spikes are about a foot tall, some sort of support will become necessary. Either stake them or mound up 6 inches of soil around the stems.

About a month after the flowers fade, lift the corms with a spading fork, cut off the foliage, and dry in a dark, dry place for two or three weeks. Remove the spent corm, divide the corms and cormels, and dust them with an insecticide-fungicide. Place in an old stocking or mesh bag and store in a very cool place over the winter.

Gloriosa
(GLORY LILY)

Surprisingly, the glory lily is a climbing vine. The 3- to 4-inch flowers are composed of long, recurved petals which may be either yellow tipped with scarlet or orange tipped with red. They are popular as house plants because they can be induced to bloom in any season, as they can when grown outdoors in the Deep South. When planted outdoors in colder areas, they bloom in summer.

For outdoor culture, plant the tubers 4 inches deep in manure-enriched soil, preferably in full sun. Apply 5-10-5 fertilizer once a month during the growing season. In the North, the tubers must be dug up in fall after the first frost.

To grow as house plants, pot glory lily tubers in a mixture of equal parts potting soil, peat moss, and clean sand. Keep the soil moist and fertilize every twelve weeks during the growing season. The dormant period usually lasts from October through January; during this time, withhold both water and fertilizer.

Propagate from the tubers in early summer.

Hippeastrum
(AMARYLLIS)

Amaryllises are most popular as winter-blooming house plants, although they can be grown outdoors in the Deep South. In late winter or early spring, amaryllises send up flower stalks which rapidly attain a height of 1 to 2 feet. Shortly thereafter, the buds open into 3 or 4 spectacular, lily-shaped flowers which may be white, pink, or red. Often, a second flower stalk appears as the blooms on the first begin to fade.

Amaryllises may be grown outdoors in the garden year-round in zones 8 and 9. For those of you in zones 5 through 7 who wish to grow amaryllis in your garden, start the bulbs indoors in pots in February. For zones 3 and 4, start the bulbs in March and set them outside in late May. In all cases, the plants should be set in light, well-drained soil in full sun. North of zone 8, the bulbs should be dug up in fall before the first frost.

Propagate from offsets. Plants grown from seed take three or four years to produce blossoms.

Hyacinthus

(HYACINTH)

The sweet spring fragrance of hyacinths makes them as popular for indoor forcing as they are for outdoor bedding. The most popular species, the large-flowered hyacinth, grows 8 to 12 inches tall and bears tight, 6- to 10-inch clusters of tiny pink, blue, white, or yellow flowers. Almost as widely known are the smaller and more sparsely flowered French-Roman hyacinths.

Large-flowered hyacinths are hardy throughout this country, but French-Roman hyacinths are hardy only in the South. All hyacinths should be planted in the fall and do best in full sun.

Plant large-flowered hyacinths 5 inches deep, French-Roman and other smaller hyacinths 3 inches deep. In the North, a winter mulch is beneficial. Although large-flowered hyacinths will survive if left outdoors over the winter, it is advisable to dig them up every fall and replace the small bulbs (resulting from division of the parent bulb) with large, new

ones. The small bulbs can be replanted in enriched soil in another bed and left there until they reach the size necessary for good bloom development.

To grow hyacinths indoors, pot them in the fall in a mixture of equal parts peat moss, potting soil, and clean sand. Set the pots in your cellar or some other dark, cool place, and leave them there for three months, or until the sprout is about 2 inches tall. Move the plant into a very cool spot that receives indirect light. In about a week, move the plant into a sunny window. When the buds begin to color, move the plant into curtain-filtered sunlight. After the plants have bloomed and the foliage matured, allow the soil to dry out. Replant the bulbs in the garden in the fall.

Hymenocallis

(SPIDER LILY)

Spider lilies, also known as Peruvian daffodils, bear fragrant, delicately exotic 4-inch blossoms in midsummer. The most popular species is white with green stripes; another species is yellow, and still another is white with very faint stripes. The flower stalks grow 18 to 24 inches in height and the straplike leaves are often 2 feet long.

In the Deep South, spider lilies may be left outdoors over the winter; elsewhere they must be dug up before frost or grown as house plants. In spring, work well-rotted or dried cow manure into the soil and plant the bulbs 4 inches deep. (In the Deep South, bulbs may be planted in fall as well as spring.)

In areas having cold winter temperatures, dig the bulbs when the foliage dries up; cut off the foliage and store the bulbs upside down in dry peat moss or vermiculite in a shady, airy place at 65°–70°F.

Propagate from offsets.

Ipheion

(SPRING STARFLOWER)

The small, bluish white flowers of spring starflowers appear in early spring above low-growing grassy foliage. They are especially charming when naturalized in low grass or clumped together in rock gardens.

Spring starflowers are hardy in all but the northernmost states. Plant the bulbs 3 inches deep in late summer or early fall. They prefer full sun, but will tolerate light shade. The plants will flourish and multiply rapidly with no further care.

For indoor culture, set the bulbs one inch deep in a mixture of equal parts peat moss, potting soil, and clean sand. Keep the soil moist until the foliage dies back in early summer. From then on, keep the bulbs dry until you repot them in fresh soil in late summer or early autumn.

Propagate from offsets in midsummer.

Iris

Only 3 groups of iris are classified as bulbous plants; the rest are perennials. *Reticulata* irises grow only 4 to 8 inches tall, and bear small purple, blue, or yellow flowers in early spring. The *Xiphium* group includes the Spanish, Dutch, and English irises, all of which grow 1 to 2 feet tall and are available in a wide variety of colors. Juno irises bear 5 to 7 blossoms on each 2-foot stalk; the blossoms may be one of several colors or bicolored.

Juno and *Reticulata* irises are hardy except in the northernmost states; *Xiphium* irises are hardy only in the southern half of the country.

All bulbous irises should be planted in late summer or early fall, and all do best in full sun. Cover *Reticulata* irises with 3 inches of soil; cover *Xiphium* and Juno irises with 5 inches of soil. When the plants appear in spring, make a light application of 5-10-5 fertilizer. Dig up and divide the bulbs during their midsummer dormancy once every four or five years.

Ixia

(AFRICAN CORN LILY)

The gaily colored, 2-inch blossoms of African corn lilies are borne on 18-inch stalks in early summer. The blossoms may be pink, red, orange, yellow, or cream; most of them have darker centers. The flowers open fully and form a star only when in full sun; under any other conditions, they will remain folded in a cup shape.

Ixias do well outdoors only in the dry regions of the West and Southwest. In warm climates elsewhere, moist soil prevents the corms from ripening as they should. Plant the corms 3 inches deep in November, and apply 5-10-5 fertilizer when the plants appear. For best results, dig up the corms in summer, after the foliage has died away, and reset them in late fall.

To grow ixias as house plants, pot the corms in equal parts potting soil, clean sand, and peat moss in the fall. Water regularly and feed once a month while the foliage stays green. When it withers, remove the corms, store them in a dry place, and repot in fresh soil the following fall.

Propagate from cormels in summer. Seeds take three years to produce flowering plants.

Leucojum

(SNOWFLAKE)

There are 3 types of snowflakes—spring, summer, and autumn flowering. All bear delicate bell-shaped flowers which are white, tipped with green, except for the autumn snowflake which bears pinkish flowers.

The summer and spring snowflake grow in all parts of the country. The autumn snowflake does not do well in very warm climates. Plant the bulbs 3 inches deep in early fall, preferably in a sunny location. Leave the bulbs undisturbed, until you wish to propagate them. This should be done in the fall.

Lilium

(LILY)

Lilies have been greatly improved in recent years. Modern hybrids are stronger, more adaptable, and more colorful than their old-fashioned ancestors. If he or she chooses wisely, the modern gardener can have a parade of different lilies beginning in June and lasting through July. With the many sizes, shapes, and color combinations now available, you need never become bored. Lilies vary in height from 2 to 8 feet and are available in every color but blue; they also come in striped and spotted color combinations.

According to the Royal Horticultural Society and the North American Lily Society, lilies can be divided into the following groups: Asiatic Hybrids, Martagon Hybrids, Candidum Hybrids, American Hybrids, Longiflorum Hybrids, Aurelian Hybrids, Oriental Hybrids, Unclassified Hybrids, and True Species of Lilies. There are also various subgroups within each of these 9 groups.

Most lilies are hardy in all areas of the country, and most need at least five or six hours of sun a day, the exceptions being tiger lilies and wood lilies which will tolerate light shade.

No lily will do well in wet soil, so good drainage is a must. It is also important that the soil have adequate organic matter, so be sure to work in a large amount of compost, peat moss, or leaf mold before planting. As soon as possible after purchasing your bulbs, plant them 4 to 6 inches deep, except for Madonna lilies which should be planted only one inch deep.

All lilies benefit from mulching, as it prevents their roots from drying out and keeps them cool. In the Deep South or in any other area where frost is rare, dig up the bulbs in the fall and refrigerate them for two months to simulate the period of dormancy. It may become necessary to stake lilies to protect them from rain and wind damage.

Lilies may be propagated in the fall from the scales that make up the bulb, from the bulbils that form in the leaf joints of some varieties, or from the small bulbs which form around the parent bulb. Plants propagated from any of the above methods will flower in two to three years; plants grown from seed usually take four years to flower.

Lycoris

(HARDY AMARYLLIS)

Very early in spring, the long, straplike leaves of the hardy amaryllis appear; in early summer, they die back. The leaves are replaced in late summer by a tall stalk topped with a cluster of large, fragrant, trumpet-shaped blossoms, either yellow, pink, lilac, or scarlet in color.

L. squamigera, the popular lilac-colored member of the family, is hardy in zones 6 through 10. All lycoris may be grown with great success in containers. To do so, set the bulbs so that their noses are at the surface of a soil mix consisting of equal parts potting soil, peat moss, and sand. Water them thoroughly, but don't water them again until the flower stalk appears. When it does, continue

to water until the flowers fade; then withhold water until leaves appear. Water and fertilize regularly until the foliage fades; then keep the soil dry until the flower stalks reappear.

Propagate from offsets.

Muscari

(GRAPE HYACINTH)

Grape hyacinths are among the most agreeable of bulbous plants. They can be grown anywhere in this country with a minimum of care, and their tiny, fragrant blossoms have long been spring favorites. They are charming when naturalized in grass or scattered about in a rock garden. Grape hyacinths may also be grown indoors as house plants. The most common grape hyacinths have sky-blue flowers. Less well known varieties come in white and purple as well as in combinations of yellow and purple, and light and dark blue. A plumed mauve variety is also available.

Plant the bulbs 3 inches deep in early fall, preferably in a sunny location. No further care is necessary. Propagate from offsets in fall.

Narcissus

Narcissuses are on everyone's list of favorite springtime flowers—and for several good reasons. With a minimum of care, narcissuses will produce great clumps of cheerful, fragrant flowers every spring. Basic narcissus colors are white and shades of orange, yellow, and red; however, they're available in many different combinations and still more shadings and variations in size and shape.

Most narcissuses are hardy in all parts of the country, the exceptions being the Tazetta types, the cyclamen-flowered narcissuses, and some of the species narcissuses.

Plant the bulbs in late summer to insure good root development before the first fall frost. All types prefer full sun or light shade. Before setting the bulbs, work bone meal into the soil at a rate of 5 pounds per 100 square feet for bed plantings or one teaspoonful per hole for individual plantings. Set each bulb 3 times as deep as its diameter at the widest point. (Depth may vary from 3 to 6 inches.) In the spring, when the bulbs begin to sprout, sprinkle bone meal around the plants again.

Propagate from offsets in midsummer.

Nerine

(NERINE LILY)

Nerine lilies are very popular as potted plants because of their striking and long-lasting clusters of long-stemmed flowers. The flowers, which may be white or one of various shades of pink and red, appear atop 1- to 2-foot-tall stalks in early fall. Long, straplike leaves appear at about the same time and continue to grow long after the flowers have faded.

Nerine lilies can be grown outdoors in the Deep South, but because they flower more profusely when crowded, they are usually grown in containers even in mild climates. In midsummer, pot the bulbs in a mixture of equal parts potting soil, peat moss, and clean sand, setting only the bottom half of each bulb below the soil surface. Don't water until the flower stalks appear; then feed and water regularly throughout the winter and spring. Cut back the watering in summer. Let the foliage die back, then cut. Move the pots indoors to a cool, bright location before frost.

Propagate from offsets during repotting, which will be necessary only once in five years.

Oxalis

There are several different species of oxalis, but all produce small blossoms atop neat clumps of foliage, which vary from a few inches to a foot in diameter. The blossoms may be pink, red, yellow, or white and appear at various times during spring and summer, depending on the species.

Plant the bulbs in spring 2 inches deep in a sunny location, and apply 5-10-5 fertilizer when growth appears. In the North, oxalises must be taken indoors in winter.

Propagate from offsets in the fall; they will flower in one year.

Polianthes tuberosa

(TUBEROSE)

The extraordinarily fragrant white blossoms of tuberoses are borne on tall (1 to 4 feet) stalks in late summer and early fall. They make excellent cut flowers, but because of their intense fragrance should be used sparingly.

Once night temperatures remain above 60°F. in spring, plant tuberose bulbs 3 inches deep in a sunny location. Fertilize them once a month from the time sprouts appear until the buds begin to color. After the foliage has been browned by frost, dig up the bulbs, remove the stems, and dry them for two weeks before storing them in a cool, dry place.

Propagate from offsets. These smaller bulbs often take two years to bloom. It's best to start out with less than full-sized bulbs to insure two or more years of flowering before division occurs, which will result in smaller blossoms. If you prefer, you can, of course, buy new large bulbs every spring.

Ranunculus asiaticus

(PERSIAN BUTTERCUP)

Persian buttercups bear large, lushly petaled blossoms in every color of the rainbow (except blue and green) as well as in various shades and combinations. A single plant may produce as many as 75 flowers in one blooming season.

In the Deep South, Persian buttercups may be planted in late fall for early spring bloom; elsewhere they should be planted in early spring for late spring bloom. To provide proper moisture conditions for the tubers (dry crowns and wet roots), knock the bottoms out of some clay pots and set them so that their rims are 1½ inches above the soil surface. Place the tubers in the pots and cover with 1½ inches of soil. Water once, then withhold any more water until growth begins; then keep evenly moist. Dig and store the tubers after the foliage withers. Tubers may be divided for propagation at this time. Spring-sown seed will reach flowering size the following year.

Scilla

(SQUILL)

The most well-known squill is blue, but pink, purple, lavender, red, and white varieties are available also. All send up 6- to 12-inch spikes of small, drooping blossoms early in spring.

The most popular varieties of squill are hardy throughout the country. Others will grow only in the southern half of the country; still others won't grow in warm climates, so make sure you know the growing requirement of the species you buy. Most squills should be planted in the fall, and all will flourish under any light conditions. Plant 3 to 4 inches deep.

Squills may be propagated from offsets, but the bulbs are so inexpensive most people buy new ones rather than disturb the original planting.

Sparaxis

(HARLEQUIN FLOWER)

Harlequin flowers are available in a wide range of colors. All have yellow throats surrounded by 6 small black triangles (one of which occurs on the inside of every petal). The 2-inch flowers appear in spring on 12- to 18-inch stalks.

Harlequin flowers do best in areas with hot, dry summers, particularly in the West and Southwest. In areas that have even a moderate amount of rain in summer, they should be grown in pots or other containers. Plant the corms 2 to 3 inches deep in fall and fertilize once a month after growth starts and until the foliage dies. Move the pots indoors before frost.

Propagate from cormels in spring.

Sprekelia formosissima

(AZTEC LILY)

If planted outdoors, Aztec lilies will bloom in summer; indoors they bloom in the spring. One 4-inch red blossom is produced on each 12- to 18-inch stalk.

Except in very warm climates, Aztec lilies should be planted outdoors, 3 to 4 inches deep, only after all danger of frost is past. They will bloom in about two months. Dig up the bulb and foliage before the first fall frost and allow it to dry completely. Then remove the foliage and store the bulb in dry peat moss or vermiculite at 55°–60°F.

To grow indoors, treat the same way as amaryllis *(Hippeastrum)*.

Propagate from offsets.

Tigridia

(TIGER FLOWER)

The 6-inch blossoms of tigridias have one very distinctive feature—brightly spotted inner petals. Tigridias come in white, yellow, pink, lavender, buff, and orange. A single plant often produces several 3- to 5-inch wide blooms with foliage collars over a period of two weeks.

Tigridias can remain outdoors through the winter only in the South; elsewhere they must be dug up in the fall after their leaves turn yellow. Dry the bulbs thoroughly and store in dry peat moss or vermiculite in a place that is cool and dry.

In the spring, when the night temperatures stay above 60°F., plant the bulbs 4 inches deep in a sunny location. Apply 5-10-5 fertilizer twice a month and keep the soil moist.

Propagate from offsets.

Tritonia

(synonym, MONTBRETIA)

The saffron tritonia, which is the most popular member of this genus, bears spikes of 2-inch blossoms in various shades of red, yellow, and orange. Other species of tritonia come in white, pink, salmon, and purple as well. All bloom in summer and grow 1 to 2 feet tall.

Tritonias will survive winter outdoors in the southern half of the country; in the North, they must be dug after the foliage is browned by the first fall frost and stored indoors. In the South, plant in the fall; in the North, plant in the spring. The corms should be planted 3 inches deep in a sunny location. Apply 5-10-5 fertilizer twice a month.

Propagate from cormels, as seeds take three years to produce plants of flowering size.

Tulipa

(TULIP)

Today there are 15 classes of tulips and over 4,000 named varieties. These include many different shapes, sizes, colors, and color combinations.

Tulips blossom at various times during the spring, from March through May, depending on the specific variety and the climate to which they are exposed. Early tulips, for example, may not bloom until mid-April in Pennsylvania or states further north.

Large-flowered garden tulips do best in the northern half of the country, where they can remain in the ground all year. Before planting, work bone meal into the soil at a rate of 5 pounds per 100 square feet. When sprouts appear in the spring, make a light application of 5-10-5 fertilizer.

Bulbs should be planted as early as possible in the fall. If you are going to discard the bulbs after blooming (to avoid multiplying and the resultant decrease in flower size), plant them 5 inches apart and 5 inches deep. It is better, however, to plant the bulbs deeper, as this slows the multiplying process and results in good flower production for up

to eight years. For deep plantings, work up the soil to a depth of 18 inches, then set the bulbs 10 inches deep and 6 inches apart.

To grow large-flowered tulips in the South, refrigerate the bulbs for two months after purchasing, then plant 6 to 8 inches deep. Discard them after flowering.

Species tulips can be grown in all but the Deep South. In the fall, plant them 3 to 6 inches deep and leave them undisturbed.

Propagate from offsets in midsummer.

Zantedeschia

(CALLA LILY)

In spring and summer, calla lilies produce large, upright goblet-shaped blossoms on tall (1½ to 4 feet) stems. The broad, erect leaves are attractive in their own right. The various calla lily species and hybrids bear flowers in white, pink, red, and yellow.

The white calla lily flourishes in mucky soil that is frequently covered with water. All the species do best in light shade. If in full sun, midday shade is advisable.

In the North, calla lilies should be planted in spring and dug up in the fall. Store in dry peat moss or vermiculite in a cool (40°–50°F.) place. In the South, they may be planted at any time of the year. Plant them 4 inches deep and apply 5-10-5 fertilizer once a month.

To grow calla lilies as house plants, plant the rhizomes in fall, setting them 3 inches deep in equal parts peat moss, potting soil, and clean sand. Water them lightly until a sprout appears; from then on, keep the soil moist and apply a good house-plant fertilizer once a month. In the summer, cut back on the watering. When the leaves wither, stop watering altogether until fall. At that time, begin watering again and growth will begin again.

Propagate by dividing the rhizomes in early fall.

Zephyranthes

(ZEPHYR LILY)

Zephyr lilies can be found blooming from spring to fall. The plants grow only 6 to 8 inches tall and produce single, upright, lily-type flowers. The many colors available include white, yellow, pink, apricot, and salmon.

In the South, zephyr lilies can be planted in the fall and left undisturbed for many years. In the North, the bulbs must be planted in spring 2 inches deep in a sunny location and dug up in the fall. Wash them in a mild solution of Fels-Naptha soap and water. Let dry and dust with medicated baby powder. Store in dry paper or sawdust. Repot them in February and outside they go in May.

Propagate from offsets.

5

Annuals

The Annual Parade

Annuals are without a doubt the hardest-working, most productive, attractive, and undemanding flower group in the whole garden. Once annuals are planted in the outside garden, a gardener seldom need spend much attention on them. (To tell the truth, they seldom get any attention from most home gardeners, and yet continue to bloom day after day throughout most of the summer and in some cases far into the fall). To top it all off, an annual lives its full life-span in one year.

They have only one purpose in life, and that is to give beauty and enjoyment to the world around them. These beauties are the elves of the flowering nation. Happy-go-lucky, carefree ramblers, they complement and help accent all of the other plants in your garden.

The annuals keep the rest of your garden in stitches most of the summer with their antics. They crawl under the pines and tickle their limbs, they snore beneath the maple, and dance with the birch. They are truly the lovable jesters of the queen's court and will try anything once. For instance, they'll try growing in the shade just because you want them to. Anyone can grow annuals if he or she will just relax and plan to have fun. There are only a few things that one needs to know to have a beautiful and successful garden full of annuals, so pay close attention and follow me down the garden path. Call out to the little ones along the way—by name, of course: Rumpelstiltskin, Thumbelina, or any leprechaun name you can remember.

PRE-PLAN

When it comes to adding annuals to our garden plan, we must stick with a pre-planned sketch. As simple as it may seem, planning a garden without a garden plan is like taking a trip without a map. A well thought-out plan allows us to get the best possible results from the flowers we select.

We must make certain that we have a place for everyone. It's embarrassing to invite a plant over to spend the summer only to find that you don't have a spare bed for him and then have to rush around and find a makeshift spot where he will be uncomfortable all season. His discomfort will be reflected in his performance, and you will have no one to blame but yourself. All it takes to have success is a little foresight, and that only costs a few minutes of your time.

Do you have a new home and want flowers right away? Or maybe you are renting and want to create a lovely effect without going to a lot of expense. Annuals are for you.

If the property already has shrubs, plant annuals between the shrubs or in front of those that are well established.

Do you love the bulb blossoms that are such a delight in the early spring and then vanish for another year? Plant annuals among them, either in the fall or early spring, and they will do much to hide the fading bulb foliage. You might try centaurea, larkspur, or phlox.

Annuals are very obliging. Use them to fill gaps in your perennial beds where they will supply lovely color all summer long while the perennials are resting. Most perennials are either spring- or fall-blooming, and without annuals in these beds, you aren't going to have very much color during the summer months.

Of course, you can also use annuals by themselves to provide a quick and inexpensive wealth of blooms in beds and borders. If you have the space, consider making a cutting garden. Actually most annuals will bloom far longer and more abundantly than perennials. Many, such as pansies, are even benefited by constant cutting.

And today, with the diversity of form, color, size, and height available, you can plan for just about any effect you feel will best express "you."

Design with a Purpose in Mind

Good-looking flower gardens don't just happen, they're made to happen by a gardener who has taken the time to study the growing habits of their favorite annuals: color, type of flower, light needs, and soil needs. Over the years, I have seen all over the world some of the most beautiful garden designs using annuals planned by world-renowned garden designers; what they all had in common was harmony. The colors, shapes, sizes, and heights were placed where they belonged, not just helter-skelter.

On pages 151–154 is a guide to the top 40 annuals that you may wish to consider for your garden. Keep in mind that *very hardy* means the plant can take care of itself, with no worry and no pampering; *tender* means you have to keep an eye on it from time to time, perhaps providing it with wind or winter protection; and *half-hardy* plants should be treated more like tender plants than hardy ones.

YOU MAKE THE BED, BUT THEY'VE GOT TO SLEEP IN IT!

You must prepare the soil for annuals just as you would for grass seed. I also want you to remember that it makes no difference whether you are planting seed or pre-grown seedlings, known as bedding plants.

Prepare the soil by spading it deeply until it is loose and will drain easily. Work as much as you can of peat moss or well-decomposed compost into the surface for best results.

Always select healthy, vigorous plants with deep green foliage. Top-quality bedding plants always pay off with a more successful and luxuriant garden.

Plant the seed or seedlings when all danger of frost is passed, spacing them according to directions. Water them thoroughly immediately after planting. You should water early in the day at ground level. Soak the soil thoroughly; don't just sprinkle the foliage.

Fertilize monthly, but be sure to follow directions and don't overfeed; this can result in too much foliage growth and not enough flowers.

Sunday Morning Snack

Feed all flowers with the following homemade mixture every two weeks on Sunday morning:

1 ounce liquid fish emulsion
1 ounce liquid soap
1 ounce household ammonia
1 ounce hydrogen peroxide
1 ounce whiskey
1 cup beer
1 tablespoon clear corn syrup
1 tablespoon Knox gelatin
4 teaspoons instant tea crystals

all dissolved in 2 gallons of warm water.

The two most important things to consider when planning a garden bed are exposure and size. Most annuals are sun-loving plants (though some will obligingly grow in shade and half-shade), so you can logically expect them to flower most vigorously and abundantly in a sunny location. Dig your bed in an area that can offer them five or six hours of sun a day, full sun if possible, and just watch them grow!

Don't make your beds less than 3 feet wide; anything narrower won't give you much of a showing. Generally speaking, 5 to 6 feet wide is plenty of space for a well-planned bed; if you make it any larger, the effect of individual flowers may be lost.

Full Sun

NAME	IDEAL SPACING (INCHES)	POTENTIAL HEIGHT (INCHES)	COLORS	HARDINESS	SPECIAL USES
Ageratum	8	8–12	Lavender, blue, white, pink	Tender	Edges, borders
Alyssum	8	3–6	Lavender, purple, white	Very hardy	Edges, rock gardens
Amaranthus	24	24–36	Colored foliage	Half-hardy	Colorful background plants
Antirrhinum (Snapdragon)	6–10	6–36	White, yellow, pink, red, orange	Hardy	Borders and backgrounds
Browallia	10	10–18	Blue, white	Half-hardy	Vines, hanging containers
Calendula	8–10	12–20	Yellow, orange, apricot, white	Hardy	Cut flowers; sometimes used as an herb
Celosia:					
Crested	24	10–18	Yellow, orange, dark red, red, lavender	Tender	Can be dried; also colorful with evergreens
Feathered	24	12–36	Yellow, orange, dark red, red	Tender	Same as Crested Celosia
Cleome	15	36–48	Pink, lavender, yellow	Tender	Set along a wall or fence
Cosmos	24	36–60	Light red, pink, white	Hardy	Nice for cutting
Dahlia	16	12–24	White, pink, light red, yellow	Tender	Blossoms profusely; good cut flowers
Dianthus (Garden pinks)	12	15–18	Pink, red, white, yellow, dark red	Hardy	For fragrance
Gaillardia (Blanket flower)	15	15–24	Yellow, orange, dark red	Hardy	Window boxes, planters
Geranium	12–14	18–30	Red, pink, white	Tender	Ideal for container plantings, window boxes

continued

Full Sun

NAME	IDEAL SPACING (INCHES)	POTENTIAL HEIGHT (INCHES)	COLORS	HARDINESS	SPECIAL USES
Gomphrena	12	18–24	White, pink, dark red	Hardy	For dried arrangements
Helichrysum bracteatum (Strawflower)	30	30	White, pink, yellow, orange, dark red, light red	Hardy	For dried arrangements
Ipomoea (Morning glory)	6	Vine	Pink, light red, blue	Half-hardy	Great climbing plant
Lathyrus odoratus (Sweet pea)	6	Vine	White, pink, light red, blue, lavender, purple, red	Very hardy	For fragrance; excellent climber
Matthiola (Stock)	15	15–30	White, pink, lavender, dark red, purple	Hardy	Excellent cut flower, fragrant
Phlox	18	10–20	White, yellow, dark red, lavender, pink	Hardy	Rock gardens, window boxes, and beds
Portulaca grandiflora (Moss rose)	10	4–6	Pink, red, white, yellow, orange	Tender	Good for rock gardens
Salvia	14–21	24	Red	Tender	Excellent for beds
Tagetes (Marigold):					
African (tall)	20	24–36	Yellow, orange	Half-hardy	
French (dwarf)	15	8–15	Yellow, orange, dark red	Half-hardy	Great for beds
Tropaeolum (Nasturtium)	15	12	Red, orange, yellow	Tender	Some can be trained to climb
Vinca (Periwinkle)	10–12	12–15	White, pink, light red, red, blue	Tender	Can stand hot or dry conditions; low maintenance
Zinnia	18	12–36	White, yellow, orange, red, light red	Tender	Superior cut flower

Sun to Part Shade

NAME	IDEAL SPACING (INCHES)	POTENTIAL HEIGHT (INCHES)	COLORS	HARDINESS	SPECIAL USES
Aster	15–24	15–36	Lavender, pink, purple, white, light red	Half hardy	Great cut flower
Begonia (fibrous or wax)	12	6–10	White, red, pink, light red	Tender	Hanging baskets, container plantings
Centaurea cyanus (Cornflower)	24	24–30	White, blue, lavender, red, pink	Very hardy	Good cut flower
Clarkia	18	24	White, purple, light red, red, lavender	Hardy	Good cut flower
Coleus	12	8–16	Colored foliage	Tender	Edging in shady garden
Cynoglossum amabile (Chinese forget-me-not)	12	30	Blue, white	Hardy	Good background for beds
Iberis (Candytuft)	12	12–18	White, pink, lavender, red	Hardy	Nice for bouquets, edging
Lobelia	8	4–10	Red, white, blue	Hardy	Edging, hanging baskets
Nicotiana	24	15–30	White, pink, dark red	Tender	For fragrance
Petunia	12	10–18	All colors and color combinations	Half-hardy	Borders, beds, hanging baskets
Salpiglossis	18	30	Yellow, lavender, dark red, white	Tender	Unusual flower, good for cut flowers
Verbena	18	8–18	White, pink, light red, red	Tender	Excellent for beds
Viola x wittrockiana (Pansy)	10	4–8	White, yellow, orange, blue, multicolor	Very hardy	Edging, rock gardens

Part Shade

NAME	IDEAL SPACING (INCHES)	POTENTIAL HEIGHT (INCHES)	COLORS	HARDINESS	SPECIAL USES
Coleus	12	20	Variegated in combinations of yellow, green, crimson, brown, salmon, and pink	Tender	Bedding, hanging baskets
Impatiens	12	8–30	White, lavender, pink, dark red	Tender	Can be grown indoors too, blooms profusely
Myosotis (Forget-me-not)	10	12	White, light red, blue	Hardy	Rock gardens, edging

The length of the bed will, quite likely, be determined by the layout of your property. And right here, in the middle of all this excitement, I will inject a sobering thought: remember, we want this flower-growing business to be a fun thing—don't bite off more than you can chew. You'll enjoy your flowers much more if you tailor the beds to what you can take care of handily in the time you have available. Gardening is fun, but it does take time to do it well. Weeds are always with us and constant vigilance is the price of liberty— liberty from a frustrating and back-breaking accumulation which can seemingly grow up overnight if you don't keep a watchful eye.

When you, in a frenzied burst of spring enthusiasm, plant too much, gardening can become a burden and defeat its own purpose, which is to give you pleasure. Especially if you are a first-year gardener, plan beds of manageable size so you can always keep them looking good and enjoy it at the same time. Don't try to grow too many different plants. Confine yourself to a few, choosing these with consideration for color, variety, and habit of growth.

The catalogs are beguiling, the descriptions glowing, and the profusion from which to choose bewildering. But you can, after awhile, begin to get your bearings and sort things out.

Knowing Your Plants from the Inside Out

When it comes to annuals, you have a choice of starting with seeds or waiting until the professionally grown bedding plants appear in your favorite garden shop. If you choose to grow from seed, you can either start the seeds indoors or sow them directly into your garden.

Let's concentrate on starting our seeds indoors. Starting seeds indoors is fine as long as you don't do it too early; seedlings grown too long indoors become tall and spindly. And don't start too many—you may run out of sunny windows. Finally, you must address the problem of damping-off up front; damping-off is a fast-spreading fungus which attacks young plants. It can cause a whole flat of your pretty baby plants to topple over and die overnight—just like that! There are a number of ways to avoid this problem. You can buy a sterilized commercial soil mix, like Pro-mix, or you can sterilize the soil you use by baking it in your oven at 250°F. until a potato bakes through. Various seed disinfectants, such as Semesan, also can help prevent this flower tragedy, or you can use vermiculite instead of soil. Vermiculite is also weed-free, holds moisture extremely well, and is so light that the delicate seeding roots can penetrate it easily. When transplanting time comes, the roots will slip out easily. Vermiculite is inexpensive and obtainable at most garden supply stores. In addition, be sure not to overwater your seedlings and do give them plenty of sun and ventilation—these cultural practices will help prevent damping-off.

Wooden seed flats now have been replaced almost entirely by plastic ones. These trays average about $2'' \times 4'' \times 12''$.

Cover up the holes in the bottom of your flats with some coarse stones, or bits of brick or broken flower pots. This must be done carefully or your seeding medium will sift out of the flats.

Fill your container to within a half-inch of the top, working the soil or vermiculite down into the corners with your fingers. Make the surface level and smooth. Soak the soil thoroughly, then let it drain. Make shallow furrows 2 to 3 inches apart; the depth of the furrows will depend on the size of the seeds. Very small seeds need no soil covering at all; larger seeds should be sown 2 or 3 times as deep as their diameter. To sow small seeds, tear a corner off the package and tap it gently with your finger to shake the seeds out. Pour larger seeds into your palm and sow them individually.

After planting, water lightly. Don't let the soil become soggy. Cover the flat with a pane of glass or a sheet of plastic film. Pots or small flats can be enclosed in plastic bags. Place the seeded pot or flat in a warm (65°–75°F.), partially shaded place.

When the seeds have germinated, remove the glass or plastic cover and put the container in the sun. But what if there is no sun, what if you are in for a spell of cloudy skies, what then?

Well, there's still a way. Actually, seedlings need a much higher intensity of light than full-grown plants; they will grow even faster and into sturdier plants under fluorescent light than they will in a greenhouse. Indoor light units, especially those designed for growing plants (such as Gro-Lux fluorescent tubes), are excellent but not essential. The fluorescent lights sold in your supermarket will work too—buy the ones labeled "daylight," "white," or "cool white."

But just suppose you don't want to buy flats or pots or fluorescent lights. Here's a really good, inexpensive way to start seedlings. Take a half-gallon milk carton, wash it carefully with warm soapsuds, rinse it out, and dry it in the sun. Staple the open end back together. Using a sharp knife or scissors, slice off one side. You now have a starting tray (see figure 1). Use a knitting needle to make several small drainage holes in the bottom. Fill with vermiculite and moisten it well. Plant the seed. Then, take a large polyethylene bag and slip it over the tray. Secure the

open end with a Twist 'em. You've got a handy little tray that cost nothing and is light enough to move from one window to another to catch the sun.

If your seedlings come up too thickly, as they almost certainly will, they will soon begin to crowd each other. If you do not correct this situation quickly, they will grow leggy and spindly as they compete for light and room. The answer, of course, is to thin and transplant them. As soon as the seedlings develop their first pair of true leaves, they are ready to be transplanted. Moisten the soil and remove the seedlings with a pencil or other small instrument. Be gentle and keep as much soil on the roots as possible.

You can transplant seedlings to larger flats, but it's best to move them to individual containers—pots, peat pellets, or planting

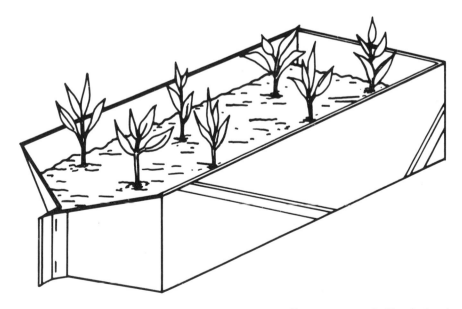

FIGURE 1. *Milk cartons cut in half make handy starting trays.*

blocks—so their roots won't become intertwined. The pots may be clay, plastic, or peat, and should be 2 or 3 inches in diameter. Peat pots, which can be put into the ground right along with the plants, are convenient and inexpensive. Clay and plastic pots are reusable.

Coldframes Aren't!

I mean coldframes aren't cold! They are, in fact, a simple, low-cost greenhouse. A coldframe is just a bottomless box that has a sash on the top. (I once used a discarded aluminum door with glass inserts for the top of a coldframe. It looked neat and worked beautifully.) The back of the coldframe should be 6 to 8 inches higher than the front so the rain will drain off. Place your coldframe so it slants to the south or southeast.

An outdoor coldframe can be used to start seeds early or to protect seeds and plants from rain. You can also use them to plant special seed all spring and summer and to carry over plants which cannot stand unprotected winter conditions. A coldframe will maintain a temperature just slightly higher than that of the world outside.

When coldframes are supplied with heat, either by the use of manure or electricity, they become hotbeds. Available on the market is the Lifetime Aluminum Coldframe. Its windows are made of fiberglass and will slide or raise for ventilation. It is 36 inches wide by 42 inches long. The back is 11½ inches tall and the front 7½ inches. This can be converted into a hotbed by the addition of a 36-foot automatic heating cable and a thermostat.

Or you can also build a hotbed yourself, supplying the heat with manure or electricity. Manure heating, however, is a bit tricky to handle. If the manure is fresh, the heat it generates may be too intense and will burn your seeds and plants. If it is too old, it will not generate enough heat to be of much consequence. However, back in the old days before the electrically heated types were available, experienced gardeners did a pretty good job with manure-heated hotbeds.

To heat with manure, fill the bottom of the hotbed with one foot of fresh horse manure, cover it with roofing paper, and set your flats of seedlings on top.

The Other Side of the Coin

I said earlier that you can sow seed directly into the garden. If you do, you must prepare your guest room ahead of time. No matter how fresh the seed you've purchased, their success depends in large measure upon how well you prepare the soil in their future bed. Break up the soil with a spading fork and remove all stones, sticks, cans, and other rubbish.

To each 100-square-foot surface, add 100 pounds of peat moss, 25 pounds of garden food and 50 pounds of gypsum, along with 6 bushels of compost, if available. Mix these into the soil, then rake the surface smooth. Moisten the soil, and after the water has soaked in, rake again. You are now ready to sow your seed or set out your plants.

Before you plant outdoors, you had better be pretty sure Jack Frost isn't going to take one more swipe on his way to bed.

It is virtually impossible to give a hard-and-fast rule for all sections of the country, since climatic conditions are so very diverse. Obviously, there can be no general rules that will apply everywhere. In some regions where there is never any frost, flowers will grow all through the year. In the North and in some mountainous sections, the frost-free season lasts only a few months. In these regions only quick-blooming or very hardy annuals can be grown.

For most of the country, however, planning and planting are directly related to the average dates of the last spring frost and the first fall frost. Accurately figuring these dates is especially difficult in the western states, where the dates may vary widely from year to year. This is due to the effect of the Rockies and the Sierra Nevada on climatic conditions.

Generally speaking, you can sow hardy annuals about two weeks before the date of the last killing frost in the spring. Half-hardy annuals can be sown a week or two later, but delay the sowing (or transplanting) of the tender annuals until the weather has settled and you are reasonably sure it has warmed up for good.

Some annuals are fussy about when they are planted and some are not. Sweet peas, for example, must be planted early so they can bloom before the weather turns really hot.

Let's suppose, just for the heck of it, that some year you are very busy and just can't get your garden planted when you planned to. You can still be tricky and have a bloomin'

good time! Concentrate on quick-blooming annuals which will germinate and grow even in hot weather.

Soak the seedbed thoroughly, plant your seed, then cover the bed with something like burlap to retain the moisture. Keep covered just until the plants peep through. The instant their little heads are above the ground (and be sure to look each day, for they may surprise you), remove the covering. I would suggest that you plant portulaca, annual baby's breath, candytuft, annual phlox, zinnias, sweet alyssum, strawflowers, and marigolds in your late beds. These flowers love the sun and are dependable bloomers.

When sowing seed in a timely manner, place the seed on the soil's surface, being careful to sow it evenly. Cover it very lightly with soil or, if the seeds are very fine, not at all. In fact, no annual seed should have a soil covering more than $1/4$ inch thick, for the delicate seedlings find it difficult to break through too much soil cover. Remember, it's better to plant your seed too shallow than too deep.

Firm the soil around the seeds, using your foot or the flat of your hoe. This will insure your seeds make good contact with the moisture in the soil. If the soil is quite dry at the time of planting, make a shallow trench and soak the soil in it. Plant your seed in the moist soil, cover lightly with dry soil, and tamp the seeds down. This will give them enough moisture to start growing.

Thinning Is a Must!

You will, at first, feel like a murderer. Steel yourself. If you do not give each plant the space it needs, it will be thin and spindly instead of straight and sturdy and you will have far fewer flowers than you would have had if you had thinned the plants properly. If you have sown your seeds quite thickly, you will undoubtedly have far too many seedlings. Decide which plants you want to keep and remove the rest.

If it will help you feel less guilty, thin them with great care. Carry a little flat with you, lay the uprooted seedlings in it, and cover their roots with a bit of soil to keep them from drying out. Many of these plants can be used somewhere else in your garden, or maybe a neighbor would like to have them. You might even arrange to trade with a friend who has something you want. Lots of times these little extras can be put in some out-of-the-way spot and used later on to fill in bare spaces where other plants have outlived their usefulness or died. If you plan ahead a bit, you won't have to throw any of your little friends away.

Some annuals, usually those with a long taproot, should not be transplanted at all. The taproot is easily broken when you dig up the plant and its survival then becomes very uncertain. However, most annuals stand transplanting very well when they are small.

PRE-GROWN ARE TIMESAVERS

If you are short on time (yours or growing season) and don't care to start your plants indoors, I suggest that you purchase pre-grown bedding plants—but Buyer, BEWARE! Here are some buying and planting tips for bedding plants:

Buying Plants

Good-quality plants can be distinguished quite easily from those that will struggle the entire growing season. A short, compact plant with good green leaves of moderate to large size has the greatest potential for producing either an abundance of blooms or a golden harvest of vegetables. Inexperienced buyers often focus attention on the size and number of flowers, which are no indications of how a plant will continue to grow. A well-grown plant, with lots of branches emerging near the soil surface, will produce flowers not only in May and June but throughout the summer and fall. The plants you buy should look crisp and fresh—this reflects adequate watering, good light, and protection from adverse weather and strong winds. Remember when buying annuals that they should not necessarily be in bloom; in fact, some grow better if planted when all green.

And also remember, the price you pay for plant materials most often reflects plant quality, newness of cultivars, and services available from the garden center operator. New improved selections, often designated as All-American winners, may bear a premium price tag. It's no bargain to purchase an inexpensive plant that has little potential for growth and production of flowers.

New Introductions

Hybridizers from around the world continue to bring forth many superior flower selections each year. The new introductions often differ greatly from older selections in terms of color, size, and shape of bloom, resistance to pests, and vigor. We now have a wide range of plant heights for snapdragons, salvia, marigolds, zinnias, and geraniums. Pay particular attention to posters at retail outlets and labels accompanying plants for information on growth characteristics and planting recommendations. Look for the All-America selections, which signal some of the new, superior introductions for our gardens.

Color

Gardeners frequently are drawn to bright colors, such as the varied shades of red. If used extensively, this color can overpower the garden viewer so that one really doesn't see pinks, yellows, or blues also present. White, often overlooked, fulfils an important role in helping to separate bold, clashing colors and highlighting blue and lavender blooms. A warm feeling can be achieved by a planting of red, yellow, and orange. Blue and green tend to create a cool setting in the border.

Planting

Having followed my directions for preparing your bed, your garden is now ready to receive your seedlings or bedding plants. Bedding plants from a greenhouse need to be "hardened off," or toughened up, before they are planted. Set them outside in a warm, protected area for about a week and bring them back indoors at night if frost or chilly air is expected.

Before planting, water both the ground and the plants. Dig a planting hole deeper and wider than the root ball and, after carefully removing the plant from the pack, fill in around the roots with soil while holding the plant at the same depth it had grown before. If the roots are tight at the bottom of the pot or pack, gently loosen them with your fingers. Firm the soil and water thoroughly. It's best to plant late in the afternoon or on a cloudy day to prevent transplanting shock and to shade the new plants from sun and wind for a few days.

Water deeply so the soil is moist to a depth of about 3 inches about once a week if it doesn't rain. Frequent light waterings will encourage shallow roots and poor growth.

Well-prepared soil should need no further feeding. If it does, however, use 5-10-5, watering it in well, or use a soluble fertilizer when watering, like Super K-Gro 15-30-15, every three weeks, and make sure it gets its Sunday morning snack every other week.

STOP THE WEEDS IN THEIR TRACKS

Don't kid yourself—your garden is not going to take care of itself. Those sneaky invaders, the weed seeds, are always lurking about, ready to rush in and crowd out your darlings if you give them a chance.

Weeds will be a problem only if you let them get the upper hand. Remember, that innocent-looking little sprig of green can quickly outgrow your flowers and take away the food and water you have so lovingly prepared for them.

When you first start gardening, you may not be able to tell flower seedlings from weeds, which often sprout at the same time. Until you become more experienced, you can overcome this situation by planting your flower seeds in rows and labeling them. When a number of identical seedlings sprout, you will just naturally know these are your flowers. After a time you will learn to recognize your flower seedlings as soon as they pop out of the ground.

The best way to outwit the weeds is to never let them get the best of you. Go over your garden conscientiously at least once a week with a cultivator—or by hand if your garden is small. Cultivation should not be more than an inch deep. Remember, annuals are shallow-rooted.

If you dislike the work of cultivating, there is a way out—one that will, in all probability, be better for your plants as well as save you a lot of work. And you do want to enjoy your flower garden—remember? The answer, of course, is mulching.

You are going to have to cut the lawn anyway, so why not save the clippings for your flower beds? It's better not to leave clippings on the lawn because they prevent air from getting to the roots of your grass. So do yourself, your lawn, and your flowers a favor! Bag up those clippings and use them in your flower beds.

But don't, I beg of you, put them on too thickly. They are green and they will heat up as they decompose. Put on a light layer each time you mow and distribute it evenly so it will dry quickly. If you have more clippings than flower beds, put them into a compost heap somewhere and let them go to work for you there. Six months later you'll be glad you did.

If you don't like the looks of clippings, hay, or straw, try buckwheat hulls or peat moss. Peat, which has a high water-holding capacity, is especially good.

You don't like any of these ideas? Well, if you like, you can avoid both mulching and weeding (or almost anyway) by placing your annuals close together so that they will shade the ground when they are well grown. Then only a few really daring weeds are likely to appear. These you will quickly notice and can exterminate with one quick pull.

Hand-weeding is slow but effective work. And, in plantings such as rock gardens, it is the most practical means of dealing with weeds. The best time to pull weeds by hand is when the soil is moderately moist. Naturally, it is easier to take out fairly small plants than big ones. When dealing with perennial weeds, it is essential to remove their roots as well as their tops.

Workless Weeders

Workless weeders, also known as the kneeless weeders, are something else. Science has come up with a real winner in the form of a pre-emergence weed killer for gardens. It eliminates the job of weeding on bended knees, which has never been one of my favorite pastimes. All the major garden product manufacturers have a pre-emergence garden weeder. They contain a chemical that will not interfere with any plant that is above the ground, but will prevent any other new growth from coming through—namely, weeds.

Apply one of these garden weeders as soon as you have planted your seedlings or as soon as your new seeds have sprouted. After you have removed any existing weeds, you will not be plagued the rest of the summer (provided you do not disturb the surface of the soil). This scientific breakthrough has saved me many hours of work that I now spend on more enjoyable projects. The best I have found is Green & Preen by Greenview Garden Products.

A GENTLE PINCH DOES WONDERS

Your little annual friends are climbers, creepers, and crawlers and it becomes necessary, from time to time, to pinch them back to keep them alert and in their own backyard. I let them bloom the first time and then I cut some of them back with grass shears to encourage more blooms. I do this again just before I go on vacation, since I won't be around to miss the flowers.

To keep your beauties blooming and to keep them vigorously healthy, also remove mature flowers and seedpods. This is known as deadheading. Doing this is particularly necessary with annuals like ageratums, pot marigolds, cosmos, marigolds, pansies, gloriosa daisies, pincushion flowers, zinnias, and petunias.

As you sit on your patio during hot, humid summer afternoons, are you looking at a bed of petunias 16 inches tall with a few flowers perched atop "leggy," almost leafless stems? What happened to that beautiful, compact, leafy plant you bought last spring?

The petunia is one of the most popular bedding plants; just walk any street and you'll find it planted in a variety of ways. But few enjoy a lush, full flower bed all summer long. Most gardeners buy their petunias in early spring, plant them, and enjoy a flowering garden until midsummer when the plants become very leggy, fall over, and remain an unattractive spectacle until frost.

A few simple tips can turn that brown thumb green and your garden into a flowering delight all summer. Petunias are "thermo-photoperiodic"; that is, their growth habit responds according to the temperature and the amount of daylight they receive. *At 62°F., the plant will always be branched, bushy, compact, and multiflowered.*

From 62°–75°F., its growth habit will vary, depending on the length of the day. With fewer than twelve hours of daylight, the plant will grow single-stemmed with only one flower. At temperatures above 75°F., no matter what the length of the day, the plant will always be tall and leggy with a single flower. This is why hot weather takes its toll on petunias.

There are ways to combat the effect long, hot, humid days will have on petunias. Many gardeners plant petunias when it's cool, and pinch (cut off) all the flowers before they bloom so that new growth efforts will be directed into branching and vegetative growth. Planting before the temperatures get warm also will encourage the petunia to branch naturally and get the plant off to a healthy start. If you must plant when the temperatures are in the 70s, the flower stem will tend to shoot straight up and should be pinched frequently.

By the second week in July, whether or not the plants were pinched at planting, they are ready to be pinched. Snip each stem about 3 to 4 inches above ground level. And don't mourn those lost blooms—in about two weeks you will have a much fuller, more beautiful display to enjoy. And while you're pinching petunias, this is also a good time to weed the beds, fertilize, and clean up dead or dying leaves.

The third pinch should be made late in the season, with the fourth at the end of September if a heavy frost has not yet occurred. Since petunias like cooler temperatures, you can have a massive bed of flowers until the first killing frost. Pinching forces the plant to branch and each branch will produce a bud.

It is important to remember that petunias don't like water on their flowers. Note that after a rain, petunias close up and appear to be wilted. So when you water, use a watering wand or soaker hose so that the plants are watered well at ground level. Once water has touched the flower, it will take several days before it is fully open again.

Proper pinching and watering are green-thumb tips to successful petunia beds all season long.

Annuals Aren't for the Birds

Newly planted seeds in your flower garden are definitely not "for the birds," as much as we may love our fine-feathered friends and appreciate their songs and friendly presence.

Annuals, which are planted right on or very near the surface of the soil, are especially subject to their depredations. Seed-planting time is really the only time when you have to think about birds very seriously, for, other than picking off an occasional insect or two, they seldom bother mature flowers. And if we act wisely, we can prevent the birds from upsetting our flower cart without harming them.

Netting is one of the best safeguards. It admits light and keeps out the birds—and often many insects as well.

Newly planted seeds can be protected with a homemade portable screen. Old window or door screening can be used for this. Cut it into 18-inch strips and nail it to an old lath to make a framework. If you think this is a bit unsightly, remember it is a temporary measure to be used only until the plants are up and well established. Hot caps, paper covers that fit over young plants, may also be used to protect small areas.

Sometimes gardeners use noise and motion to frighten away birds and small animals. You can make all sorts of devices from inexpensive materials. For instance, the discarded tops and bottoms of empty tin cans may be strung together to wave in the breeze, creating noise, shine, and movement. Crumple thin sheets of aluminum foil into balls and suspend them here and there above your beds. Sometimes fluttering strips of cloth will scare birds away from newly planted seeds. Small mirrors are sometimes left on the ground to discourage crows. Birds will usually become accustomed to any device if it is used constantly, so you might try different approaches on alternate days.

The family dog often acts as a defender of your garden, chasing away small unwelcome creatures such as rabbits and mice. Sound will often discourage animals from entering. Moles especially do not like noise. If you are troubled with them, set several toy pinwheels into their runs. I've had good luck setting empty bottles in the runs. As air passes over the mouths of the bottles, it creates a vibration that moles find very irritating.

There are all sorts of commercial traps on the market now for rats, rabbits, skunks, minks, raccoons, and other small marauders. I prefer the ones that capture the animals without injuring them. Once caught, the animals should be taken far enough away from the site of capture to make sure they do not return.

You might also consider using plants repellent to certain animals. Moles and shrews can be discouraged by plantings of daffodils, spurge (or annual poinsettia), and castor bean plants. The castor bean plant is an annual which will grow quite large in one season. It is rather coarse but has an interesting tropical look about it. Its large root system takes so much water from the soil that this, in turn, will decrease the insect population upon which the moles depend for food. The beans, placed in their burrows, are also believed to act as a repellent.

Shoo, Fly!

Shoo, fly—and away they go, but not when it comes to trouble with bugs in your garden. Insect and disease control can be a worry.

Annuals are prone to attack from the wiggling and winged warriors, so it is important that they get the soap-and-water treatment, and that you keep your eyes open for insects. At the first sign of an invasion, use Malathion or Sevin.

If it's something nibbling at their feet, use Diazinon. From time to time, a little rash or mildew will appear on the foliage, especially on zinnias. A soapy shower and an after-bath powdering with rose dust will help.

Some people use empty beer cans to trap snails and slugs. Halved cantaloupe hulls can be used to trap sow bugs, which will eat plants' roots. Another way to control these bugs, sometimes called pill bugs, is to save used corncobs. Put them under pans or flower pots that are tipped just slightly. Go out early in the morning and carefully lift the pans or pots and tap the bugs off into another container. They can then be destroyed.

Newly set-out plants can be protected from cut worms by putting little cardboard collars around them. The thin cardboard that the laundry puts in your shirts is fine for this. Cut strips about 3 inches wide, press one inch into the ground, and leave 2 inches extending aboveground.

One of the best ways I know to keep plants healthy is to plant garlic cloves among them. The small flower heads that develop from them (which in turn contain many more tiny bulblets) are not unsightly. Since garlic multiplies quite rapidly, you can quickly increase your stock and plant some around your fruit trees to repel borers.

No matter how carefully we plan and try to carry out good cultural practices, there are times when things simply get out of control. Sometimes we find our garden suffering from a sudden insect invasion. An explosion of army worms may seem to materialize out of nowhere and march pitilessly on our defenseless flowers, devouring everything in their path. Sometimes grasshoppers appear in inordinate numbers. Of course, on such occasions, you must take whatever measures are necessary for control. However, such times are infrequent, and the gardener must learn to distinguish between a moderate amount of insect life and the buildup of insect population to the proportions of a real infestation.

For a few insects, there are probably enough natural controls at work in your garden, such as birds or ladybugs, to keep things in balance. For other pests there are organic remedies which may give relief. Kelp is very useful as a soil additive and works well as both a preventive measure and an emergency treatment for soil insects.

Use ground rock phosphate against flea beetles and striped cucumber beetles. You may prevent attack by insects, mites, and fungi by using granite meal or dust. Even such dry, powdery materials as lime, tobacco, and road dust have been used to advantage against striped cucumber beetles. Dust these substances on the leaves every few days when they are wet with dew, covering the undersurfaces of the leaves as well as the tops.

An effective control for red spider (often seen on columbines) is wood ashes, dusted on the foliage.

And one of your best and safest bets is simply water! Turn a forceful spray on the infested plants—you may succeed in dislodging so many aphids that you won't have to use anything more toxic. Aphids so rudely dislodged generally will not return.

If you also have a vegetable garden, grow some hot peppers. Ground, dried hot pepper will make a very effective spray against ants, spiders, caterpillars, fleas, and many other small insects. You might even try grinding some onions and garlic with your hot pepper;

cover the mash with water and let it stand overnight. The next morning drain off the vegetables. Add this liquid to enough water to make a gallon of spray. You can use it as an all-purpose spray on roses, azaleas, chrysanthemums, and other flowers. If you have a heavy rain you must, of course, repeat your spraying.

When it's necessary to use a chemical control, I mix 6 teaspoons of Tomato and Vegetable Dust into a paste and add it to a gallon of water with one ounce of liquid soap. Spray your flowers with it after 6:00 P.M. If problems continue, take the insect to your local garden center for identification and for recommendations on how to combat it.

OTHER WAYS TO GROW ANNUALS

There are a lot of folks who don't have a lot of room to grow annuals in beds—so why not try potting, hanging, or letting them climb?

Hanging Baskets

Hanging basket gardens allow you to grow attractive plants in the most unlikely places. A basket or suspended planter can add a vining tomato, cucumber, or flowering annual to your porch or balcony without really taking up any space. Hanging baskets display color-

ful blooms at eye level and can disguise a plain or unsightly view.

Numerous types of containers are available for hanging gardens. Any of these, whether a plastic, wood, or wire basket lined with peat moss, will work fine. The containers should be lightweight and have good drainage. Baskets hanging outdoors will require watering at least once a day, so check them frequently. Larger containers, such as 10- to 12-inch pots, will need less frequent watering than the smaller ones. In addition to watering, fertilize your plants with 15-30-15, following the manufacturer's instructions, and make sure they get their Sunday morning snack every other week. Be sure the baskets are attached securely with strong hooks; a basket plus plants and moist soil can be quite heavy.

Special varieties of plants have been developed specifically for use in hanging baskets and can be found at any garden center. Most bedding plant annuals make attractive instant baskets. Purchase the plants and design your own baskets, or buy them pre-planted. If you decide to plant your own basket, choose one color and one type of flower for a bright, showy splash of color, or design a mixed planting.

When mixing different plants in one basket, start with more upright plants at the center, such as marigolds, ageratum, or coleus; then add trailing plants around the edge of the pot. Some suggestions for vining plants are fuchsia, vinca, alyssum, or black-eyed Susan vine. You might also want to add some variegated foliage, such as English ivy. Be sure the plants in combination baskets have similar sun requirements. For example, in a shady location a good combination might include fibrous begonias with English ivy, coleus, or impatiens. In a semi-shady to sunny spot, try browallia, alyssum, fuchsia, tuberous begonia, lobelia, or pansy. Good sun-loving companions include ivy geraniums, petunias, spider plants, alyssum, dusty miller, lantana, nasturtium, and black-eyed Susan vine. Fibrous begonias can be used in shade, semi-shade, or sunny locations.

Set your basket plants in a porous planting mix rather than garden soil. Commercial potting soil is sufficiently porous to allow good drainage, whereas garden soil may be too heavy to drain properly and may contain insects, weed seeds, and disease. Plant the plants as soon as possible after purchase and keep them well watered and out of direct sunlight for a couple of days. For a spectacular, full basket, plant the annuals rather close together, allowing only a little extra space for continued root growth.

Of course, basket gardening isn't limited to just flowers. Vegetables can be attractive in baskets and provide homegrown food, too. New varieties are being developed especially for basket or container culture. Ask for them at your local bedding plant outlet. Vegetables such as cherry tomatoes, lettuce, radishes, and dwarf cucumbers make fine, productive baskets. Herbs like parsley, chives, rosemary, and thyme are very attractive in baskets and mix well with flowering annuals.

Don't crowd vegetables in pots. They need plenty of space so that each plant and its produce can develop properly. Tomatoes, especially, require plenty of room so that the sun can reach the developing fruit.

This spring is a good time to spruce up your home with a few baskets of flowers and vegetables.

Colorful Climbers

Need to cover an unattractive fence? Want privacy at one end of your porch—or perhaps some shade? Consider the colorful climbers—annual vines—that will provide cover, shade, flowers, or fragrance almost instantly.

For color and fragrance, it's hard to beat a trellis or fence covered with sweet peas. Plant them early, as they are a cool-climate crop. However, the blooming period and geographic range of sweet peas have been extended by new hybrids. If the old types didn't do well in your area, the newest ones may.

If morning glories charm you, rig up an invisible zigzag support of nylon fishing line from floor to ceiling at the sunny end of your porch. Put 8- to 10-inch pots containing several morning glory seedlings at the base of each line and watch them grow! The vines will reach the ceiling in a few weeks, affording privacy and color. Remember that this type of pot culture is intensive, so water and feed frequently.

If your preferred color scheme is orange and yellow, try a patch of climbing nasturtiums. In addition to enjoying the beauty of the flowers, you can eat the young leaves in salads, and pickle the green seeds to use like capers.

The black-eyed Susan vine is another yellow or orange beauty. More fragile in appearance than the other annual vines, it is particularly suitable for sunny hanging baskets or window boxes.

Whatever your need, there's a vining annual that fits the bill.

Going to Pot in the Garden

If the gardener can't get to the garden, then the garden can come to him through the versatile world of containers. More and more people are trying their hand at growing flowers, vegetables, and herbs in containers, as they realize that this method of gardening allows for the best of all possible worlds. Just think of all the places that exuberant, plant-filled containers would add a special touch—balconies, patios, decks, rooftops, poolsides, or steps.

Anything that will hold a planting mix can be used as a container, from purchased plastic, stone, or clay pots to improvised containers made from bird cages, wheelbarrows, tires, fruit crates, or wooden barrels. The experts at Bedding Plants, Inc., an educational group that disperses information on flower and vegetable gardening, recommend that your container has adequate drainage holes and is filled with a soilless mix of one half peat moss or bark mixed with one half perlite or vermiculite.

Buying bedding plants at the garden center or greenhouse is the way to have an instant container garden. Choose plants for the shade or sun as your conditions dictate. Flowering annuals may be of any size or shape—erect, mounded, or trailing—but should be in proportion to the size and shape of the container, compact, and floriferous. Vegetables should be one of the dwarf or bush types. Your container planting can be as simple as a pot filled with glorious geraniums, petunias, or marigolds for the sun or impatiens or begonias for the shade, or as complex as a mixed bouquet of a half-dozen different annuals in different textures and colors. Whatever you choose, space the plants more closely than you would in the ground. Most important in caring for containers is to check the moisture at least daily during hot weather, as containers can dry out rapidly. Increased watering will also increase fertilizer needs; give your plants their Sunday morning snack every weekend instead of every other.

OTHER WAYS TO USE ANNUALS

Don't just gaze at them longingly in their beds; bring them in to admire a little longer.

Annuals for Arranging

Behind the fence or in a sunny spot beyond the vegetables, plant a cutting garden this year.

No need to pay lots of attention to the design or other aesthetics—simply grow neat rows of annuals in the colors and forms that please you best.

If you have space for only a tiny cutting bed, try tall zinnias and snapdragons. Their white, yellow, orange, red, and pink colors blend well and their forms contrast nicely. Zinnias provide rounds and the snaps, vertical lines. Both are long-lasting as cut flowers and the plants will continue to bloom and provide color until frost.

More space? If your color scheme calls for pinks and blues, raise larkspur, canterbury bells, asters, bachelor buttons, felicia daisies, or stock. In this cutting garden, be sure to add some dusty miller for its gray foliage—it's most compatible with pink tones.

For vivid reds, yellows, and oranges, grow marigolds, plumed celosia, geraniums, gloriosa daisies, and gazanias. The taller varieties are best, so read the labels to be sure you're buying tall plants. Coleus makes a fine foliage filler with these flowers.

Poppies—both the Shirley and the Iceland types—are great additions to mixed bouquets. They are long-lasting if you sear the stem ends after you cut them. Taking a lighted candle or disposable lighter into the garden in full sunlight may look ridiculous, but any flower arranger will understand.

And for airy fillers, grow some annual baby's breath or dill. The latter plant is dual-purpose, useful both in arranging and cooking.

Dry Annuals for Lasting Beauty

Your beautiful garden won't last forever, even in warm climates. How sad to watch the advance of cold weather and the end of the gardening season. Vegetables and fruit are easily preserved for the future by freezing and canning, but what about your lovely garden flowers? Must their lives be limited to a few days? Not if you take a little time to preserve them.

The easiest way to dry flowers is by air-drying. The first step is to choose a place that is dry and dark, with good air circulation. An attic is usually good, a basement usually too damp. Harvest before the flowers are fully open and strip the foliage from the stems. Tie small flowers in bunches so that their flower heads do not touch, then hang them upside down. Most will dry in two to three weeks.

The most popular annual for drying is probably the strawflower. It grows up to 2 feet tall with flowers in all shades of red, pink, and gold. The showy, stiff bracts surround and conceal the tiny flowers inside.

If you like vivid purple or fuchsia-colored flowers, try drying globe amaranth or statice. The $\frac{3}{4}$-inch round flower heads of globe amaranth dry quickly and are long-lasting. Purple statice and sea lavender, like the florists use, are easy to dry at home. Rat-tailed statice has 18-inch-long, pencil-thin spires of tiny lilac-colored blossoms and should be cut when the flowers are fully open.

For warm colors—yellows, golds, and reds—grow calendula (also known as pot marigold), marigolds, yarrow, and cockscomb. All retain their colors when dried; but the bright, clear colors of cockscomb (*Celosia cristata*) are unsurpassed. Its distinctively shaped flowers come in brilliant shades of yellow, orange, red, and purple. Other types of celosia are plumed or feathered.

Bells of Ireland (*Molucella laevis*) are delicate green spikes which enhance any arrangement. Pick off most of the leaves so that the bells will be more conspicuous. Dusty miller dries to a delicate silver-white and complements soft pink and purple flowers.

For a light, airy touch, add dried grasses. Just about any ornamental grass will do, especially animated oats, quaking grass (*Briza maxima*), squirrel-tail grass, and rabbit-tail grass.

Air-drying is quick and easy; when the flowers are dry, use them generously in flower arrangements, bud vases, door swags, or wreaths. Viewing these flowers through the winter will remind you of how beautiful your garden will be next spring. Consider adding even more flowering annuals to your garden just for drying. Listed below are annuals which can be dried by hanging them upside down.

A SEED SAVED IS A DOLLAR EARNED

You can save seeds from your own plants if you want to and know what you're doing. When saving seeds, remember that many hybrids which are developed by intercrossing one kind with another do not breed true to type from seed. Most of the original species or wild types of plants do breed true provided the flowers have not been cross-pollinated. To prevent cross-pollination, enclose the flowers in muslin bags and artificially pollinate them with pollen from flowers of the same plant or from the same species of plants. Unless protected in this manner, the flowers may be cross-fertilized by wind or insects.

As soon as the seeds are ripe they should be gathered and spread out to dry in a well-ventilated room. When quite dry, the seeds may be packaged and stored in a cool, dry place.

I have done some pretty exhaustive research on the best method of storing seeds and I have not, as yet, come up with a com-

Baby's Breath	Chinese lantern	Larkspur (annual)	Plume poppy
Beebalm	Chives	Lavender	Sage
Bells of Ireland	Cockscomb	Lemon verbena	Salvia
Blanket flower	Dusty miller	Marigold	Statice
Butterfly weed	Globe amaranth	Okra	Strawflower
Calendula	Grasses	Onion	Yarrow
Castor bean	Honesty	Plumed celosia	

pletely satisfactory answer. This applies both to seeds saved from my own plants and to those purchased from a nursery. The life span or viability of different flower seeds varies so much that there simply cannot be any hard and fast rule to cover all varieties.

However, if you do get carried away with your purchasing and find yourself in possession of partial or full packets of perfectly good seed when the spring planting season is over, give some thought to storing these seeds properly. You may lengthen their life-span.

I seal my leftovers in their original packets, put them in small, dry, airtight jars, and place them in my refrigerator. Small baby-food jars are just perfect for this or, if you have several packets, put them in a pint jar with a tight lid.

The best storage temperature is between 36° and 45°F. Check your refrigerator with a thermometer and adjust the setting as necessary.

Larkspur and dwarf hybrid marigold seeds do not keep well. Buy these fresh annually from a reliable seed man.

Generally speaking, oily seeds quickly lose their vitality, whereas those with hard seed coats are the longest lived.

The seeds of ageratum, alyssum, summer forget-me-nots, snapdragons, asters, begonias, coleus, coreopsis, cyclamen, blanket flowers, flowering tobacco, schizanthus, sweet Williams, violas, and wallflowers will remain viable about two years.

Chrysanthemums, clarkia, nasturtiums, and papaver are viable for three years; sunflowers for four years; and sweet peas for ten years.

Knowing Your Annuals

Getting to know your plant can mean the difference between success and failure. The more you know, the less chance there is for surprises that could result in disappointment for both you and your annuals. So let me begin with the top three contenders for annual popularity and then continue with the introductions.

THE MOST POPULAR ANNUALS IN THE CLASS

Let's just suppose that this first year you are going to plant only three different kinds of flowers—marigolds, petunias, and zinnias. These are three of the most popular and they remain so, year after year. There are sound reasons for this. They come into flower quickly, they have an immense and evergrowing color range and, perhaps most important, they flower gloriously even during hot, dry summers when other blossoms go limp and droop. These girls can take it.

It's hard to get into trouble with marigolds; since the color range is largely confined to yellow, orange, and blending shades of copper red, there are no clashing colors. Of course, Burpee, who has done such marvelous things with marigolds, is still searching for that elusive white one which has not yet been found. The 'Whitemost Marigold' is, so far, the nearest-to-white.

However, what we are really concerned with here is a glorious bed of golden color and in this there is ample range to choose from. Let us consider the Burpee Lady Marigolds, an ideal bed or border plant 18 inches high. These are carnation-flowered semi-dwarfs, fully double with some blooms measuring 3 1/2 inches across. They spread about 20 inches, making almost round, bushy, compact plants that retain their neatness all season long. Wouldn't these look lovely bordering a walk?

You can also choose from 'First Lady,' a clear light yellow; 'Gold Lady,' fully double and golden; and 'Orange Lady,' an exciting bright, deep orange. The Gay Ladies packet is a blend of all three colors.

In the French marigolds we find orange, yellow, and mahogany shades, 9 to 18 inches tall and fully double. There are also dwarf single French marigolds and extra-dwarf double French marigolds that are just 6 inches tall with a spread of 10 inches. 'Petite Gold,' 'Brownie Scout,' and 'Gypsy' are outstanding varieties.

Lastly, let's find out what a "mule" marigold is. This is the name given to triploid hybrids, crosses between the big American marigolds and the little French.

Because the little French marigolds have twice as many chromosomes as the big Americans, they cannot mate normally. The resulting triploids have their chromosomes out of balance. That makes them mules, and like the mule animal, they cannot reproduce themselves. But like all living things, they try to do so. They keep on blooming and blooming and BLOOMING but never go to seed, and they are the earliest blooming of all marigolds.

Petunia

Petunias are one of the showiest and most versatile garden flowers. The range of colors and forms available is tremendous, and they are one of the easiest flowers to grow, with the longest season of bloom of any annual.

Petunias will grow well with minimum care even in poor soils. Fertilizer, 15-30-15, should be added to the soil when the plants are set in the garden, and the addition of peat moss or compost is also helpful, although not absolutely necessary, unless you have very poor soil indeed.

Two or three light applications of fertilizer can be made during the summer. Once the plants are established, they should be watered deeply at one- to two-week intervals, depending on the weather, and should get their Sunday morning snack every other weekend. Excessive water and fertilizer or too much shade can reduce flowering.

Some gardeners prune the plants back in mid-season to encourage a heavier flush of blooms. Even without this grooming, they perform better than almost all other annuals.

Petunias have practically no pest or disease problems (snails and slugs will eat newly set out plants—collaring them with cardboard cut to stand 2 or 3 inches high sometimes helps protect them).

Petunias flower heavily over a long season, from three to four months in northern states and Canada to more than six months in milder climates. Plants should be set out after the danger of heavy frost has passed. They can also be planted later—almost until midsummer—and still make a colorful show.

Petunias can be used in almost any sunny spot in the garden, large or small, where you want a bright splash of color. Medium or large beds or border plantings of one or two colors give the most striking effect. Ten plants will quickly make an 8- to 12-foot border of color.

Petunias can also be used to provide color in front of permanent shrubs. They are especially useful in new landscapes to fill in bare spots between small shrubs. Any spot a foot or more in diameter with at least a half day of sun is sufficient.

There are both single- and double-flowered petunias. Both types are divided into two classes or categories: multiflora (many-flowered) and grandiflora (large-flowered). The color range in both types includes red, violet blues, purple, shades of pink, white and pale yellow. There are also interesting striped or starred bicolors in red and white, blue and white, purple and white, and pink and white. Two-tone pinks, blues, and purples with an interesting veined or lace pattern are among the newest colors available.

The multiflora single petunias have flowers 2 to 3 inches in diameter. Although the flowers are smaller than those of the grandiflora, each plant produces more of them, so the color effect is equal to, or greater than, that of the grandifloras. They are sometimes called "carnation-flowered" because of their resemblance to that frilly blossom.

Multifloras are useful in climates with wind or heavy summer rain because the flowers are more resistant to adverse weather. They are often used in parks for mass plantings and a clever home owner can use them the same way.

The large, or grandiflora, doubles have the showiest individual blooms in the petunia kingdom. Its flowers are 3 to 4 inches in diameter and most varieties have delicately fringed, ruffled, or serrated petals. The choicest variety, having the most consistently top-quality flowers and the widest range of color, is 'Fanfare.' 'Bridal Bouquet' is a brand-new pure white with a light spicy fragrance. 'Princess' is a medium pink with very large flowers.

Zinnia

In the plant world, zinnias got off to a slow start, but no one looking at them now would ever recognize these Cinderellas as the plants called *Mal de Ojos,* or eyesore, in their native Mexico!

Zinnias are now one of the most favored and best-performing annuals. Easily grown in full sun in almost any soil, they will make a striking and dramatic garden display in even the hottest weather.

The flowers are available in an enormously wide range of bold colors, which now even includes an exciting apple green—'Envy' (available from Park Seed). This lovely variety adds something never to be had before in a zinnia planting—coolness. It grows 2 to 2 ½ feet tall and has perfectly formed 3- to 4-inch wide dahlia-flowered blooms of good, long-lasting quality.

Until a few years ago, zinnias were all boldly colored, but now they are also available in soft pastel shades. Don't pass them up just because you thought they came only in harsh colors.

You may find that the habits of some of the plants are not entirely fixed. Occasionally they revert to single and semi-double forms. The colors may not be entirely true, and once in a while the flowers may have little cones or "Mexican hats" in the center. This is because zinnias hybridize readily and because plant habits may vary greatly among seedling plants obtained from the same flower head. Don't let this dismay you—if an occasional plant shows undesirable characteristics, simply discard it.

Another slight disadvantage of zinnias is that late in the season the foliage may become a bit unsightly from mildew or may shrivel because of prolonged dry weather. But in the face of so many advantages, none of these problems seems significant. Consider their long, continuous, prolific bloom, the ease of culture, and their adaptability to just about any climatic condition. They are extremely effective as bed or border plants.

Would you have a zinnia still smaller? Try 'Thumbelina'; these make the neatest possible edging for a walk or border. They grow only 4 inches tall, and the fully double flowers are 1 ¼ to 2 inches in diameter. They bloom early and continue through the season. If you want a low-carpet color, these are your

zinnias. Try some of these adorable elves and you will never be sorry!

HERE IS THE REST OF THE CROWD . . .

We have talked about a number of annuals, their good qualities and their special uses. The ones I have mentioned are by no means the only ones you should consider trying—there are many others just as worthwhile, just as beautiful, just as interesting.

Even here, there are so many annuals that I can attempt only a partial list, but the ones I will now try to describe are generally considered to be the most popular, primarily because they are both lovely and easy to grow.

Ageratum

This is a multipurpose, everblooming flower. Ageratum is equally at home in semi-shade or full sun. There are both dwarf types for borders, edgings, or rockeries and tall types for cutting. By potting a few plants in fall, you may enjoy the bright blooms in winter. Ageratum begins to bloom three months after sowing. It is easily grown from seed, and a packet contains about 1,000 seeds. Plant tall varieties 12 inches apart, dwarf varieties 6 inches apart. Germination time is six to ten days.

'Blue Mink' has 6-inch trusses of powder blue blossoms on strong upright plants.

'Blue Cap,' an elfin ageratum, grows 4 to 5 inches tall. The foliage is literally smothered with rich, blue flowers; it's a fine dwarf for edging.

'Fairy Pink,' 5 inches tall, is a dainty fairy princess and blooms from early summer to late frost. Flowers are a delicate, soft, salmon-rose-pink.

'Midget Blue,' a 4-inch dwarf with exquisite, tiny, blue flowers, is just perfect to plant in front of 'Fairy Pink.'

'Snow Carpet' is very dwarf. It forms 4-inch mounds of pure white loveliness and is an extremely free-blooming strain. It makes an excellent dividing plant to put between bright-colored annuals.

Alyssum

Even beginners will find this plant delightfully easy to grow. It will germinate and flourish under almost any conditions and is tolerant of both cold and of hot, dry summers. It can be planted early in the spring, and will begin blooming in early summer and continue right up to frost.

Alyssums are particularly recommended for the hot, dry sections of the country. They are good for edgings, for bedding, to cover sunny banks and terraces, for pots, and as a quick filler for rock gardens.

They may also be used for indoor winter blooming. Sow some seeds in a flower pot in late fall and keep the container in a sunny window. For anyone who longs for a bit of June in January, this obliging flower could be the answer.

Dwarf varieties should be planted 6 to 8 inches apart, larger varieties 8 to 10 inches apart.

'Carpet of Snow,' a new extra-dwarf spreading white, grows only 3 inches tall, as does 'Tiny Tim'; it, however, blooms several weeks earlier than other whites.

'Royal Carpet,' as its name implies, is a deep, vibrant purple. It makes a neat and well-behaved edging and is a perfect companion for 'Tiny Tim.' It grows only a few inches high but will be about 10 inches across.

'Rosie O'Day,' a deep rose-pink, grows 3 inches high. This one is not only ideal for edgings but is also delightfully fragrant.

'Violet Queen' is one of the older varieties—first introduced in 1941—but is still deservedly popular. It grows 5 inches tall, is neat and compact in habit, and deliciously fragrant.

Antirrhinum

(SNAPDRAGON)

Ah, here's something to get really excited over! What's been happening to snapdragons is incredible, simply incredible.

Goldsmith's 'Little Darling' received the 1971 All-America and the All-Britain award, and this isn't an easy accomplishment. 'Little Darling' has the same leaves and spikes as normal snapdragons, but the flowers look like rows of butterflies rather than dragons' jaws. Because the flower petals have actually been opened up by the change in shape, there is more color exposed on each spike. What this really means is that there is more "flower" and less "snap"!

'Little Darling' plants grow only 12 inches high and have a vigorous, basal branching growth habit. Each plant grows several short spikes suitable for cutting without time-consuming pinching or staking. Each time a flower is cut, the plant will produce several new ones, giving continuous color in the garden throughout the summer.

The new azalea-flowered type, 'Madame Butterfly,' is also excellent. It has the showiest flowers of all the snapdragons. Each floret resembles a double azalea flower. Plants grow 2 to 2½ feet high.

The original variety of the butterfly type was 'Bright Butterflies,' which grows about 2½ to 3 feet high and is excellent for background planting in flower beds. It's also choice as a cut flower.

All three of these new snapdragons belong to the elite class of F_1 hybrids that are sold as bedding plants. Because of careful selection and cross-breeding, they have increased vigor and stamina. If you are looking for a garden conversation piece, try some of these "butterflies."

If you want to grow snapdragons from seeds instead of—or along with—purchased plants, start them indoors or in a coldframe. With the coldframe method, make your sowing a month before the earliest outdoor planting date. Sow the seed thinly on the surface of the ground, in rows 3 inches apart. Press down with the palm of your hand. Do not let the soil get too dry. They won't germinate

until the soil reaches 50°F. On fair days raise the sash so the plants get plenty of fresh air. These seedlings can be set directly into a sunny spot in the garden without any intermediate transplanting; space them 6 to 10 inches apart.

Infant snapdragons are demanding, but once in the garden, they are very little trouble. Pinch back the tops to make the plants bushier. Rust was once a serious snapdragon problem, but it has been largely eliminated in the newer varieties.

Aster

Asters are among the most glorious flowers in the garden, but you will have to try them out for yourself in your own particular section of the country. Many people grow them without the slightest difficulty; others find it impossible to raise them. This is not because of any actual difficulty with the asters themselves, for they are easy to grow. The trouble lies with two diseases which may attack them, fusarium wilt and aster yellows.

Fusarium wilt is caused by a soil-inhabiting fungus and aster yellows is a virus disease transmitted by leafhoppers. I don't mean to frighten you away from asters by telling you this but, rather, to alert you to the need for extra care. As a safeguard against both of these troubles, do not plant asters in the same place more than once every three years. Rotation may enable you to grow fine asters every year. Sow seeds in spring in a spot that gets full to partial sun. Thin the seedlings 15 to 24 inches apart, 15 inches for dwarfs, 24 inches for giants.

Asters are offered in a bewildering and seemingly endless profusion of colors and sizes. They come in white, pink, blue, purple, creamy yellow, red, or lavender. Many have yellow centers. There are dwarfs such as the 6- to 10-inch high 'Kirkwell,' which has fully double 2-inch flowers; 'Giant Princess Aster,' with flowers 3½ to 4 inches across on long stems; and 'Massagno Cactus Asters,' with well-formed flowers having airy, needlelike petals. And then there are the 'Super Giants,' which are wilt-resistant. These, the largest fully double asters known, grow 3 feet tall. Their huge, "ostrich-feather" flowers are very striking and they are superb for cutting.

Begonia

Looking for a colorful, graceful plant for that shady spot—why not try one or more of several types of begonia? In recent years, hybridizers have been making major improvements in begonia breeding both in fibrous-rooted and tuberous types.

The fibrous-rooted, wax begonias have come a long way from the small-flowered, shade-loving bedding plants of grandmother's day. Today we can grow wax begonias with flowers up to 3 inches in width, profusely covering neat mounds of green, bronze-tinged, or dark bronze foliage.

New varieties have been developed to be weather-resistant and to perform well in sun or shade. They will bloom outdoors until frost and can then be whisked indoors to pro-

vide color all winter as house plants—they're truly everblooming.

European hybridizers have come up with the newest innovation in tuberous begonias. These seed-grown tuberous begonia hybrids produce vigorous and uniform plants that are abundantly covered with 3-inch, semi-double flowers in delicious colors. They have a neat habit, stay small and mounded—perfect for hanging baskets.

While the fibrous begonias are undemanding and will grow in almost any garden soil, they do prefer to dry out slightly between waterings. Space them 12 inches apart.

Outdoors in sun or shade, for neat bedding plants or spectacular specimens, take another look at begonias—there's one that's right for you.

Calendula officinalis

(POT MARIGOLD)

Calendulas are the marigolds, or "Mary's-gold," flowers that come to us from Europe, having been grown there in Scots and English gardens. One of the best annuals for the garden or greenhouse, they are easy to grow and will thrive almost anywhere. In the South, they will bloom almost all year and in the North from May until frost. They are attractive as either border or bedding plants.

Plant them early in the spring in a spot that receives full sun so you can enjoy their long-blooming period. Just barely cover the seeds with ¼ inch of soil. As you will be planting them in the soil while it is still cold, growth will be slow at first. Plants should be ready for thinning or transplanting in about a month. Thin them so they stand 8 to 10 inches apart.

If possible, transplant on a cloudy day or in the late afternoon. When first transplanted you may notice the plants have a tendency to wilt, but be patient. Keep them watered. Also, shading with a shingle the first day or two will help, especially if the weather turns sunny and hot.

Calendulas require little care beyond keeping down the weeds and watering them during dry, hot weather. Cut off the old blooms so they won't run to seed.

A pixie you will love is 'Dwarf Sunny Boy.' The 6-inch, mound-shaped plants are covered with 3-inch, fully double, bright orange flowers. It makes a perky pot plant too.

Another small fry is 'Zvolanek's Crested,' which grows just 1½ feet tall. Each flower has a crested center made up of tiny tubes or quills, some dark-tipped. The centers are framed by overlapping guard petals, and the effect is lovely.

Celosia

These are easy-to-grow, old-fashioned annuals that have been magnificently improved in recent years by selective breeding. Late-summer bloomers, celosias provide long-lasting flowers in fresh arrangements and may be dried attractively for winter enjoyment. Use them for edgings and window or porch boxes and the tall ones for solid beds or in the middle area of a mixed border.

Both the crested *(C. cristata)* and the plumed *(C. plumosa)* varieties are extremely easy to grow. Just give the plants plenty of room to branch properly. This means pretty drastic thinning and it must be done early. Water if the weather turns dry, but otherwise no particular care is necessary.

After danger of frost is past, sow the seed directly in your garden in a spot that receives full sun and cover with ¼ inch of soil. Transplant the extras when the seedlings have 4 to 6 leaves. Thin them so they are 24 inches apart.

Celosias are very rapid growers, enjoy the heat, and resist drought—they are great for warm climates where the summers are long and hot.

The crested types, or cockscombs, include dwarf and extra-dwarf sprites. They range in height from 10 to 18 inches. Among these are 'Empress,' 10 inches in height, with dark bronzy foliage and huge combs of crimson purple; 'Gladiator,' also 10 inches tall, with yellow combs up to 10 inches across—a sort of "Mr. Five by Five" of the plant world; and 'Fireglow,' a fairly tall type growing 20 inches high with 6½ inch balls of the brightest color.

Among the plumed celosias are the extra-dwarf or lilliput varieties, 'Golden Gem' and 'Scarlet Gem.' Among the dwarfs are 'Fire Feather' and 'Golden Feather.' The semi-dwarfs include 'Forest Fire Improved,' which is 2 feet tall and early flowering.

One of the most unusual now offered (by Park Seed) is 'Silver Feather,' a 16-inch, sparkling silver-white. Who said celosias only came in loud, bright colors?

Centaurea cyanus
(CORNFLOWER)

These hardy favorites are showy in the garden and make beautiful cut flowers for the house. Growing from 12 inches to 6 feet high, there are over 500 species of centaurea.

You can sow the seed in the fall, or early in the spring. Pick a spot that gets full to partial sun and just scatter the seeds on the surface—the way self-sown seeds get planted—or cover them with about 1/4 inch of soil. If you are planting the taller varieties, it is better to cover the seed to give the roots better anchorage later on. Sow where you want them to grow, for they don't transplant well. Thin them to stand 24 inches apart so they will have plenty of space.

These undemanding plants will just about take care of themselves. They are hard workers and will bloom abundantly. To keep them from going to seed, remove the faded flowers—you will enjoy their blossoms over a longer period of time. However, you might like to save some of the seed. In order to do this, you will have to let the plant have its own way and go to seed. It may do so anyhow if you aren't very watchful.

Varieties offered include 'Blue Boy,' a bright cornflower blue; 'Pinkie,' an exquisite light pink; 'Red Boy,' a deep, glowing red; and 'Snow Man,' a glistening pure white; they range in height from 24 to 30 inches.

The dwarf variety, 'Snowball,' a delightful pure white, grows just 12 inches tall, is very free-blooming, and makes an excellent border plant. It's also good as a cut flower, both fresh and dried.

Cleome hasslerana
(SPIDER FLOWER)

Cleome is a most unusual-looking plant, being, in a way, both bulky and airy in appearance. The flowers are actually quite small. New petals form on the tops of the stems as the old ones fade and die. As this happens, long, narrow seed pods develop and stand rather stiffly outward. Someone thought these pods looked like spiders' legs, hence the name spider plant. Every afternoon a new whorl of airy, orchidlike blooms opens on every stem.

Sow the seeds in May where they are to bloom and give them full sun and sandy soil. When the seedlings get big enough, thin them so they stand 15 inches apart. They are the easiest of all flowers to raise and will self-sow lustily, even in poverty-stricken, waterless soil where you wouldn't think anything would have the courage to grow. And they'll bloom from June until frost.

Because cleomes are so tall, they are principally used as a background or bedding plant, and are unequaled in either use. Even though some of the colors are not brilliant, the flower heads are so immense that they may be seen from a distance to good advantage.

Probably one of the oldest, but still an excellent, variety, is 'Pink Queen,' which will blend beautifully with lavender asters and white alyssum in a bed on border. It grows 3 to 4 feet tall and bears huge trusses of bright pink all summer.

'Helen Campbell Snow Crown' is a new, orchid-flowering, pure white cleome with even larger, fuller heads than 'Pink Queen.'

'Golden Sparkler' grows 3 feet tall and is a bright, golden orange—a most unusual and attractive cleome color.

Coleus

Coleus are grown chiefly for their ornamental leaves. Available in various combinations of yellow, green, crimson, chocolate brown, salmon, and pink, coleus grow about 20 inches tall. Fringed varieties have also been developed.

Coleus are easily grown from seed. Plant them in full to partial sun after all danger of frost is past or start them in the house and transplant. When the seedlings get big enough, thin to 12 inches. They will grow in shade, in any kind of soil, but their coloring is more brilliant if grown in full sun. Pinching back the central spire will make the plant stay compact and bushy.

Cosmos

These are summer-blooming plants which will go right on making flowers into the fall. They are graceful and especially good for cutting, growing from 3 to 15 feet tall, depending on the species. The early-flowered types are of special value where growing seasons are short.

All varieties are easy to grow and will thrive in average soil or even in light, poorly textured soil. They're nice for first-year gardeners who have not yet had time to build up a supply of compost. They will do well either in sun or partial shade. Sow out-of-doors after danger of frost is past. Thin the seedlings so they are 24 inches apart. When the plant is about half-grown, pinch it back so it will form numerous side branches. This will make the plant bushier and more symmetrical, and the additional branches and shoots will also bear flowers.

Here are some of my favorite varieties: 'Radiance,' with deep rose flowers; 'Pink,' a nice shade of rose-pink; and 'White,' noted for its purity.

The 'Klondike' strain is a bright mixture of yellow, golden orange, and vermilion red. 'Sunset' bears semi-double flowers of bright vermilion red over a long period and grows 3 feet tall.

Cynoglossum amabile
(CHINESE FORGET-ME-NOT)

These form graceful, loose sprays of large flowers similar to forget-me-nots that are freely produced on strong plants 30 inches high throughout the summer. Of easy culture, sow their seed in good garden soil in a spot that gets full to partial shade. When the seedlings get big enough, thin to 12 inches. *C. amabile* comes in white and shades of blue and is excellent in borders, edgings, and rock gardens. They are particularly useful in the cutting garden; like baby's breath, they add lightness and grace to bouquets, corsages, and nosegays when used in combination with larger flowers.

Dahlia

It is easy and fascinating to grow annual dahlias from seed. They should be sown directly in the garden in a spot that receives full sun and has well-drained soil after all danger of frost is past, or they can be started in a coldframe for earlier bloom. Thin the seedlings so they stand 16 inches apart. Dahlias will start blooming in ten to twelve weeks and continue right up to frost and are virtually disease- and pest-free. The plant will produce a small tuber which can be stored indoors during the winter and replanted the following spring. However, new plants grown each year from seed are more satisfactory.

There are over 15,000 varieties of dahlias, available in all types of colors, both solids and combinations. They can grow from 6 to 20 feet high, with flowers that range from 3 inches in diameter to the size of dinner plates. The elvin 'Pompom' dahlias form bell-shaped flowers that come in a wide range of colors. Dwarf dahlias include varieties such as 'Coltness Single Mixed,' 'Sunburst Mixed,' and the extra-early 'Early Bird Mixture.' Tall, giant-flowered dahlias are cactus-flowered and large-flowered doubles.

Delphinium

(LARKSPUR)

Something you must always keep in mind when growing these lovely spires is that larkspur is a cool-weather plant. It needs cold weather for germination and while the seedlings are young. Plant the seeds either in the fall or very early spring in a spot that gets full sun. It reseeds itself profusely year after year so it is a good idea to plant it, if possible, where it can self-sow. The double varieties will eventually revert to single-flowered strains, but for the first year or two, you will have many doubles in many colors.

The 'Giant Imperials' grow 4 to 5 feet tall with long spikes of closely spaced delphiniumlike flowers. The colors are azure blue, violet-purple, scarlet, and salmon. The 'Regal' strain includes pink, white, and rose. Both bloom in July.

Dianthus

(PINKS, CARNATION)

Dainty, fragrant dianthus are among the most adorable little people of the Flower Kingdom, blooming from June until frost. And, like so many annuals, their culture is a simple matter. Dianthus may be grown from seed or purchased as pot plants and actually do best in poor soil with plenty of sun. They are considered to be half-hardy and can be either sown right in the garden about the date of the last spring frost or grown in the coldframe and transplanted. In some mild climates (or with adequate protection), they will live over winter, and the second-year plants will bloom very early. Thin seedlings so they stand 12 inches apart.

Their 'Queen of Hearts,' an F_1 hybrid of brilliant scarlet red, grows 12 to 15 inches high, becomes covered with blossoms, and will overwinter in most climates.

Their 'Snowflake' is an outstanding dwarf

single dianthus suitable for borders, edgings, mass beds, and pot culture. This new hybrid grows 6 to 8 inches high with a spread of 12 inches. The serrated white flowers are 2 to 2½ inches across.

'China Doll,' the 1970 All-America winner, has double flowers in clusters. The color range includes shades of crimson red, red and white, and salmon. The plants have heavy, attractive leaves and a compact, basal branching habit.

Eschscholzia

(CALIFORNIA POPPY)

This carefree, spring-flowering annual grows just 1 foot tall. Sow the seed in fall in well-drained soil where the plants are to bloom, as this little sprite, who loves to nod in the wind, resents transplanting. Just stir the top of the soil to make it rough enough to hold the seeds, broadcast as evenly as possible, and you're all set.

The original California poppy, *E. aurantiaca*, has single, rich, bright yellow blossoms. 'Mission Bells' have lovely double and semi-double flowers, many with crinkled petals and picotee edges. Color combinations include rose and white, scarlet and yellow, orange and gold, pink and amber, as well as the usual solid colors.

Gaillardia

(BLANKET FLOWER)

These flowers, reaching heights of 15 to 24 inches and producing flowers of yellow, orange, and dark red, also thrive on heat and sun—in fact, they grow wild all over the Southwest, blooming during the summer and reseeding themselves profusely every year. Just sow the seeds in full sun and step back. When seedlings get big enough, thin so they stand 15 inches apart.

The annuals include the 'Lollipop' series, sweet 2½-inch, ball-shaped double flowers, each resembling a lollipop. These compact plants grow 10 inches high.

Other mixtures include 'Butterscotch Bronze,' 'Lemon Delight,' and 'Raspberry Red.'

Gazania

For summer-long brightness, start these fellows early. They are fearless little warriors who will overcome the most adverse growing conditions, including drought and hot sun. Put them in pots and use them freely in beds and borders—they're an especially good choice for busy people who have little time but still want flowers. They are evergreen south of zone 5.

The 'Sunshine' hybrids will fill your garden with splashes of dazzling color. The 'Colorama' mixture includes such shades as white, bright yellow, gold, cream, yellow-orange, red-yellow, and pink.

The 'Fire Emerald' mixture contains another profusion of colors, most of which have an emerald green center ring which adds depth and pleasing contrast to their fiery outer colors. Have you ever seen a real Russian fire emerald (Alexandrite)? If you have, you will know these gazanias are very aptly named.

Geranium

Chances are every gardener has enjoyed the clear, lively colors of geranium flowers in their own garden—planted in window boxes, pots, hanging baskets, or beds.

These popular plants have showy, bright flowers in clusters held proudly above handsome foliage. They're available in a range of leaf shapes and flower colors, including red, white, pink, salmon, and fuchsia. Geraniums are compatible with almost any plant and can be mixed with garden perennials and annuals for quick color additions or grouped with other plants in container gardens.

There are many types of geraniums to choose from: zonal, ivy, scented-leaf, and Martha Washington. The zonal, or common, geranium is the most popular garden geranium, with many varieties and colors to choose from. Named for its interesting "zoned" leaf markings, it's subdivided into two categories determined by the method of propagation: cutting geraniums and seed geraniums.

Cutting geraniums are propagated vegetatively from stock plants and are generally noted for their tall height, great early-season floral display, and flower heads with large florets. They are usually considered early spring potted plants.

Seed, or hybrid, geraniums are grown from seed by commercial growers. They tend to be shorter than cutting geraniums, with beautiful flowers that last throughout the growing season. These relatively new plants are heat-resistant and thrive in summer and early fall when many other garden plants have begun to decline. Since their introduction in 1965, seed geraniums have become true bedding plants. Available as small plants, seed geraniums can be used like petunias in mass plantings.

Whichever type you decide to grow, buying small bedding plants will give your garden colorful blooms early in the season. Start with healthy plants that have well-developed, dark green foliage. Bedding plant labels provide lots of information, so be sure to read them before you buy. The chosen location should provide at least five to six hours of full sun each day. If you cannot plant on the day of purchase, water thoroughly and place them in the shade. Evenings or cloudy days are the best times to plant any bedding plant.

To prepare your flower bed, spade to a depth of 6 to 8 inches; loosen heavy clay or clay-loam soils by adding peat moss, ground bark, or compost. Fertilize with 2 pounds of 5-10-5 or one pound of 10-10-10 fertilizer per 100 square feet. Turn the soil over and rake smooth. For containers, fill the pots or window boxes with lightly moistened commercial potting soil. Do not use straight field or garden soil, since it may drain poorly and contain insects, disease, or weed seeds.

When planting, remove each geranium

from its container with the root ball intact. Plants not in individual containers should be gently separated to retain as much soil around the roots as possible. Set them 12 to 14 inches apart. Water thoroughly immediately after planting and then whenever the soil feels dry. Water early in the day, soaking at ground level; sprinkling the foliage isn't enough and may lead to disease problems.

Maintain geraniums by cutting off faded blooms to encourage more flowers and by pinching the long stems occasionally to keep the plant compact and bushy.

In window boxes, containers, and gardens, the popular, showy geranium outshines and outblooms many other sun-loving plants. However they're used, versatile geraniums add a bold accent to any garden setting.

Gypsophila
(ANGEL'S BREATH)

This is a charming little fellow, similar to the perennial gypsophila, baby's breath (*G. paniculata*). The small flowers appear as a light cloud in early summer and last till the frost and are graceful when mixed with other flowers in bouquets. Gypsophila is not too showy, so grow it in your cutting garden. It comes in white, rose, and red. Sow seeds outdoors in well-drained soil in spring after danger of frost is past.

Heliotropium
(HELIOTROPE)

This 30-inch-tall plant is topped by huge (one foot in diameter) flower clusters in early summer. Best of all, this plant is very fragrant. 'Blue Bonnet' is the deepest blue. 'Marine,' a 2-foot-tall, semi-dwarf strain, has giant umbels of pure dark violet. Seeds may be sown in pots of sandy, well-drained soil in full sun in early spring and then transplanted into the garden.

Impatiens

Step outdoors to the shimmering colors of impatiens in those shady spots this year. Impatiens is the botanical name for the popular and pretty old-fashioned flower often called busy Lizzie and sultana. Few other bedding plants bloom with so little sunlight; no other bedding plant offers the glowing, luminescent colors of impatiens.

Their radiant colors range from cool white to lavender-rose, intense pinks to brilliant orange-reds. 'Harlequin' bicolor flowers add spice to the sunshine-in-shade of impatiens. The 'New Guinea' hybrid impatiens add attractively variegated leaves, too; plant these hybrids in partial shade, since they need more sunlight than their shade-loving cousins.

Impatiens grow into colorful mounds that bloom all summer. They come in several heights, from 8 inches up to 15 or 20 inches tall. The shorter ones make fine edging, hanging basket, or small-container plants; use taller impatiens for larger bedding displays.

It's best to wait until the weather is settled on the warm side of spring before planting impatiens. They are tender plants that grow fast in warm and hot weather. Ready-to-plant impatiens are available in spring and summer at your garden center and greenhouse. The young plants are offered in flats, trays, or peat or plastic pots.

Before transplanting them to your garden and outdoor planters early in the growing season, condition all bedding plants by placing the flats or pots outdoors in a shady spot during the day; bring them in at night, if it's going to be cool. And be sure to water them every day; plants in small containers dry out rapidly.

Impatiens are adaptable plants, not caring unduly about the type of soil in which you plant them, provided it's well drained. To give them the best start in your garden, dig the ground to a depth of 6 to 8 inches. Work in plenty of organic matter such as peat moss, leaf mold, or compost; add perlite or ground bark to improve drainage where soil is heavy and compacted.

You may need to replace the exhausted and root-laden soil under established trees with a fresh supply from elsewhere in the garden, or with a commercial soil mix. For hanging baskets, window boxes, and planters, use equal volumes of potting soil, peat moss, and coarse sand or perlite; or buy a ready-prepared mixture for your containers.

As you dig or mix the soil, add some 5-10-5 fertilizer at the recommended rate—about 2 pounds per 100 square feet—to boost fertility levels for your bedding plants. Feed 'New Guinea' hybrid impatiens every month to maintain their vibrant colors. As growth slows in late summer, all impatiens will benefit from an extra shot of fertilizer.

Transplant impatiens in the late afternoon or evening, or on a cloudy day, so that the new plants aren't immediately subjected to full noonday heat. Carefully separate the plants from one another and from their containers. The stems are brittle, so handle them gently. Space impatiens 12 inches apart. Plants grown in peat pots can be set in the prepared ground, pot and all, but be sure to cover the whole peat pot with soil, folding under the top rim that rises above soil level. If the top of the pot rises above the soil, the pot will act as a wick—drawing moisture away from the plant's roots.

Water well to settle the transplanted roots into their new home. Check every few days and water again when soil starts to dry out.

Your colorful impatiens will blossom and flourish all summer long in the shade and even in moderate sunshine when you provide enough water. At the end of summer, dig up your favorite ones and replant in pots—or take cuttings—for indoor decoration.

Lathyrus odoratus
(SWEET PEA)

If I were awarding prizes, I would certainly say that those pretty dancing girls, the sweet peas, deserved one of the best. Though most can't bear hot summer weather, sweet peas are a spring and summer delight. Many think them temperamental, but this is not really true if their requirements are understood—

and these vary in different sections of the country.

Here are a few tricks worth knowing. First, of course, it goes without saying that for the climbing kinds you must provide support—wire or even thin shrubs or climbing roses. Planted on the latter, they won't be noticeable when they start to die back in the heat of summer, leaving, as they would, a bare spot at a time when it is difficult to start something else.

Those who live in the South and have a heavy clay soil should be especially careful to lighten it with sand and compost. Northern gardeners with light loam or sandy soil will need to make very little preparation when sowing in the early spring and can do so just as soon as the soil has started to warm up. Southern or southwestern gardeners are best advised to grow their plants through the winter to obtain earlier flowers. October is a good month in which to plant the seeds. Sow the seeds in a spot that gets full sun. When the seedlings get big enough, thin them to stand 6 inches apart.

Here is a good recipe for preparing the soil for sweet peas. Dig a special 2-foot trench (it may be quite a narrow one), and move the soil to a low spot you want to fill in somewhere else.

Now make a mixture of one part soil, one part peat, and one part sharp sand. To each bushel of this mixture, add 2 ounces of bone meal, $1/5$ ounce of potassium sulphate, and $1\frac{1}{2}$ ounces super phosphate. For areas that are not alkaline, add 4 ounces ground dolomite limestone and 3 ounces of ground chalk limestone. With a preparation like this you will get earlier and far superior results. For sustained performance, try one of the foliage applications of fertilizers suitable for sweet peas and fairly low in nitrogen.

There are a number of frilly-skirted beauties, in almost any color, from which to choose:

The 'Galaxy' strain produces many-flowered giant sweet peas which will create a lovely massed effect, each stem usually carrying 5 to 7 well-formed, well-placed, fragrant flowers.

Other varieties include Burpee's 'Giant Spencer' sweet peas, which come into bloom after the spring-flowering type, thus extending the blooming period. They have large, long-lasting flowers.

'Knee-Hi' sweet peas are early, large-flowered and heat-resistant, and staking is not necessary.

'Little Sweetheart' makes small, compact, bushy mounds only 8 inches high and these minis are just covered with ruffled blossoms.

'Bijou' sweet peas are a delight because of their low growing habit. They may be used in borders, beds, and window boxes and make excellent cut flowers. The profusion of flowers produced literally covers the foliage. The plants grow only a foot tall, but produce 4 to 5 ruffled pretties on each 5- to 7-inch stem.

If you are feeling patriotic and would like some majorettes, try the 'Americanas.' This is a new class of sweet peas, growing only 18 inches tall. They can be grown without staking, but if used as bedding plants may be trained on 3-foot stakes. The summer-flowering 'Americanas' do better than the 'Bijous' in eastern gardens and will flower longer.

They are vigorous and prolific and, yes, these American beauties of the sweet pea world do come in red, white, and blue.

Mirabilis jalapa
(FOUR O'CLOCK)

Here's a comical fellow for you—a late, very late, sleeper who refuses to get out of bed until four o'clock in the afternoon. Once open, however, he remains that way quite a while into the evening, and the blooms are abundant. This is a tuberous-rooted annual available in many colors and of easy culture. It grows 2 to 3 feet tall, blooming in June north of the Mason-Dixon line and a little earlier further south, and develops best in the warmth of summer, planted in full sun to part shade. The name "mirabilis" means "wonderful" and refers to the color of the flowers. Sow the seed directly into the garden in spring.

'Jingles' is a mixture of striped colors of yellow, red, white, pink, and salmon. A bit on the dwarf side and well branched.

'Petticoat,' 3 feet tall, has a flower-in-flower effect and is a lovely rose color.

The little gnomes are well represented by the 'Pygmy' mixture, which grows just 20 inches tall and comes in many magnificent colors.

Molucella laevis
(BELLS OF IRELAND)

I have often wondered why this utterly charming flower is not more widely grown. It is superb as a cut flower, both fresh and dried. The graceful 2-foot-long branching stems are literally surrounded by 2-inch flowers. The bell-shaped calyx, which is green and delicately veined, contains a pure white corolla.

This lovely plant is easy to grow. Sow the seeds directly outdoors in the early spring. If you prefer, raise them indoors and transplant. They need a well-drained, fairly fertile soil, and a position in full sun. You'll love these little leprechauns.

Papaver rhoeas
(SHIRLEY POPPY)

Shirley poppies are truly number one among the beautiful people of the garden, with their delicate silken petals in midsummer and their bluish green foliage on plants that grow $1\frac{1}{2}$ feet tall. And their colors, usually sold in mixed packets, are particularly lovely, ranging from bright yellows to pinks, reds, and scarlets.

You may have 'Sweet Briar,' double, deep rose-pink, or 'Ladybird,' marked like a ladybird. This last is an amusing one—it is a brilliant scarlet, with a shiny black spot at the base of each petal, and is very free-flowering.

Poppies of this species are hardy annuals which can be sown in fall or early spring. The seed must be sown where it is to bloom, since no poppy likes transplanting.

Poppies are easily grown in a sunny location. Their only drawback is that the blooms do not last very long. But if you fall in love with them and feel you must have them, willy-nilly, here's a suggestion. Remember some of those seedlings I told you to save to fill in bare spots later on? Pull out your spent poppies some late evening or on a cloudy day and do a bit of transplanting; presto—your beds will look lovely again.

Phlox drummondii

(ANNUAL PHLOX)

Here's an easy one for the beginner that's beautiful enough for the experienced gardener to grow. No other flower can surpass its brilliant colorings—reds, yellows, pinks, and white. It is obliging enough to thrive and grow in a sunny location in almost any type of soil. When seedlings get big enough, thin so they stand 18 inches apart.

Annual phlox begins to bloom in early summer and continues until fall if the faded flowers are removed. It's great for bedding, borders, edgings and cutting, growing 10 to 20 inches high.

Portulaca

Often called moss rose or sun plant (*P. grandiflora*), this is one of the very best annuals for a brilliant and continuous display of color—pink, red, white, yellow, and orange—over a long season, starting in early spring. Portulaca is great for rock gardens, growing 4 to 6 inches high, but will grow in almost any well-drained soil in full sun. Try using it between stepping-stones.

Portulaca has a lot going for it, but you must not expect everything—it doesn't work well at all as a cut flower.

Sow its seeds in a place that gets full sun. Thin seedlings so they stand 10 inches apart.

Scabiosa

(PINCUSHION FLOWER)

The old varieties of scabiosa were not particularly attractive, but the hybridizers, who just can't seem to leave anything alone, went to work on this ugly duckling and have come a considerable distance toward turning it into a swan.

The 'Giant Imperials' are tall, with double, ball-shaped flowers 2½ to 3 inches across. The blossoms are made up of broad, wavy petals without the usual pincushion center.

The 'Dwarf Doubles' are pretty, compact, rounded, free-blooming plants, with flowers that grow from 1 to 1½ inches across.

Plant seed about the date of the last frost in a spot that receives full sun and has well-drained soil, and cover with ⅛ inch of soil. They can be thinned or transplanted. Scabiosa is usually insect- and disease-free.

Verbena

Verbena, or vervain, is a deliciously fragrant flower, in bloom from summer till frost. Fine for beds or borders, this little creeper will make a beauty spot wherever it is planted. The impish blossoms, available in white and shades of red and pink, are borne on terminal shoots which raise their perky heads 6 to 7 inches off the ground. The flower clusters are about 2 inches across, each composed of a dozen or more tiny florets.

Verbenas love the sun, though they will grow in partial shade, and will grow quickly and easily when the seed is planted directly in the garden about the time of the latest of the spring frost dates. Cover the seed lightly with about ⅛ inch of soil.

Give it plenty of growing room; 10 square inches of space is about average for most plants. In mild climates the plants, if given a light mulch, will sometimes live over winter.

'Sparkle' is a dwarf, compact strain; varieties available are 'Crystal,' white; 'Delight,' coral; 'Splendor,' royal purple; and 'Dazzle,' red.

'Amethyst' is that lovely and much sought after shade of medium-blue. The 8- to 12-inch plants are very dwarf and compact.

Finally, there are the giant-flowered varieties, 'Ruffled Pink' and 'Ruffled White.' These are the multiflora gigantea type which bear semi-double, ruffled flower clusters 3 inches across.

Viola

(PANSY, VIOLET)

These are the real court jesters of the garden. Both flowers are so similar in culture that I will treat them together. Pansies succeed best in fairly rich, well-drained soil in a sunny position and produce their finest flowers in the cool, early days of spring.

Keep the flowers well picked and the plants pinched back during the summer to produce new growth and flowers in early fall. Seeds may be sown outdoors when the soil has become warm. For earlier blooms, start seed indoors or in a greenhouse eight weeks before your usual outdoor planting time. When seedlings are big enough, thin so they stand 10 inches apart.

In mild climates pansies will not winter-kill. Even in colder climates, they may winter over if given some protection, such as leaves or hay.

Pansies come in all sorts of giant strains and many, many different colors. They bloom so profusely that you will be doing your plants a real service if you pick them often—very often. Enjoy their funny "little old man" faces indoors.

6

❧ ❧

Roses

Everything Is Coming Up Roses

Whenever I sit down to write about roses, I always find my mind going in a million different directions all at one time, looking for just the right introduction, just the right words, that will motivate all of you new gardeners to include as many roses as possible in your flower garden plan. I am also hoping to interest those of you who have heard how hard roses are to grow to try them for yourself and see how wrong that warning is.

On an overall scale, roses are by far the most popular plant sold in garden centers year after year. It is true that many, many roses are lost each year, but in most cases it is the rose grower's fault, not that of the rose, because in most cases a rose dies trying.

Like any other plant you select for your portrait of posies, there are some basic rules you must follow to insure growing success. The rose is no exception.

Here again, as in each of the other sections, I will give you a rather broad overview of the plant group referred to as roses, including background material, information on their needs, and possible problem areas. I will also describe the agreed upon techniques of rose care by the professional rose growers, amateur growers, and the U.S. experimental stations, along with my own tips and tricks.

I will not try to complicate life for you and your roses, since I want you to become lifelong friends.

THEY'RE NOT ALL CALLED ROSE BUSHES

☙ ❧

Roses are separated into two main classes—bush roses and climbing roses—according to their habits of growth. Full-grown bush roses are 1 to 6 feet high and require no support. Climbing roses produce long canes and must be provided with some kind of support.

Bush Roses

The bush roses are further subdivided according to their flowering habit, winter hardiness, and several other traits. The types of bush roses are hybrid tea, floribunda, grandiflora, polyantha, hybrid perpetual, shrub, old-fashioned, tree or standard, and miniature. All of them will require winter protection.

Hybrid Teas

Hybrid teas are the so-called monthly, or everblooming, roses. They are grown more widely than all other types of roses combined. When the word "rose" is used, a hybrid tea variety generally is meant.

Mature hybrid tea rose bushes are 2 to 6 feet high, the height depending on the variety and pruning frequency. The flowers vary from singles, which have but one row of pet-als, to doubles, with many rows. In general, the buds are pointed and long, and the flowers are borne one to a stem or in clusters of 3 to 5 from July till the fall. Hybrid tea varieties are available in a wide range of colors, including pure white and many shades of red, yellow, pink, and orange. All the varieties are good for cutting.

Most hybrid teas have some fragrance. This characteristic, however, is variable. When fragrance is present, it is usually most intense in the early morning before the fragrant oil (a complex of at least 30 essential oils) has evaporated from the base of the petals.

Most hybrid teas are winter-hardy in areas where the winter temperatures do not often go below zero, but varieties differ in cold resistance.

Floribundas

Floribunda roses bear their flowers in clusters from late June till fall, and the individual blooms of many of them closely resemble those of hybrid teas. They are increasing in popularity, especially for bed plantings, where large numbers of flowers are wanted. Floribundas will tolerate more neglect than any other type of rose, with the possible exception of some of the shrub species.

Grandifloras

Grandiflora roses resemble hybrid teas in bloom—single on long stems—and in hardiness. Though the flowers are somewhat smaller than those of hybrid teas, grandifloras bloom more abundantly. The flowers are good for cutting.

Polyanthas

Flowers of polyantha roses are smaller than those of the grandifloras and are borne in rather large clusters. The clusters are similar in form and in size of individual flowers to many of the climbing roses, to which the polyanthas are closely related. The polyanthas are hardy and may be grown in many areas where hybrid teas are difficult to grow. Their chief use is in bed plantings or in borders with perennials. They are excellent for mass plantings. They tend to flower only once a year in early summer.

Hybrid Perpetuals

Hybrid perpetuals are the June roses of yesterday's garden. Their flowers are large. Generally they lack the form of hybrid teas; an exception is the white-flowered variety 'Frau Karl Druschki,' which many consider the finest white rose in existence.

Before the development of modern hybrid teas, hybrid perpetual roses were very popular. As their name indicates, they are considered everblooming types, although most of them do not bear continuously through the growing season as do hybrid teas. They usually develop into large, vigorous bushes if provided with good care and proper pruning. They are very hardy and can stand low winter temperatures without protection.

Shrub Roses

Shrub roses are actually a miscellaneous group of wild species, hybrids, and varieties that develop a large, dense type of growth that is useful in general landscape work. They are hardy in all sections of the country, blooming from June till the end of the season. While their flowers do not equal in size or form those of other types of roses, many bear very attractive seedpods in the fall. They have fine-textured foliage and some are quite useful for hedges or screen plantings.

Old-Fashioned Roses

Old-fashioned roses include the varieties and species that were popular in Colonial gardens. Though the flowers of old-fashioned roses are not as attractive as those of the newer varieties, they usually are much more fragrant. These roses are all very hardy, require little care, and furnish an abundance of flowers in June.

Among the varieties occasionally found in gardens are:

Rosa centifolia (cabbage rose)	Light pink
Moss roses	Pink
'Cardinal de Richelieu'	Purplish red
Rosa mundi	Striped white and red
'York' and 'Lancaster'	Pink and white and variegated

Tree, or Standard, Roses

Tree, or standard, roses are distinctive because of the form of the plant rather than the type of flower. They are made by grafting any of the bush-type roses onto upright trunks. Many of the better-known varieties of bush roses are available as tree roses. Tree roses are used in formal plantings or to accent a particular part of the garden. In sections where winters are severe, these plants need special protection.

Miniature Roses

Miniature rose plants, including their leaves and flowers, are very small; for some varieties the maximum height is about 6 inches. They are available in all the colors, forms, and fragrances of the large-flowered plants. Miniatures are used mostly for rock gardens, edging beds, and borders. They also may be grown in containers in a window or inside under fluorescent lights. Miniature roses should be brought in for the winter; if you make this effort, they will oblige you by blooming year-round.

Climbing Roses

Climbing roses include all varieties that produce long canes and require some sort of support to hold the plants up off the ground. They are often trained onto fences or trellises, and some are used without support to cover banks and aid in holding the soil in place. Climbing roses are hardy. They are becoming more popular with the development of finer varieties.

Climbing roses, like bush roses, are grouped into several types. There is much overlapping among types, and some varieties could qualify under several. Most rose catalogs list the following types: ramblers, large-flowered climbers, everblooming climbers, climbing hybrid teas, climbing polyanthas, climbing floribundas, and trailing roses.

Ramblers

Rambler roses are very rapid growers. They sometimes develop canes as long as 20 feet in one season. The flowers are small—less than 2 inches across—and are borne in dense clusters. The plants flower only once a season, in June, and on wood that was produced the preceding year. The foliage is glossy and the plants are very hardy; unfortunately, however, many varieties are very susceptible to mildew. They are being replaced by other climbing types that bear larger flowers during a longer growing season and are less subject to mildew.

Large-Flowered Climbers

Large-flowered climbers grow slowly in comparison with ramblers. They are often trained on posts or some other type of support, and may require rather heavy annual pruning to keep them in bounds. These roses are well adapted to small gardens, where they may be trained against a wall, fence, or small trellis. When the plants are grown well, the flowers are rather large and are useful for cutting.

Everblooming Climbers

Everblooming climbers usually bear an abundance of flowers in early summer. After this period of heavy bloom, the plants continue to produce a few scattered flowers until fall. If growing conditions are favorable, the plants may then bear heavily again.

Plant breeders are rapidly improving this type of rose. Some everblooming climbers are available that bloom as continuously as hybrid teas and are more winter-hardy.

Climbing Hybrid Teas

Climbing hybrid tea roses have originated as seedlings and as chance sorts (mutations) of bush varieties.

When a bush hybrid tea produces a cane that has climbing characteristics, the new type of plant is usually given the same name as the bush variety from which it originated—for example, 'Climbing Crimson Glory' from a 'Crimson Glory.'

The climbing forms of hybrid teas, in general, do not bloom as continuously as their bush parents. The flowers, foliage, and other characteristics, however, are usually identical. The climbing hybrid teas are just as susceptible to winter injury as the bush forms.

Climbing Polyanthas and Floribundas

These types, like the climbing hybrid teas, originated as sports (or mutations) and seedlings from polyanthas and floribundas. The flowers of these sports are generally identical with the bush form from which they originated, and they are also fairly continuous in blooming. They are hardier than the climbing hybrid teas, but not hardy enough to withstand severe winter climates unless protected.

Trailing Roses

Trailing roses are climbers adapted to planting on banks or walls. They produce long canes that creep along the ground, making a pleasing ground cover. Their flowers are not as attractive as those of the other types, but they are hardy and have a place in some gardens.

Rose Buyers, Beware!

Buy your rose plants from reputable sources. Generally, local nurseries and garden centers are good sources of planting material. Retail stores—drug stores, supermarkets, and department stores—are also good sources if their stock has been kept dormant and has been protected from drying.

You can also get a good selection of high-quality plants from mail-order nurseries and nursery departments of mail-order houses. Reputable mail-order organizations will send you catalogs listing the plants that they sell. They will guarantee their plants to grow and bloom if given normal care.

For help in deciding which of the many varieties of roses to buy, get catalogs from several of the large nurseries. The varieties listed in these catalogs generally are favorites with rose growers, and you are likely to be satisfied with any of them. See the Appendix for my list of favorite rose catalogs and for the address of the American Rose Society (they also put out a catalog).

Members of local garden clubs and rose societies are sources of specific information on the varieties that do well in your area.

THEY'VE GOT TO LIKE WHERE YOU PLANT THEM

Roses grow best where they have full sunshine all day. They will grow satisfactorily, however, if they have at least six hours of sun a day.

If you must plant roses where they are shaded part of the day and you have a choice as to morning sun or afternoon sun, plant them where they have morning sun. If plants are shaded in the morning, their leaves will remain wet with dew a few hours longer than if they were in morning sun. Moisture on the leaves is favorable for the development of several leaf diseases.

There Is a Right Time and a Wrong Time to Plant

The proper time to plant packaged roses depends on the severity of winter temperatures in your area. Use this as your rule of thumb:

- If winter temperatures do not go below 10°F., plant any time the bushes are fully dormant.
- If winter temperatures do not go below −10°F., plant in fall or spring.
- If winter temperatures regularly go below −10°F., plant in spring only.

Some nurseries and garden centers sell roses that are planted in containers. These container-grown roses can be transplanted at any time from spring to fall.

They All Need Room to Grow

When planting hybrid teas, grandifloras, polyanthas, and floribundas, space them about 2 feet apart where winter temperatures are very cold (−10°F. or below), about 2½ feet apart where winter temperatures are moderate (10° to −10°F.), and at least 3 feet apart where winter temperatures are mild (above 10°F.). In all areas, space hybrid perpetuals, rose trees, shrub roses, and old-fashioned roses 3 to 5 feet apart. Climbers should be planted 8 to 10 feet apart; with miniatures, the spacing is up to you.

Any Old Dirt Won't Do

If you are planting only a few roses, dig individual planting holes for them. Make the holes 12 inches deep and at least 18 inches in diameter. If you are planting a large number of roses in one bed, prepare the bed by spading the soil to a depth of about 12 inches. Then, dig planting holes in the prepared bed.

Any good garden soil will produce good roses. If you can grow good grass, shrubs, and other plants, your soil probably needs no special preparation for roses. If your soil is very heavy, or if it is light and lacking in fertility, or if the builder of your house has used subsoil from the basement excavation to level your lot, you can improve your soil by adding organic matter, like peat moss, leaf mold, or manure. Most gardeners prefer to use manure. But remember, never add fresh manure to the soil—you'll burn your plants' roots. Dehydrated cow manure is available from garden-supply stores. If you use it, add about one-half pound of superphosphate (it increases root growth) to each bushel.

Spread a layer of organic matter 2 to 4 inches deep over the spaded bed. Work the organic matter into the soil to spade depth.

If you are digging planting holes in unprepared soil, mix soil from the holes with organic matter. Use one part peat moss or leaf mold to 4 parts soil or one part manure to 6 parts soil. Mix thoroughly.

After the planting holes are dug, either in beds or unprepared soil, loosen the soil at the bottom of the hole and work in about half a spadeful of well-rotted manure.

Prepare the beds and dig the planting holes well in advance of planting so the plants can be set out as soon as you get them. It's best to prepare the soil in fall, whether for a fall or spring planting. If the soil has to be completely reworked, do it at least four weeks before planting.

You Don't Need Kid Gloves to Handle Roses

Unless your rose plants are frozen when they are delivered, unpack them at once. If they are frozen, store them where they can thaw out gradually; do not unpack them until they are completely thawed.

Inspect the roots for drying. If they are dry, soak them in warm (100°F.) water for an hour or two.

The plants are best planted as soon as they are received. If you cannot plant them immediately, moisten the packing material and repack the plants. They can be kept this way safely for two or three days.

If you must hold the plants for more than two or three days before planting, heel them in a protected spot in the garden. That is, place them in a trench and cover the roots with moist soil. If the canes are dry, cover them with soil also.

When you are ready to set out the plants, examine their roots. Cut off all dead or injured growth. Remove broken or dead canes and, if necessary, cut the canes back to about 12 inches in length. Nurseries usually cut the tops back to about 12 inches before shipping the plants. If the tops have been cut back, do not cut them further; flowering usually is delayed if canes are cut back to less than 10 inches.

Protect the roots from drying at all times. Never expose them to sun or drying winds. Move the plants to the garden with their roots in a bucket of water or coat the roots with a thin clay mud and keep them covered with wet burlap or some other protection until planted.

If Planted Right, They Grow Right

Place a small, cone-shaped pile of soil in the center of each planting hole. Set the plant on the peak of the cone and spread the roots down the slope (see figure 1).

If winter temperatures in your area regularly go below −10°F., make the top of the cone low enough so the bud union of the plant is about 2 inches below ground level. If the temperatures go below 10°F. but not lower than −10°F., set the bud union one inch below ground level. If winter temperatures are warmer than 10°F., set the bud union at ground level or just slightly below it.

Carefully work the soil about the roots so that all roots are in contact with it. When the roots are covered, add water to help settle the soil about the roots. Then fill the hole.

Mound the soil 8 to 10 inches high around the canes of bush and climbing roses, and 3 to 4 inches high around the canes of miniature roses. Remove the soil mound when all danger of frost is past.

After setting tree roses, drive a sturdy pole into the soil beside the upright trunk and tie the trunk to the pole. This prevents the trunk from whipping in the wind and loosening the roots.

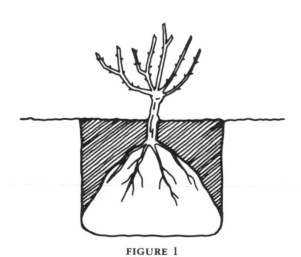

FIGURE 1

Weeds Don't Need to Be a Worry

Cultivate roses carefully; their roots may grow close to the surface and can be injured by deep cultivation. The main purpose of cultivation is to remove weeds. This can also be accomplished by hand-pulling the weeds or cutting them at the soil's surface.

Use a mulch to aid in controlling weeds, conserving moisture, and providing additional fertility. Peat, ground corncobs, ground tobacco stems, buckwheat and cottonseed hulls, spent mushroom manure, and well-rotted, strawy manure are effective mulching materials.

Apply mulches about a month before the roses bloom. Remove all weeds and rake the soil lightly before applying mulches. Then spread the mulching material evenly around the plants to a depth of 2 or 3 inches.

Keep the mulch on the soil throughout the year. The mulching material decays and becomes incorporated in the soil. Add new material as the mulch settles and becomes thin about the plants.

They Are Drinkers

Roses need large amounts of water. Even where rainfall is plentiful, occasional waterings are beneficial. Roses should receive the equivalent of one inch of water every seven to ten days throughout the growing season.

Soak the soil thoroughly to a depth of 8 to 10 inches. Direct a small, slow-moving stream of water from a garden hose around the bases of the plants. A heavy stream usually is wasteful; most of the water runs off and fails to penetrate the soil more than a few inches.

They Just Can't Live without Food

Roses are the hardest-working flowering plants in your garden. No, I'm not kidding. Roses bloom only for the sake of showing off, as much as they can, for as long as they can. And let me tell you, folks, it takes a whole lot of work and work builds up an appetite—that's where you come in.

You are the provider. Roses are fed first in the early part of the growing season when the new growth is well established and the danger of freezing is past.

I make a mixture of one cup ordinary 4-12-4, 5-10-5, or 4-8-4 dry fertilizer, one cup Epsom salts, and 4 cups bonemeal. Apply one liberal tablespoon per bush or 4 pounds per 100 square feet of rose bed.

Then I feed my roses one pint of the following mix every three weeks, in the morning, after I've watered.

> ½ teaspoon 15-30-15 Super K-Gro water-soluble plant food
> ½ capful of fish fertilizer
> 1 ounce of hydrogen peroxide
> 1 cup of beer
> 2 teaspoons of instant tea granules
> ½ ounce of liquid soap
> mixed in 2 gallons of warm water.

Roses should never be fed after July 15 in the North or August 15 in the South.

If the foliage turns a yellowish white (a sure sign of iron deficiency), spray with an iron chelate as directed on the package.

It Only Looks Like It Hurts

For large single blossoms or single-stemmed roses, disbud the plants when the buds are very small. Remove all but the terminal bud on each stem. The terminal bud then develops into a much larger flower.

The flower clusters of polyanthas and other roses bearing many flowers per stem also will be improved by disbudding. Remove some of the buds from each stem—the more buds you remove, the larger the remaining flowers will be.

Don't Be a Rose Hack

Cutting roses is an important cultural operation. Improper cutting can injure the plant and decrease its vigor.

Use only sharp tools to cut flowers. Breaking or twisting off flowers injures the remaining wood.

It probably is best if you do not cut any flowers during a plant's first season of bloom. If early flowers are not cut, the plants usually develop into large bushes by fall. You may cut some flowers then.

If you do cut flowers during the first season, cut them with very short stems—snip off only the flowers. Removal of foliage with long-stemmed flowers robs the plant of its food-manufacturing capacity and cuts down on its growth and subsequent flower yield and its chances for survival the following winter.

Even when plants are well established it is unwise to cut stems any longer than is actually needed. At least 2 leaves should remain between the cut and the main stem.

Hybrid tea roses usually have 3 leaflets at the top of the rose stem, and below that a spray of 5 leaflets. If the stem is weak, make the cut just above the topmost spray of 5 leaflets. If the stem is strong—as thick as a pencil—the cut may be made above a higher 3 leaflet spray.

If you do not cut the flowers, remove them when their petals fall. Cut them off with sharp shears or a knife just above the topmost leaf. A withered individual flower in a cluster should be removed to give the remaining flowers more room to develop. After all flowers of a cluster have withered, cut off the entire stem just above the top leaf. This insures that the new side shoots will begin to develop.

Roses that are cut just before the petals start to unfold will continue to open normally and will remain in good condition longer than if they are cut after they are fully open. Roses will keep best if they are cut in late afternoon.

BE A CONTROLLED CUTUP

You must prune roses annually to improve their appearance, to remove dead wood, and to control the quantity and quality of flowers produced by the plants. If roses are not pruned, they soon grow into a bramble patch with small flowers of poor quality.

Sometimes undesired shoots develop from the understock (usually the shoot has many small, dark green leaves). These should be removed as soon as they appear (cut them right off at the ground) or they are liable to dominate the plant.

Rose bush before pruning . . .

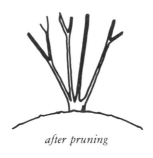

after pruning

Rose pruning is not difficult. As when cutting flowers, use only sharp tools. A fine-toothed saw is useful for cutting dead canes. All other pruning can be performed with pruning shears.

Do not leave bare stubs when pruning. Make all cuts even with a cane, to the point on the crown from which the pruned member originated, or to a strong outward-facing bud.

Bush Roses

Prune bush roses in early spring, just before growth starts. First remove the dead wood; be careful to cut an inch or so below the dark-colored areas. If no live buds are left, remove the entire branch or cane.

Next, cut out all weak growth and any canes or branches growing toward the center of the bush. If two branches cross, remove the weaker.

Finally, shape the plant by cutting the strong canes to a uniform height. In mild climates, strong plants can be pruned to a height of 24 to 30 inches.

In some areas, the winters are so severe that much of the top of the plant is killed. Under these conditions it is not possible to do much toward shaping the plants. Just cut out the dead wood, saving all the live wood you can.

Tree Roses

Tree roses require heavy pruning in spring and some pruning during the growing season to keep the tops from becoming too large for the stem. After removing the dead wood, cut back the live canes to a length of 8 to 12 inches and shape the overall structure of the plant. Most of the shrub roses should be pruned after they have bloomed. As a rule, these plants are very hardy, so pruning is needed primarily to thin out and remove old canes. They do not require shaping; in almost all instances shrub roses are most attractive when they are allowed to develop their natural shape.

Climbing Roses

Remove all dead canes and weak branches in spring, but don't prune hardy ramblers until after they have flowered; otherwise you will reduce the production of flowers. This pruning stimulates new cane growth and the development of new laterals on which the next year's flowers will be borne.

Where ramblers are trained to a trellis or support so high that one season's growth will not cover it, cut off some of the older shoots and shorten the strong, vigorous canes. This pruning will stimulate laterals to develop and continue to elongate and eventually cover the trellis.

Many of the large-flowered climbers, especially the everblooming types, do not produce as much growth each year as the hardier climbers. As a result, your pruning should be less severe.

WRAP THEM UP FOR THE WINTER

Roses must be protected not only against low winter temperatures but also against fluctuating temperatures. Occasionally, rose varieties that are hardy in the North, where winter temperatures are constantly low, are injured during the winter in areas farther south, where the temperature fluctuates considerably.

As the first step in avoiding winter injury, keep your roses healthy during the growing season. Roses that have been sprayed to control diseases and have been properly nourished are more likely to escape winter injury than plants that have lost their leaves because of diseases or nutrient deficiencies.

Bush Roses

Immediately after the first killing frost, while the soil can still be easily worked, pile soil 8 to 10 inches high around the canes. It is best to bring in soil from another part of the garden for this; if you dig it from the rose beds you may injure the roots of the rose plants. After mounding the soil about the canes, tie all the canes together to keep them from being blown about and loosening the root system.

Inspect the plants frequently to be sure the soil is not washed away before the ground freezes.

Protection by mounding usually is effective if the temperature does not drop below zero.

Where the temperature regularly goes below zero, further protection is necessary. Pile hay, straw, or well-rotted, strawy manure over the mounded canes. Hold it in place by throwing on a few shovelfuls of soil.

Remove covering materials—straw and soil—in spring as soon as danger of severe frost has passed. Remove the soil mound carefully to avoid breaking off any shoots that may have started to grow beneath the mound.

Tree Roses

In areas where the temperature does not often go below zero, wrap the heads of the plants in straw and cover with burlap.

Where the temperature goes to 10°–15° below zero, protect tree roses by covering the plants with soil. Do this by digging carefully under the roots on one side of the plant until the plant can be pulled over to the ground without breaking all root connections with the soil.

Cover the entire plant with several inches of soil.

In spring, after the soil thaws and danger of severe frost is past, remove the soil cover and set the plants upright again.

Climbing Roses

Climbing roses need protection in areas where the temperature regularly drops below zero. Lay the canes on the ground, hold them down with wire pins or notched states, and cover them with several inches of soil. Remove the soil in spring after danger of severe frost is past.

Start Your Own Rose Family

Most varieties of roses can be propagated from cuttings taken during the summer or in fall.

Take 6- to 8-inch cuttings from the stems after the flowers have fallen in summer. Remove all the leaves except one or two at the top. Then plant the cuttings, with half their length below the ground. Water them, then invert a fruit jar over them. Remove the fruit jar the following spring.

Take fall cuttings after the wood has ripened well. Cut the stems into 8- or 10-inch lengths, remove all the leaves, and plant the cuttings in a well-protected sunny place with only the top bud above the ground. When freezing weather approaches, cover cuttings with a mulch of vermiculite several inches deep to keep the ground from freezing.

FACE TROUBLE STRAIGHT ON

I have never known a rose grower who has never had to face a bug or a blotch in his growing career. If you are to take your roses seriously, you must be ready to act or react to a problem as soon as you notice it.

What follows are the descriptions of just about all the known insects and diseases that the homeowner might come in contact with and the chemical recommendations of the U.S.D.A. Keep in mind, however, that if you give your roses a bath with a mild solution of soap and water or Flea and Tick Shampoo once a week, odds are you won't need any chemical controls!

Many different diseases and insects attack

roses. These pests vary in type and severity from area to area. You can control most of them effectively—no matter where you live—if you follow these general recommendations:

- Buy plants that are free of diseases and insects.
- Keep your rose garden cleaned of weeds, fallen rose leaves, and diseased or insect-infested canes.
- Apply pesticide sprays or dusts as needed.

Three types of pesticides are used on roses: fungicides for diseases; miticides for spider mites; and insecticides for insects. You can use them in dust or spray forms. Ready-to-use dusts are available from pesticide dealers. Few sprays come ready to use on roses. It is usually necessary to prepare sprays by mixing wettable powders or emulsifiable concentrates with water.

Select the pesticides by studying this section and the pesticide container labels. Follow label directions for dilution and care in handling.

Diseases

Of the many diseases that can attack roses, black spot, powdery mildew, rust, crown gall, and the cankers are the most serious.

Black Spot

Circular black spots, frequently surrounded by a yellow halo, appear on the leaves. Infected leaves turn yellow and fall prematurely. Severely attacked plants may be almost completely defoliated by midsummer. The plant is weakened, becomes subject to winter injury, die back, and stem cankers.

Black spot is spread by water, which must remain on the leaves for at least six hours before the infection can take place.

Severe pruning in spring eliminates some infected canes on which the disease overwinters. Begin spraying or dusting when leaves are half grown. Spray or dust weekly throughout the growing season.

Maneb, Zineb, and Folpet are effective for black spot control. Follow the label directions.

Powdery Mildew

White powdery masses of spores appear on young leaves, shoots, and buds. Young shoots become swollen or distorted. Foliage may be stunted.

This disease is spread by wind. It overwinters on fallen leaves and in infected bud scales and flower stems.

For control during growing season, apply Folpet or Dinocap. Do not apply Dinocap when the temperature is above 85°F.

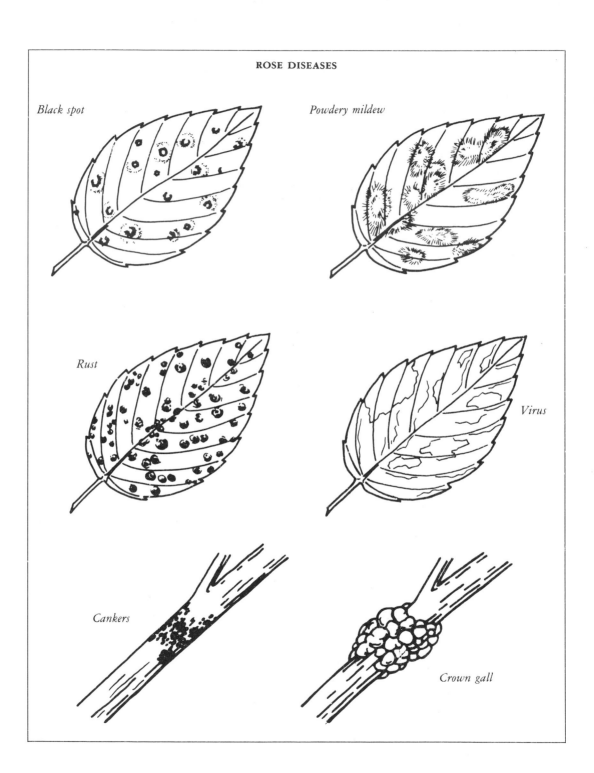

ROSE DISEASES

Black spot

Powdery mildew

Rust

Virus

Cankers

Crown gall

Rust

Yellow or orange pustules appear on leaves. The plant may become defoliated. The disease may also attack young stems. Spread by the wind, rust overwinters in fallen leaves. Cool, humid summers and mild winters are conducive to the development of rust. It is troublesome primarily along the Pacific coast.

For control, apply Zineb or Maneb (registered for use on rust in California only).

Cankers

Cankers occur commonly in plants that have been weakened by black spot, winter injury, or lack of nutrients. They first appear as small reddish spots on the stem. They enlarge and eventually encircle the stem, causing the cane to die.

For control, keep bushes free of black spot and provide them with proper winter protection. When pruning, make clean cuts near a bud. Prune out all cankered canes. Disinfect pruning tools with alcohol after use on a cankered shoot.

Crown Gall

Galls begin as small swellings, usually at ground level but sometimes on the upper part of the stem or on the roots, and slowly increase in size. Infected plants become stunted and may die.

Control is a matter of prevention; buy plants free of crown gall and plant them in soil that has been free of crown gall–infected plants for at least two years. If crown gall appears, remove the infected plants and burn them.

Virus Diseases

Rose viruses are spread by the propagation of infected plants. The diseases do not seem to be spread by insects or by handling.

Viruses cause small, angular, colorless spots on the foliage. Ring, oakleaf, and watermark patterns also may occur. Infected plants may be otherwise unaffected or they may be slightly to severely dwarfed.

The only control for viruses is prevention; buy plants that are free of the symptoms of virus diseases.

Insects

Roses are attacked by a large number of insects. The most common ones are the Japanese beetle, rose chafer, rose leaf beetle, rose leafhopper, flower thrips, rose aphid, rose scale, rose midge, leafcutter bees, two-spotted spider mite, rose stem girdler, mossy rose gall, and rose root gall.

When preparing blooms for exhibition, it may be desirable to protect prized plants and flowers from insect attacks by covering them with cheesecloth or other coarsely woven cloth on a light framework.

Japanese Beetle

The Japanese beetle attacks rose flowers and foliage during July and August. This beetle is about ⅜-inch long and metallic green with coppery brown wing covers. In areas of moderate infestation, plants can be protected against the Japanese beetle by frequent applications of Carbaryl or Malathion.

In heavily infested areas you may have to cover the flowers with cheesecloth cages or bags to protect them from injury.

Rose Chafer

Yellowish brown beetles, known as rose chafers, are often abundant in the North during June and early July, especially in areas of light, sandy soil. They are about ½ inch long and have long, spiny legs. They appear on the rose petals on which they feed. They may destroy the entire flower. For control apply Methoxychlor to newly opened flowers as needed.

ROSE LEAF BEETLE

Rose Leaf Beetle

The rose leaf beetle is a small, metallic green beetle that feeds in the buds and on the flowers of roses, often riddling them with holes. The insects are most numerous in suburban gardens near uncultivated fields. There are no pesticides registered for use against this pest.

Rose Leafhopper

The rose leafhopper, a tiny greenish yellow jumping insect, is frequently found on the underside of rose leaves. It sucks out the contents of the leaf cells, causing a stippling of the leaves that resembles the injury inflicted by spider mites. For control, apply Carbaryl, Malathion, or Diazinon to the underside of the foliage.

ROSE CHAFER

ROSE LEAFHOPPERS

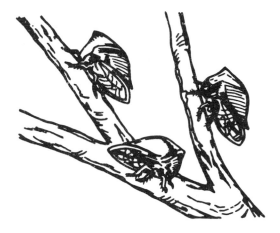

Rose Slugs

Rose slugs, the larvae of three species of sawflies, feed on the leaves of roses. Their injury is recognized by the skeletonized effect on the leaves. For control, use Carbaryl. Treatments must be applied promptly; the insects appear suddenly and do their damage quickly.

Flower Thrips

For several weeks each summer the petals of garden roses, especially white varieties, may turn brown. This injury is caused by the flower thrips and related species that enter the opening flower. These tiny yellow or brown insects can be seen if an infested flower is shaken over a sheet of white paper.

No fully satisfactory control is available because of the daily influx of thrips to the rapidly expanding varieties of flowers, which cannot be kept adequately covered with an insecticide. Carbaryl, Diazinon, Acephate, or Malathion spray applied to flowers and buds every two or three days will destroy many thrips as they alight on flowers. Cheesecloth cages or bags around prized blooms may help to protect them from damage.

Aphids

Several species of aphids may infest the stems, leaves, and buds of roses. By sucking its juices, they stunt the plants. They often occur in large numbers on rosebuds. The insects also secrete a sticky honeydew, which accumulates on foliage.

For control, apply Acephate, Diazinon, or Malathion spray as needed.

Rose Scale

Old rose stems sometimes become encrusted with white insects known as rose scale. These insects suck sap from the plants.

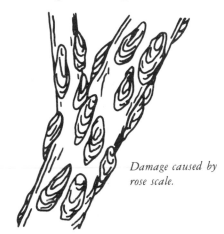

Damage caused by rose scale.

Acephate or Carbaryl spray applied at least once every two weeks during the summer will reduce the number of scales by killing the young rose scale crawlers. If scales persist until fall, prune out the stems that are most severely infested. During the dormant season, spray the remaining stems with a summer-oil emulsion; this should kill the scale.

Rose Midge

The rose midge can sometimes be a serious pest of roses. This tiny yellowish fly lays its eggs in the growing tips of the rose stems. The maggots that hatch from the eggs destroy the tender tissue, killing the tips and deforming the buds.

Cut and destroy the infested tips daily for one month to eliminate the maggots before they complete their growth and drop to the ground. Nicotine sulfate applied to the soil surface will control adult midges as they

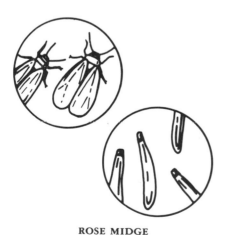

ROSE MIDGE

emerge from their pupation sites in the soil. Soak the ground thoroughly with it. Apply in mid-May and again in seven to ten days.

Leaf-Cutter Bees

Leaf-cutter bees cut circular pieces from rose leaves and other plants and store them as food for their young in burrows dug in the pith of rose stems, broken branches, or in plant crevices. The tunneled stems usually die back for several inches.

LEAF-CUTTER BEES

No satisfactory insecticide control is available for these bees, which are valuable as pollinators of alfalfa and other plants. A carpet tack pushed into the end of the cut stem at pruning time will prevent the bees from entering and tunneling the stems. Tree-wound paint can also be applied to the ends of the cut stems as a deterrent.

Spider Mites

The two-spotted spider mite and related species suck the juices from rose leaves, which soon become stippled. As the injury progresses, the leaves turn brown, curl, and drop off. When the mites are abundant, they spin a web over the leaf surface. Infested plants are unthrifty.

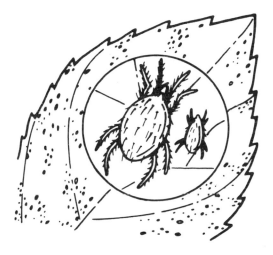

Spider mites and the damage they cause to a leaf

These spider mites usually are greenish colored with two brown spots, although some are dark red. They are almost too small to be seen without a magnifying glass. The mites overwinter as adults on leaves of living weeds or perennial garden plants. They quickly multiply during hot, dry weather.

When Carbaryl is used to control other pests, it destroys the insect enemies of spider mites and the mites tend to become more numerous. To control spider mites, clean up trash and living weeds in early spring and make weekly applications of a spray containing either Diazinon, Dicofol, Hexakis, or Tedradifon.

Rose Stem Borers

The stems of garden roses are occasionally infested with one of several kinds of borers. These stems usually die back, and those infested with the stem girdler develop a marked swelling at the point of injury.

Cut and destroy infested stems.

Rose Galls

Several species of wasplike insects lay their eggs in the stems of roses and their larvae cause large swellings or galls. One species makes a gall on the stem resembling fibrous moss. Another causes a large wartlike gall near the ground surface. These galls may be confused with crown galls, which are caused by bacteria. However, if insect galls are cut open, numerous larvae—or the cells in which they develop—will be visible.

No insecticide known will control the insects that produce these galls. The best control is to prune the infested stems, removing the galls, and to bury them promptly, destroying the larvae in the galls before they emerge.

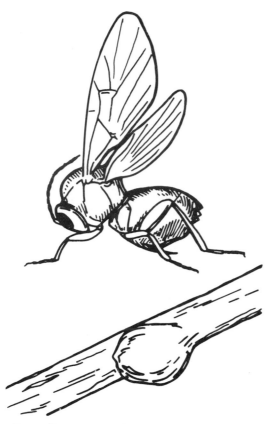

Rose gall on a stem and (above) the wasplike insect that causes them

For those of you who insist that the only effective control of insects and disease is rose dust, then by all means continue your application. However, I have always found this to be an unsightly solution, especially when you have lots of visitors in your garden.

I mix my rose dust at a rate of 6 teaspoons per gallon (mix 3 drops of liquid soap and a little water to make a paste) and apply it in the evening with a 6-gallon Super K-Gro Shrub Sprayer (put a golf ball into the spray jar as an agitator).

Lastly, an early application of Super K-Gro Systemic Rose and Flower Food is a good insurance policy against aphids and other sucking insects.

Sources

The following are my favorite sources for mail-order plant material or information about the following types of plants:

Shrubs

Emlong Nurseries
2671 West Marquette Woods Road
Stevensville, MI 49127

Four Winds Growers
Box 3538
42186 Palm Avenue
Fremont, CA 94539

Inter-State Nurseries
P.O. Box 208
Hamburg, IA 51640-0208

Also look to their catalog for a nice listing of roses.

Kelly Nurseries of Dansville, Inc.
19 Maple Street
Dansville, NY 14437

Stark Brothers Nurseries & Orchards Co.
Highway 54 West
Louisiana, MO 63353-0010

Also have an outstanding listing of fruit trees and berries.

Wayside Gardens
P.O. Box 1
Hodges, SC 29695-0001

Also a wonderful source for ornamental trees, perennials, and roses.

White Flower Farm
Route 63
Litchfield, CT 06759-0050

There is a $5.00 charge for the catalog, but the money is credited to your first order. I think it's worth the price just to get the catalog; it's a great source for perennials, also.

Perennials

W. Atlee Burpee Company
300 Park Avenue
Warminister, PA 18974

They're a great source of perennial plants in packs of six.

Bulbs

Breck's
P.O. Box 1757
Peoria, IL 61656

Bakker of Holland
U.S. Bulb Reservation Center
Louisiana, MO 63353-0050

Your connection for Dutch bulbs.

Park Seed Company, Inc.
P.O. Box 46
Highway 254 North
Greenwood, SC 29648-0046

North American Lily Society
P.O. Box 476
Waukee, IA 50263

They can provide you with information on lilies and they also sponsor seed exchanges.

Roses

Jackson & Perkins Company
P.O. Box 1028
Medford, OR 97501

Armstrong Roses
P.O. Box 1020
Somis, CA 93066

American Rose Society
P.O. Box 30,000
Shreveport, LA 71130

Index